THE OSAGE INDIAN MURDERS

*The true story of a multiple murder plot
to acquire the estates of wealthy Osage Tribe members*

BY LAWRENCE J. HOGAN

THE OSAGE INDIAN MURDERS
The true story of a multiple murder plot to acquire the estates of wealthy Osage Tribe members.
BY LAWRENCE J. HOGAN

Published by:**AMLEX, INC.**
P.O. BOX 3495
FREDERICK, MD 21705-3495

Telephone: 301- 694-8821
Fax: 301-694-0412
E-Mail: amlex@radix.net

Library of Congress Catalog Card Number 97-95334
Hogan, Lawrence J.
The Osage Indian Murders
1. The true story of the multiple murders of members of the Osage Indian tribe of Oklahoma
2. True crimes.
3. Osage Indians
4. Indian murders

ISBN 0-9659174-1-x

Printed in the United States of America

SECOND EDITION

COVER: Bacon Rind, respected Osage leader at the time of the murders. He was reputed to be the wisest and most popular person of the Osage Tribe. He went to Washington to talk to "The Great White Father" about the problems of the Osages.

This story is true. The Osage Indian Murders was the FBI's first big case and it helped to establish the FBI's reputation as one of the world's great investigative agencies. The names[1] of the federal investigators have not been used, but all other names are accurate, and the story adheres faithfully to the true facts of the case.

---

[1] Among the federal agents on the case were John Vincent Murphy, who was also involved in the shootout with John Dillinger several years later; Thomas F. Weiss, Sr., later an Oklahoma City attorney; and Thomas B. White, Sr., a former Texas Ranger.

.

.

Dedicated to:

The men and women of the
Federal Bureau of Investigation who carry on today
the noble tradition of service exemplified
by the investigation chronicled herein
and
To the noble people of the Osage Tribe.

ACKNOWLEDGMENTS

I have been fascinated by the Osage murders for more than 45 years. In the early 1950's, while I served with the Federal Bureau of Investigation, Director J. Edgar Hoover and Associate Director Lou Nichols assigned me the task of reviewing all the FBI files relating to this case and writing a summary for a proposed motion picture. The movie was never made, but Don Whitehead in his book, "The FBI Story," devoted a chapter to the case and it was featured in a movie based on this book.

My subsequent research has convinced me that, although much has been written about the case in periodicals, no one has ever given the investigation and the trials the comprehensive treatment which I feel is warranted.

The cruel and monumental injustices done to the Osages cry out for exposure. That is why I have written this book.

Many people have reacted very enthusiastically to this project and have rendered invaluable assistance to me: Ilona M. Hogan, my editing/proofreading wife, Amy Wokasien of Publication Concepts, Billie Ponca of the Oklahoma Historical Society's White Hair Memorial, Catherine Wilson and Connie Rencountre of the Osage Tribal Museum, Arlena and Joe Trumbly of the Clifton's Osage Prairie Gift Shop in Pawhuska, Peggy Sanford of the Osage Emporium in Pawhuska, Sean Standing Bear of the Bison Bison gift shop in Pawhuska, artist Bill Alsabrook of Tulsa, the staffs of the Pawhuska and Tulsa public libraries, the staff of the *Tulsa World* Library, Roxanne Shenker of Whitehall Printing Company of Naples, Florida, and numerous others who have given me encouragement and help.

In my research I sometimes found contradictory information. I have tried to resolve these discrepancies, but I accept full responsibility for any errors the discerning reader might find, and I will gratefully welcome any clarifications or additional information which can be sent to me in care of the publisher.

Lawrence J. Hogan

SUMMARY OF CONTENTS

SYNOPSIS

The investigation of the brutal Osage Indian murders was one of the most difficult investigations ever conducted by the FBI.

The Osages, who were forced to sell their reservation in Kansas to satisfy the white man's hunger for more land, bought a reservation in Oklahoma in 1872 which was almost worthless for agricultural purposes. Serendipitously, oil was discovered on the worthless land and virtually overnight the Osages became the richest people per capita in the world. The tribe's wealth earned from oil and natural gas bonuses and royalties was divided into headrights with each of the 2,229 tribe members receiving an equal allotment of the income, the equivalent of about $1 million per year in 1998 dollars. Each tribe member also received 657 acres of land. The total number of headrights was fixed permanently at 2,229. These shares in the tribe's wealth passed on in fractional or undivided headrights to heirs of the tribe members.

Unscrupulous white men and women, attracted by the oil money, moved into Osage County and devised countless ways to cheat the Indians out of their money. Many married the Indians so they could acquire their wealth. The greed of the whites also spawned a scourge of murders. Nearly two dozen Osage Indians died under suspicious circumstances. The entire Osage Tribe, as well as their white neighbors, was horror-stricken and in desperate fear for their lives.

On May 27, 1921, a hunting party found the body of Anna Brown in a ravine about three miles from Fairfax, Oklahoma. On February 6, 1923, an Indian boy found an automobile in a rocky swale a few miles northwest of Fairfax. On the front seat was the bloody body of Anna Brown's cousin, Henry Roan, a bullet hole in his head. At about 2:50 am on March 10, 1923, W.E Smith's home at Fairfax was demolished by an explosion. His wife, Rita — Anna Brown's sister — and their 17-year old servant were killed instantly, their bodies blown asunder. Smith himself was rescued from the debris and lingered in agony, dying four days later.

The Osage tribal council passed a resolution requesting the aid of the federal government in solving these murders, and the FBI's investigative machinery went into action. The FBI began its investigation in 1923 and spent years of painstaking effort to unravel the mystery surrounding these brutal murders and accumulating the necessary evidence to convict the guilty parties. Special Agents, carefully selected because of their knowledge of Indian and frontier life, drove thousands of miles day and night in all kinds of weather, running down innumerable leads, many of which were planted to confuse them. Some Agents assumed undercover roles, including an insurance salesman, an Indian medicine man, a cattleman, a prospector and a rough Texas cowboy. Since the area abounded with robbers and killers, the lives of the investigating agents — especially those undercover — were constantly in danger.

Who committed these murders and why?

This is the true story of the federal investigation and the trials which brought the murderers to justice.

BACKGROUND

❧ Chapter 1 ❧

History and Culture of the Osage Indians

The name "Osage" is a French corruption of the tribe's name, "Wazhazhe," which, in turn, is an extension of the name of one of the three bands of which the tribe was composed.

The Osage Indians are part of the Siouxian-speaking Indians, belonging to the Dhegiha group and were said to be the most important tribe of this division. Their nearest kindred tribes are the Omaha, Ponca, Quapaw, and Kaw. Their languages are so similar that they have little difficulty understanding each other.

The Osage Tribe is divided into two great divisions, one to symbolize the sky and the other the earth. The division symbolizing the sky is called Tsi-zhu, a word interpreted as "Household." The division symbolizing the earth is called Hon-ga, "the Sacred One." The great division symbolizing the earth is subdivided so that one part represents the dry land of the earth and the other part the waters. In accordance with the religious significance of these two great divisions, the men of one division were obliged to choose wives only from the women belonging to the other division. (This rule was strictly and religiously observed until the tribe became so reduced in number that this was no longer feasible. The influx of the white race in later times, of course, was also a disturbing influence to this marital pairing as well as in so many other aspects of the tribe's life.)

The Osages were divided into a clan-and-band system and were scattered throughout Arkansas and Missouri. The bands later became known as the Great Osage and the Little Osage which were further divided into smaller groups led by subchiefs and heads of families.

These two great divisions were further subdivided into 24 clans or ton-won-gthon, membership in which was inherited through the father. Each clan was associated with a set of zho-i-ga-the or life symbols which included animals, plants, heavenly bodies and natural phenomena such as clouds and lightning. Clans were referred to by their life symbols. Collectively, the 24 clans symbolically represented all of the various forces of the universe. The clans were grouped into large units. Nine clans formed the sky or tsi-zhu people and together they symbolized the forces of the sky. The sky people were divided into two groups. One was simply called the Sky people and one was called "those-who-came-last."

The other 15 clans formed the Earth or hon-ga People. The Earth People were divided into three overall groups. Seven formed the Land People, symbolic of the land forces on the earth, another group of 7 clans formed the water (wa-sha-she) people, symbolic of the water forces of the earth. The remaining clan of the Earth People was simply called the Isolated Earth Clan.

About 1802 a third division, the "Arkansas Band," was created by the migration of nearly half of the Great Osage to the Arkansas River under a chief known as Big-Track. By that time, the Little Osages had moved from the Missouri River to within about six miles of the Great Osage River.

Religion of the Osages

To the Osage people, their tribal rites were both their law and their religion, keeping them in constant touch with Wa-kon'-da (God).

Dr. Francis LaFlesche, an authority on the Osages, wrote:

"Under the new conditions and the new ideas introduced among the people by the white race, these rites will soon fade from the memory of the coming generations and be lost beyond recovery...."

"Every rite to which the Osage people clung from the earliest times of their tribal existence is regarded by them as religious and supplicatory in character. Those relating to war, to peace, and to life are held with equal veneration. The thoughts embodied in the symbolic tribal organization and in the formulated rites were gathered by the 'holy men' from the open book of nature, not in a single season nor in a single lifetime, but through years of patient mental toil."

From these ancient tribal rites the Osage people learned to depend always upon Wa-kon'-da (God) for their continued existence. Although they were sometimes described as a peace-loving people, they often marched against their enemies in defensive or offensive warfare. At such times, the warriors pleaded for divine aid in over-coming their enemies. Their first act in preparing for war was to choose a man whose duty it was to appeal constantly to Wa-kon'-da. This officer was called Do-don'-hon-ga, a title which may be freely translated as "The-sacred-one-of-the-war-movement." If the war party achieved success, this mediator was given the credit and great honors were heaped upon him.

The people also learned that, as a tribe, they must daily appeal to Wa-kon'-da for a long and healthful life. Therefore, at dawn, when the reddened sky signaled the approach of the sun, men, women, and children stood in the doorways of their houses and prayed. As the sun reached midheaven, they repeated their prayers and at sunset they again prayed.

Men who traveled in the far West in 1806 and 1811 mentioned this daily praying.

In the year 1829, Governor Miller stated in a letter:

"These Indians have a native religion of their own and are the only tribe I ever knew that had. At break of day every morning, I could hear them at prayer for an hour. They appeared to be as devout in their way as any class of people."

In 1840 a Baptist missionary, Reverend Isaac McCoy, said:

"It has been reported that the Osages did not believe in the existence of the Great Spirit. I was astonished that anyone who had ever been two days among them or the Kansas, who are in all respects similar, should be so deceived. I have never before seen Indians who gave more undoubted evidence of their belief in God."

Later, a visitor from the Omaha Tribe said:

"My father and I visited them (the Osages) when they had moved to their new reservation (in the early 1870's). Before sunrise in the morning following the first night of our visit, I was awakened by the noise of a great wailing. I arose and went out. As far as I could see, men, women, and children were standing in front of the doors of their houses weeping. My parents explained to me that it was the custom of the people to cry to Wa-kon'-da morning, noon and evening. When I understood the meaning of the cry, I soon learned not to be startled by the noise."

In this way the Osages kept in contact with Wa-kon'-da, whom they believed to be present in all things.

Not only are the thoughts of the ancient tribe's wise men incorporated into the rites, but they are also given expression in other aspects of tribal life, including the tribal organization. The idea was perpetuated that the part of the universe which is visible is a great unit and that life issues from the combined force and influence of the various bodies that compose this unit. This expression is emphasized in some of the rituals which describe the descent of the people from the sky to take possession of the earth and make it their home.

Their ancestors were always remembered in the daily prayers of the tribe and the hills surrounding villages which contained the graves of their ancestors were considered sacred ground.

The Plains Indians' Culture

The Osage Tribe belonged to the culture group of American Indians categorized as "Plains." Like other woodlands and long-grass prairie people, the Osages were village-dwelling agriculturists and hunters.

The Osages settled in the midwestern part of North America and their culture is that of the Plains Indians. They formerly hunted over much of the northern and northwestern parts of what is now Arkansas, claiming all lands which are now included in that state as far as the Arkansas River.

Although tradition indicates a prehistoric seat of the Osages on the Ohio River, data gathered from the brief references to the Osages made by early travelers reflects that, during the seventeenth century, these Indians lived on the banks of the Little Osage River near where it joins the main Osage River, but from a very early period one group was on the Missouri River, along which they established trade routes.

Rev. Jacques Marquette (1673) was the first traveler to mention the Osages. He did not personally visit the Osage people in their villages, but guided by information obtained from members of other tribes, he located the Osages upon his map as living at the head of the river bearing their name. It is not known how long prior to that time they lived there, but it is certain that for more than a century before this first mention of them, they had made this place their fixed home. This area is now part of Vernon County, Missouri. From here the Osages went forth on their excursions and war parties, but they always returned to this location. ,

In the later 17th Century, lodge villages were built along the Missouri and Osage rivers where women would plant corn, beans and squash in small fields along the river bottoms. The men would form small hunting parties. In addition to buffalo meat, the Osages supplemented their diet with roots, nuts and berries. These were not only eaten in season, but were dried and stored for winter, together with beans and corn.

Buffalo Hunting

The existence of the Plains Indian was almost completely dependent on the buffalo, and the lives of the two were very closely entwined. The Osages considered the buffalo one of the greatest gifts from God (Wa-kon'-da) since it filled so many of their needs: food; robes for warmth in winter; hides for teepees, parfleches, clothing, cooking pots, ornaments, and boats; and horns, bones, sinews, and hoofs for weapon points, implements, tools, fluid and glue. Sometimes buffalo hair was spun and woven into bags to hold sacred items. Wherever the buffalo moved, the Indian also moved. Therefore, life on the plains was a continuous, suspenseful journey in search of the buffalo herd.

Before the coming of the horse, the buffalo was hunted on foot. During those days these Indians lived for the most part in permanent villages of round earth lodges. Twice a year in winter and summer, every able hunter in the tribe left the village for the hunt. On these trips they lived in small conical hide tents.

The tribe would set up camp near a buffalo trap which they had previously constructed. Fire was commonly used to drive the buffalo into a surround, a river or other confined area where the buffalo could be easily killed with bows and arrows. One technique used by Plains Indians was to make a trap on a cliff. An open area ended narrowly at the edge of the cliff. At each extremity of the entrance to the trap, running out vertical to the cliff in a "V" formation, the Indians lined piles of stones spaced about 15 feet apart for about two miles. At the point where the lines were furthest apart the distance was about two miles wide, and the smallest end of the "V" — at the lip of the cliff — was about 100 feet across.

When a herd of buffalo was located by the tribe's scouts, a medicine man would approach the herd and annoy the nearest bulls who would follow him into the entrance of the trap. The rest of the herd would then follow the bulls into the area of the trap. Once the buffalo had been lured between the two lines of piles of stones which formed the "V," hunters would take up positions between the stone piles along the sides of the "V" and behind the herd. These hunters would then shout and wave robes to stampede the herd. The buffalo were forced into progressively closer quarters by the "walls" of the "V" and were headed toward the narrow end of the trap at the edge of the cliff. As the buffalos toppled over the cliff, they were killed with spears and bows and arrows by other hunters waiting for them below.

During these buffalo hunts the Osages were highly vulnerable to attacks from their enemies — the Comanches, the Kiowa and other plains tribes.

When the Osages received guns from French traders they were able to drive out many of their rivals and expand their hunting territory. By the end of the 18th Century, the Osages controlled all the land now comprising the states of Missouri, Arkansas and southeastern Oklahoma, including what is now Osage County.

As they returned home from the hunt, everything had to be transported on the backs of the Indians or on a dog travois. A travois consisted of two poles, attached at one end to a harness on a dog and the other end left to drag on the ground. In between them and spreading out in a "V" was fastened an oval or square frame netted with rawhide. Onto this arrangement, baggage and the assets from the hunt were fastened.

Travel and transportation in those days was very difficult and hunting, therefore, was carried on close to home until horses later afforded the Indians more mobility.

Horses Change Their Lives

By 1541 DeSoto had reached the Mississippi and about the same time Coronado and his army swept across the Southern Plains of Kansas. Both left stray horses in their wake. Spanish settlements spread many more horses throughout the Southern Plains and the horse became the Plains Indians' main mode of transportation and hunting. That was the beginning of the "golden age" of hunting and travel for the Plains Indian. One tribe after another began to ride horseback. Within one hundred and fifty years these Indians of the Plains were rarely seen on foot. Their entire life changed and, since every member of the community rode horses, life became nomadic.

The buffalo could then be followed with greater ease over greater distances. It was no longer necessary to stampede whole herds over the cliffs with the resulting waste of food and decimation of the herd, and much larger quantities of meat could be transported home. The Indian had moved into a life of plenty.

The Indian's horsemanship was unexcelled. He trained his mount to single out one buffalo in a herd, ride alongside it until the beast was felled with an arrow or a spear, then to continue cutting other buffalo out of the herd in the same manner. Since the horse was so well trained, the hunter was able to keep both of his hands free for the use of his weapons.

The horse also made the Indians more effective warriors. Riding bareback, the fighter could hang sideways from his horse by hooking one leg over the horse's back and his bow arm around and over the animal's neck. Reaching underneath with his bow, he could then shoot an arrow at an enemy with a minimum of his body exposed. Dead and injured comrades would often be removed from the battlefield on the run by this same technique of hanging low on one side of the horse to lift up a fallen comrade.

The horse gave the entire community mobility, since family tents and belongings could be moved quickly on horseback and brought close to the hunting grounds. Many tribes gave up living in permanent homes and what little agriculture they had formerly practiced many gave up completely. Distances which formerly took weeks were now covered in a single day. It was not uncommon for a tribe to cover 600 miles in one hunting season, and during this time, they had to be prepared to make or break camp at a moment's notice.

The Large Teepee Is Invented

This spawned the invention of a large teepee which was unexcelled in beauty, lightness, comfort, and serviceability. The framework of the teepee consisted of about 13 slim, rigid wooden poles about 18 feet long. The ends were tied together with thongs and the poles were raised and spread until the bottom ends formed a circle about 15 feet in diameter. Buffalo hides were then sewn together to fit the frame neatly. The hides were spread over the frame and the ends of the covering were laced together. The bottoms of the skins were pegged into the ground. A doorway, covered with a flap of skin, was provided and a collar-like flap held open by two poles was installed in the top for a chimney. This flap could be adjusted to take advantage of changes in the wind for the best removal of smoke and it could be closed completely when it rained or snowed. In summer, the bottom pegs were removed and the covering rolled up for additional ventilation. In winter, an interlining of skins was used for extra insulation. The teepee could be quickly erected and dismantled. Two women could set one up completely in about 15 minutes.

The sides of these teepees were very colorfully decorated with symbolic designs which had religious or historical meanings. In some

An Osage Indian Village. The Osage teepees were unexcelled
in their lightness, comfort and serviceability.

cases these designs depicted the family totem or portrayed important and heroic events in the history of the tribe.

Teepee villages were arranged in a circle, or circles, depending
on the size of the village and the space available. The order in which
families were arranged in these villages was not haphazard. Each
group of relatives had its own fixed place. The women who built the
village knew exactly where each teepee was to be erected in a pattern that never varied.

As with barn building by their white neighbors, building a new
teepee was a community affair. Friends and neighbors were invited
to a feast and afterwards the women would work together sewing
and assembling the teepee. The cutting of the skins required a great
deal of skill and was usually assigned to the woman with the most
experience. The woman with the happiest disposition was chosen
to work on the smoke flaps since it was believed that her personality would influence the satisfactory removal of smoke.

Since the buffalo herds never remained in one grazing area, the
village was always on the alert for the signal to break camp, a very
exciting operation. Scouts would return to the village with news
that the herd was on the move. Within a few hours, the complete
community was dismantled, the baggage was packed and men,
women and children were mounted and on the move.

At the head of this column rode the chiefs, at the flanks and in the rear were the armed warriors. Scouts rode up ahead in the distance, searching for signs of enemies or the buffalo herd.

Everything which the Plains Indians owned was designed for easy transport, another example of their ingenuity. The baggage, constructed of stiff, light rawhide in the form of bags, envelopes, and boxes, was folded away when not in use. These were called parfleches and were adjustable in size. All furniture was collapsible.

The teepee itself was transformed into a vehicle for transporting family baggage. This was known as the horse travois, similar to the dog travois, which could be quickly assembled and attached to a horse as soon as the teepee was dismantled. The poles were divided into two equal bunches which were then fastened at their thin ends, one bunch on either side, to a rawhide harness worn near the horse's neck. The other ends were left to drag on the ground. The teepee cover, along with the parfleches, was fastened on a frame installed between the poles.

Water for the trip was carried and stored in buffalo paunches and fire was carried in a buffalo horn slung over the shoulder. This horn was lined with moist rotten wood. Before extinguishing the final camp fire, an ember was placed inside the horn, together with a piece of fungus punk. The horn was then sealed with tight- fitting wood cork. The punk smoldered over a long journey and brought warmth to the new village from the old one.

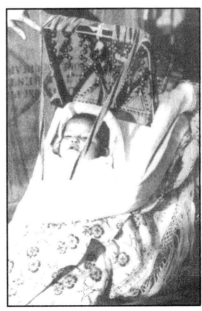

An Osage papoose.

Food

Buffalo meat was the principal food. Fish, very abundant in the well-stocked streams along which the tribes camped, were ignored. When a buffalo was killed, the meat was sometimes roasted, sometimes broiled over an open camp fire. Sometimes a stew consisting of pieces of meat and often vegetables was made by the stone-boiling method, which was another example of the Indian's ingenuity. Meat was eaten raw until the stone-boiling method was adopted. Hot stones were dropped into water in a hole in the ground shaped like a bowl and lined with water-tight skins or hides. The stones were heated in the fire, then picked up with sticks and dropped into the pot until the water or stew boiled. The adoption of this stone-boiling method changed their way of life. Food could now be cooked and preserved through periods of poor hunting and the health of the Indian improved by eating more easily digested food. Entirely new menus were developed. Meat was preserved by first drying thin strips of it in the hot sun or over a smoky fire. Next, it was beaten into shreds with sticks. Buffalo tallow was melted and mixed with it and then the meat was packed tightly into a bag of buffalo skin which was sewed up tight. Sometimes marrow fat and dried berries were added to the mixture. Indians called this condensed food pemmican. It was said to have been very nourishing and lasted for a long time.

Eventually, the glorious days of the buffalo-hunting tribes of the plains were gone. The life-giving buffalo had been killed off and the Indian hunter's way of life was substantially changed. With the white fur traders, came disease, moral degradation, whiskey and guns for tribal warfare. With the later arrival of white settlers, hungry for land, came complete economic and military defeat for the Indians and, finally, humiliating confinement on reservations.

The Osage Roach

The Indians of the plains usually wore their hair in long braids over their shoulders or loosely down their backs. The Osages wore their hair in roaches on ceremonial occasions. The roach was a strip of hair made to stand straight up in the middle of the head with the rest of the head shaved clean. Porcupine hair and deer tail were used to make the roach stand up straight.

Clothing

Clothing consisted of breech cloth, moccasins and fringed jackets. The moccasins of the Plains Indians, as opposed to others, were

Each feather represented a deed of valor.

hard-soled, made of tough buffalo hides or other tough rawhide. Buffalo robes were the most important items of the wardrobe and, even in the coldest winter, most Indians went about clad only in moccasins, breech cloth and robe. The women, however, wore loose dresses of skin in place of the breech cloth. The decorations painted and embroidered on clothing and parfleches were in many bright colors and always followed an angular, geometric pattern.

Awards for Valor

The beautiful, wide-spreading, feathered war bonnet later worn by most Indians was developed by the Plains Indian. In the old days it was worn only on special occasions and was very symbolic. Its beauty was only of secondary importance. Its real value was in its supernatural power to protect the wearer. The bonnet had to be earned through brave deeds in battle. The feathers themselves signified the deeds which had been performed to earn them. Some warriors might only be able to obtain two or three honor feathers in their entire lifetime because they were so difficult to earn. These war honors were called coups. The Osages also called them d-don. There were several ways in which they could be earned. The highest honor to be won was the touching of a live enemy with the bare hands or a coup stick in the midst of battle. This might seem strange, but the honor was not for the harm done to the enemy, but for the courage it displayed in doing it. Being the first to touch an enemy who had fallen in battle was another high honor.

Warfare had to have a meaning and was strictly controlled by the clan's priests who had to sanction the organization of the war party. There were 13 war honors (o-don) awarded for various acts of valor during an organized war party.

The feathers were notched and decorated to designate the nature of the deeds they represented. The feathers told an individual story of killing, scalping, capturing an enemy's weapon or shield and whether the deed had been done on horseback or on foot.

The eagle was considered the greatest, most powerful of all birds and the finest bonnets were, therefore, made of the eagle's feathers. When about ten honors had been won, the warrior was sent to secure the eagle feathers with which to make his bonnet.

Eagle hunting was very dangerous and time-consuming. The warrior had to leave the tribe and travel to high country where eagles nested. When the destination was reached, ceremonies were conducted to appeal to the spirits of the birds to be killed. A satisfactory spot on a high hill was selected and a hole large enough for the warrior to stand up in was dug in the ground. To allay the suspicions of the eagle, the earth taken from the digging of this hole was scattered over a wide area. This hole was then covered with twigs, leaves, stones, and earth and, while it was still dark, the hunter crawled into the hole and covered his hiding place from within the hole. On top of the camouflaged cover, a piece of meat was placed. A thong (a strap, or strip of leather used for fastening things) attached to the meat was held in the hunter's hand. When an eagle swooped down for the meat, it found that it could not be removed. At the exact instant the struggle for the bait began, the hunter quickly reached up through the covering, grabbed the bird by both legs, pulled it into the pit and broke its back by crushing it with his foot to prevent breaking the wings in the struggle.

The War Shield

The war-shield of buffalo bull hide was the warrior's most sacred possession and it was as valued as the war bonnet for its power of "protective medicine." Its practical use, of course, was to ward off arrows, spears, and even bullets, but as far as the Indian was concerned, the real protection was from the design painted on its front and on its buckskin cover. Permission to possess and use a shield came through a dream in which an animal appeared and told the warrior how many shields he could make and how they were to be decorated. Along with this information, he was also told how he must paint himself and decorate his horse. The shield decorations took the form of animals and the elements of nature.

Communication

Although all of the American Indians used sign language to communicate with those they did not understand, the Plains Indians, who came into constant contact with other tribes and encountered many strange tongues, developed a greater ability to use this method of communication. The Plains Indian's sign language vocabulary was the greatest of all Indians and the highest developed. They also used smoke signals more widely and more often than other Indians since the open country of the plains was ideal for this long-distance transmission of messages. They set up signal stations at strategic high points and messages were relayed over distances of many miles by controlling the smoke of the smoldering fire with a blanket. At night fire signals were used.

With puffs of smoke and the blinking of lights, the speed, slowness or number of signals told of the enemy's approach, defeat or victory in battle, or the movement of a buffalo herd.

Horse Stealing Was Commendable

Warfare and horse stealing were constant on the plains. When game became scarce, it was necessary to invade the territory of a neighbor to secure food. Many times this resulted in conflict which was perpetuated by revenge.

Revenge was often carried out by small raiding bands whose purpose was to scalp enemies and steal horses. Horse stealing, however, was not always the result of revenge. Stealing horses was a consuming passion with the Plains Indians and they preferred getting them by raiding than by any other method. They often scorned the many wild herds of horses in favor of those already trained and belonging to someone else. A young warrior was taught that, to steal the horse of a stranger, was one of the most commendable acts he could commit.

The Sun Dance

In June, during buffalo breeding season and when the summer grass of the prairie was high most tribes assembled far from home to celebrate the greatest religious ceremony, the Sun Dance. The Sun

Dance was the highest and most meaningful emotional experience of the year.[2] From all directions, came small groups of the tribal family, which had been separated from each other for the past year, to assemble in a reunion. They gathered in a large circular encampment around the tribe's sacred teepee. The great circle was symbolic of tribal brotherhood, warmth and a time for joyful activities. Among the men, ceremonial pipes were smoked. There were great feasts, mock battles, ceremonial hunts, and recounting the past year's experiences. The Osages were remarkable for their social organization.

The Word "Osage" Meant "Enemy"

During the 18th century and the first part of the 19th Century, the Osages were at war with practically every other tribe of the Plains, and a large number of those of the Woodlands. To many of these tribes the word "Osage" was synonymous with "enemy." Among all the tribes of the southern plains and many of those of the Gulf region, the Osages attained a great reputation as fearless fighters. The Quapaw Indians proved to be a strong bulwark against the Osages, but they suffered many casualties as a consequence and part of them were forced to move to another location. The town they established in this new location was also attacked by the Osages who inflicted such heavy losses on its inhabitants that the Quapaw again were forced to migrate.

Apparently the Osages, the Kansas, the Quapaws, Omahas and Poncas once lived together east of the Mississippi River as one nation, but separated following a western migration. As early as 1698, British-sponsored tribes of the Illinois country launched raiding parties against the Osages and the Kansas, seeking fur pelts and slaves. The governments of Spain, France, Britain and the new United States were in almost constant competition for domination of the Osages and other tribes.

Trade Changed Osage Life

The Osages' trade with the European nations had a profound impact on Osage culture. It brought them some of the conveniences of western civilization. Woven goods, blankets, cloth, silk ribbon, beads, knives, axes, kettles, guns and metal tools were traded to the Osages for hides and slaves. Native industries were altered because

---

[2]The Osage Tribe still holds its dances in June.

Ready for the warpath. To many tribes the word "Osage"
was synonymous with "enemy."

of trade, but so was warfare. With the military advantage of guns
and the French demand for more slaves, the Osages increased their
war-making against other tribes and expanded Osage territory
through these conquests. Hunting and warfare to control prime hunting grounds became increasingly important and, as a result, the little
agriculture the tribe engaged in declined.

Trade with the French had begun at the end of the seventeenth
century and developed rapidly. During the last quarter of the 18th
Century, the most important export items for the Osages became
furs and hides.

Caught between French and Spanish traders, some Osages
formed an alliance with the French trader Chouteau in 1802 and
moved near where the Neosho and Arkansas rivers meet. This was
a very rich, productive area. Zebulon Pike (discoverer of Pike's Peak)
reported that 'the borders of the Arkansas River may be termed the
paradise of our territory.... Of all the countries ever visited by the
footsteps of civilized man, there was never one that produced game
in greater abundance." General Pike visited the Osages in their villages along the Osage River in Missouri in 1806. When he made his
western exploratory trip at the request of Thomas Jefferson, he took
many Osages with him as guides. When Pike battled the Spanish in
southern Kansas, Osage Indians served as scouts.

No serious change was made in the social organization of the Osages until a rivalry arose between certain traders, who, to further their own enterprises, recognized as chiefs certain influential and ambitious men who were not within the established order of chieftainship. A breach was created in the tribal organization and gradually the authority of the real chiefs was weakened.

General Zebulon Pike, who used Osage scouts.

❧ Chapter 2 ❧

The Osages Become Reservation Indians

Osage Land, Part of the Louisiana Purchase

The land of the Osages was included within President Thomas Jefferson's Louisiana Purchase from France in 1803 and, in the early wars, the tribe had fought with the French against the British. Like most tribes, its subsequent migrations coincided with the western trend of the white man's exploration. For every step forward taken by the white pioneers, the American Indian had to retreat one step. In describing the westward migration of white settlers, one Osage elder said, "They just kept coming like ants." The first impact of the whites' westward expansion was felt by the Osages as displaced eastern Indian tribes such as the Delaware, Sac, Fox, Kickapoo and Shawnee, who were pushed out by the white settlers, entered Osage territory, frequently with the encouragement of the federal government's representatives.

The year 1806 marked the beginning of a gradual process by which the Osages relinquished their territorial possessions to the United States. On November 10, 1808, the Osages signed a treaty ceding to the U.S. Government all their territorial claims to land which now constitutes the present states of Missouri and Arkansas. The remainder of their land was further curtailed by a treaty signed in 1818. The treaty of 1825 required them to give up their ancient home along the Little Osage River.

Kansas Reservation

By this 1825 treaty, the Osage Tribe ceded to the U. S. Government its "title, right and interest to land in Missouri, Arkansas, and further west" in exchange for a large reservation in Kansas. (Under the treaties of 1808, 1818 and 1825, the Osages ceded 96,800,000 acres

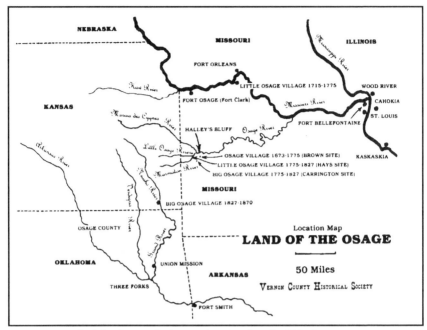

Land of the Osages before ceding land to the U.S. Government.

to the U.S. government, receiving in return $166,300 in cash, annuities, cattle, horses, farming equipment and merchandise — approximately one cent for every six acres.)

Enactment of the Indian Removal Act of 1830 allowed for the removal of southeastern Indians into Osage territory, causing the Osages' reservation in Kansas to be overrun by other tribes and later by white settlers. As a result, the game animals were largely decimated, leaving the Osages short of food to eat and furs for trade. Fortunately, at about this time two things occurred: a new market for buffalo robes developed and peace was made with the Comanche and the Kiowa. This gave the Osages renewed access to large buffalo herds around the salt plains in eastern Oklahoma and new trading partners. The Osages acted as middlemen between these other plains tribes and European traders, exchanging goods of European-American manufacture for buffalo robes and horses.

Through this Indian Removal Act of 1830, the U.S. government had succeeded in moving to the Indian territory out west the five civilized tribes when they were removed from the fertile east coast land which white farmers wanted. The Cherokees got most of the northeast corner of the territory. The Seminoles and the Creeks were sent to the southern one third.

Washington Irving Describes the Osages

Writer Washington Irving visited the Osages in 1832 and described them as "stately fellows" and as "the finest looking Indians I have seen in the West.... They have fine Roman countenances, and broad deep chests... like so many noble bronze figures." All observers described the Osages as being exceptionally tall, most of them standing well over six feet and some reportedly as tall as seven feet.

With the Osages now located on a reservation, the U.S. government and missionaries began to implement a policy to "civilize" and "Christianize" the Osages. This program, conducted by the Jesuits and the Sisters of Loretto, religious orders of the Catholic Church, was designed to make the Osages into farmers and to teach them to become manual laborers. The American Civil War ended what little farming the Osages had begun. The Jesuits urged the Osages to support the North and trader John Matthews urged them to support the South, but few Osages actually got involved in the Civil War. However 244 Osage Indians did serve with the Union armies.

The greatest impact the Civil War had on the Osages was that it stimulated more encroachment by white settlers. Immediately following the war, there was a rush of white families to the rich farmlands of Kansas who looked enviously on the Osage lands. Between 1860 and 1870 the European-American population of Kansas tripled. These white settlers ignored reservation boundaries and stole Osage horses and food. They argued that, since the Osages did not make productive use of their land, it should be sold and the Indians sent elsewhere. Railroads, too, stretched out grasping, hungry tentacles toward Osage land. This encroachment on Osage land pressured the U.S. government to negotiate a new treaty with the Osages.

Responding to that pressure from white settlers who were invading the Osages' Kansas territory, Congress enacted a law in 1870 which authorized — forced is a more accurate word — the sale of the Osage land holdings in Kansas, some five million acres. The proceeds of the sale — $8.5 million — were to be used to purchase a new reservation in what was then the Indian territory for $1 million and the balance deposited in the U.S. Treasury for the tribe's account.

A strip of land along the Kansas border called the Cherokee Outlet had been set aside to give that tribe a corridor to the plains for buffalo hunting. However, the Cherokees did not use the land for this purpose. They stayed closed to home and farmed. Because the Cherokees had supported the Confederates during the American Civil War, the U.S. government decided to put the Osages between the Cherokee land and the Cherokee Outlet. So, arrangements were made for the Osages to buy this land which, ironically, they had previously ceded to the U.S. government in 1825.

The new reservation was purchased from the Cherokee Indians and the federal government conducted the negotiations for the Osage Tribe. After the winter hunt, the Osages began their migration to their new home. When they left Kansas they were told their new lands would cost them 25 cents per acre. Once they arrived in the Indian territory, however, the Cherokees demanded more money since several other tribes who were making similar purchases from the Cherokees had created a seller's market. President Ulysses S. Grant settled the common dispute by setting the price of the land at 70 cents per acre.

Oklahoma Reservation

The new reservation consisted of 1,470,058,980 acres and extended from Bartlesville on the east to Ponca City on the west, from the Kansas State border on the north along the meandering Arkansas River to Tulsa on the south. Although the tribe consisted of only 3,956 members, the new reservation was larger than the State of Delaware. The land was very poor and almost worthless for agriculture. Many of the Osage leaders wanted to move farther west to a more fertile area, but Chief Pawhuska (White Hair) counseled otherwise. He reasoned that, if the Osage moved to good farm land, eventually the white man would want it and they would be forced to move again. He argued that it was better to take land the white man would never want. His view prevailed. In 1872 the Osages moved to their new home.

The Commissioner of Indian Affairs, in his report for the year 1872, speaking of the Osage and their new home in the Oklahoma territory, said:

"Their reservation is bounded on the north by the south line of Kansas, east by the ninety-sixth degree of west longitude, and south and west by the Arkansas River, and contains approximately 1,760,000 acres.... By the act of July 15, 1870, provision was made for the sale of all the lands belonging to the Osages within the limits of Kansas and for their removal across the line into the Indian territory.... They still follow the chase, the buffalo being their main dependence for food.... They have since their removal begun farming to some extent, having already about 2,000 acres under culti-

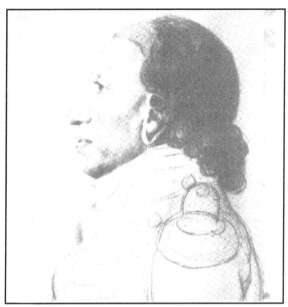

Payouska, or Paw-hui-skah, or Pawhuska, or White Hair , the wise Osage chief
after whom the capital of the Osage Nation — Pawhuska — was named.

*vation. Their agent reports the reservation 'poorly adapted for civilizing
purposes,' there being only one small valley of fertile soil, barely affording
enough good farming land for 4,000 Indians. Having just located, they
have at present but one school in operation, with an attendance of 38
scholars."*

The Osage Nation's capital was established at Pawhuska. They
established a second settlement at Hominy and a third at Gray Horse
(near what is now Fairfax). Three branches of the tribe settled in
those three communities. In 1872 there were actually five bands (divisions) of the Osage Tribe.[3] These bands settled in five areas corre-
sponding to the five traditional villages to which they had belonged.

How the Clans Were Created

The Osages historicaly lived in three village communities, thus
perpetuating the story of a tribal division that was forced by accident. The story handed down concerning this division was that the
Osage people had built their village upon the banks of a large river
where they lived for a long period of time. When this river over-
flowed its banks, the flood forced them to flee in panic toward a

---

[3]Today there are three: The Pawhuska, Hominy and Grayhorse districts.

high hill, taking with them only the absolute necessities of life. Many tribe members continued their flight until they reached the summit of the hill where they established a temporary camp. From that time on, this group was referred to as Pa-cui'-gthin, Dwellers-Upon-the-Hilltop. Another group halted and pitched its camp in a forest. This group was spoken of as the Con-dseu'-gthin, Dwellers-in-the-Up-land-Forest. A third group was caught in a thicket of thorny trees and bushes, where the people set up their temporary dwellings. They became known by the name Wa-xa'-ga-u-gthin, Dwellers-in-the-Thorny-Thicket. A fourth group stopped and camped near the foot of the hill, and were known by the name Lu-dse'-ta, The Dwellers-Below. In later times the people of this group united with the Dwellers-in-the-Thorny-Thicket and lost their identity.

When they moved to the Indian territory which is now Oklahoma, the Dwellers-Upon-the-Hilltop established their village at Gray Horse, the Dwellers-in-the-Upland-Forest at Hominy; and the Dwellers-in-the-Thorny-Thicket at Pawhuska.

(When Oklahoma became a state in 1907 Pawhuska became the county seat of Osage County, the largest county in Oklahoma and the third largest county in the United States, and the Osages became Oklahoma citizens.)

Osages Face Near Starvation

The buffalo was by now almost extinct and the Bureau of Indian Affairs tried again to convert the Osages into farmers. The Osages did settle down to a life of farming, even though the soil with too many hills, too much poor timber and too much underlying stone, made farming very difficult. The Osages lamented that farming in Oklahoma was much worse than it had been in Kansas. For many years, the life of the Osage Indians was very hard. Occasionally, the federal government would give members of the tribe a small check, money paid to the government by cattle ranchers who grazed cattle on Osage land.

Loss of the buffalo herds (largely from white hide hunters) brought the Osage to near starvation, reducing the tribe's population by two-thirds. Coinciding with this decline, the power of the chiefs was also undermined by the federal government and competing traders' support of rival chiefs.

The Osages lived quietly and modestly in huts on the scant supplies furnished by the federal government from the Osages' own money on deposit in the U.S. Treasury. For 25 years there was little interference from the white man. When they moved to their present reservation in Oklahoma the U.S. government paid them $10 per year each in cash and supplied limited rations. When the tribal body was organized in 1878 and Big Bill Joe was chosen Chief, the Osages were changed from a ration to a cash income of $160 a year.

Constitution Adopted in 1884

In 1884 the tribe adopted a constitution which was recognized by the federal government. By the late 1880's many full blood Osages were leasing their farms to white tenants. Also, annuities increased from interest on the Osage Tribe's money in the U.S. Treasury. All land was held in common by the tribe, but the white tenant farmers and ranchers, as well as some mixed-blood Osages, wanted to buy the land outright so they began pressing for abolishing the reservation.

℘ Chapter 3 ℘

Oil is Discovered

Edwin B. Foster of Westerly, Rhode Island, who was then building a railroad from Kansas City, Kansas, to Coffeyville, Kansas, thought there might be oil on the Osage land. It was his son, H. V. Foster, however, who reaped the benefit from his father's foresight. In 1896 James Bigheart, then Principal Chief of the tribe, executed a lease of the entire Osage Nation land to the Foster Oil and Gas Company of New York for a nominal sum. The lease was approved by Hoke Smith, Secretary of the Interior under President Grover Cleveland. Foster drilled two dry holes near the Kansas line and then sublet a portion of the Osage Nation land to other oil and gas developers, who succeeded in drilling producing wells. On October 28, 1897, the first producing oil well on the Osage reservation yielded 20 barrels of oil per day. Foster held the main lease and later incorporated the Indian Territory Illuminating Oil Company. This company also owned and developed the famous Oklahoma City field. The I.T.I.O. made millions for Foster and others associated with him in developing the Osage fields. They held a monopoly until 1916 when Osage leases began selling for fabulous sums to other oil operators.

Headrights System Adopted

On June 28, 1906, the federal government enacted a law under which the 2,229 members of the Osage Tribe were to receive, through the government, an equal number of shares, known as headrights, in any income growing out of the tribe's property. This number of headrights remained constant whether the number of the tribe increased or decreased. In other words, an Osage Indian born after that time could inherit only his or her proportionate share of the headright of one of the 2,229 members of the tribe who were en-

An Osage maid. A headright and often a greedy, vicious white husband.

rolled as of June 28, 1906. Various Osage Indians drew revenue from or were allotted tracts of land based upon these headrights. The original allotment of a homestead to each Osage Indian consisted of 160 acres, but this was later supplemented by various land grants until each headright allotment consisted of approximately 657 acres.

This Act of 1906 practically abolished the reservation, but unlike similar acts, it reserved the mineral rights to the tribe, creating in effect an "underground reservation."

The discovery of oil eventually brought hundreds of thousands of dollars to the Osages, but this wealth proved to be a mixed blessing.

Distribution of funds to the Osage Indians differed somewhat from other tribes in that a common pool was made of all earnings derived from the tribe's land and divided among tribe members on the basis of the 2,229 headrights which had been established in 1906.

Money in such abundance astounded the Indians, but even greater wealth was to follow which made the first small checks look insignificant.

The federal government stipulated that the tribe was to receive one-sixth of all the oil that was extracted. In 1916 oil was flowing from numerous wells, but even more wells would come on line. The number of actual producing oil wells on the reservation as of June 30, 1920, was 5,859. As of June 30, 1922, the number had increased to

8,579. Nearly all of the reservation land was leased for oil or natural gas production.

It is interesting to compare the Osages' wealth in former times with their wealth after oil was discovered on the reservation. The net per capita payment to each Osage who was entitled to receive income from the tribe's common fund in 1880 was $10.50 per year; in 1900, $200 per year; in 1910, $250 per year; in 1915, $221.31 per year; in 1920, $8,090 per year; in 1921 (the year of the first pertinent Osage Indian murder), $8,600; in 1923, (the year of multiple murders), $12,440 per year (equivalent to more than $980,000 per year in 1998 dollars). Every time a new well was drilled, the Osages became richer.

The average Indian family numbered four persons. Two or three members of the family often owned one or more of the 2,229 Osage shares. This meant a family income of more than $25,000, (about $2 million per year in 1998 dollars).[4] Since the tribe's rolls had been closed at 2,229, each tribe member — man, woman and child — who possessed a headright received one share or 1/2229th of the tribe's quarterly bonuses and royalties from the production of oil and natural gas.

When an Osage died, the headright passed to his or her heirs, making it possible for one individual to hold several headrights, or a fraction of a headright.

The Osages, through this oil income, became the richest people per capita in the world. This attracted a horde of vicious outlaws determined through every means possible, including murder, to separate the Indians from their money. Never has one group of people been more cruelly and more openly exploited.

Osages Face Absorption

Dr. Francis LaFlesche, an authority on the Osage Tribe, said in 1921 that the Osage Tribe was rapidly approaching extinction by absorption into the white race. The 1910 census showed that out of the 2,100 persons enrolled as Osages only 885 were full-blooded, and it was believed that many of those counted as full-blooded were in fact mixed-bloods. The 1910 census gave the entire population of the Osage Tribe as 1,373 with 591 full-blooded.

Along with this process of absorption, the Osage language was

[4] Note: For an approximation of what the dollar amounts mentioned in the book would be in 1998 dollars, multiply the figure by 80.

also becoming obsolete. Most of the Osages could speak English, but in their conversation some preferred to use their native language. LaFlesche reported that Osage children attending public schools freely associated with the white students, speaking with them in English, but when they were at home, they spoke both languages, "often dropping from one to the other in their conversation without a break in the sentence or flow of thought, both languages being spoken with equal fluency."

❧ Chapter 4 ❧

The Osage Indians in 1923[5]

In 1923 alone, the Osage Tribe received $27 million. In two decades the Osages would receive more money from oil than all the old west gold rushes combined had yielded!

As a train entered Osage County, a visitor watched the area's scenery flash across the windows like a silent movie on prairie life. In the few areas where there was pasture land, outcroppings of stone showed through the grass. Now and then on the creek bottom in a small valley, an isolated cornfield was under cultivation. Suddenly there appeared on the horizon hundreds of oil wells. The train passed a small farmhouse surrounded by oil wells. Three pipe lines, one of which ran into a cornfield choked with weeds, crisscrossed the neglected and overgrown yard. When they struck oil in that farmer's fields he took the money and let his corn go to grass.

The train stopped at a village which was peppered with wells. Oil tanks lined the roadway and there were wells in front yards and back yards and even one in a churchyard.

Finally, the train[6] arrived in Pawhuska, county seat of Osage County and the vortex of all the swirling activities of oil men, federal government representatives, unscrupulous parasites who had come to prey on the Indians, and the Osage Indians themselves. Named for the great Chief Paw-hui-skah

---

[5] This narrative is based in part on an article which appeared in the April 3, 1926, issue of the *Literary Digest* (which in turn drew on an article by Homer Croy which appeared in Liberty magazine) and an article by William G. Shepherd from the August, 1920, issue of *Harpers* magazine.

[6] The trains stopped running to Pawhuska in the late 1970's.

or White Hair[7] who had led a delegation to Washington to meet with President Thomas Jefferson, the town of Pawhuska, which lies 25 miles south of the Kansas border and 100 miles west of the Missouri border, was aswirl with activity and excitement. People of Pawhuska frequently boasted that the first Boy Scout Troop in America was established in Pawhuska in 1909 for both Indian and white boys.

Old trees lined the streets, and old stone buildings of the Civil War era and older, testified that Pawhuska had been a U.S. government Indian center for several generations. Red brick buildings and costly concrete-and-steel buildings were under construction and others had obviously been completed recently.

One tree in Pawhuska, "the million dollar elm," became famous because on 18 separate occasions 160-acre tracts of land were auctioned off for more than a million dollars under that tree. The auctioneer, Colonel (his real name) E. Walters from Skeedee, Oklahoma, also became famous.[8] Walters would manipulate his voice and his gavel while his sharp eyes instantly spotted the slightest nod from a bidder, usually raising the price in $100,000 increments. One auction on a hot summer day drew $10,888,000. Walters, exhausted from the grueling activity, was soaked with perspiration. That day he more than earned his usual $10 fee, but the Osages had previously given him a large diamond ring to show their gratitude for his work.

---

[7] Chief White Hair was originally called Gra-to-moh-se (Iron Hawk), a six-feet-seven inch or six-feet-eight inch Osage brave. He got the name Paw-hui-skah or White Hair in an interesting way. At the Battle of Wabash on November 4, 1791, one of the worst defeats the Americans ever suffered from the Indians, General Arthur St. Clair led 3,000 American soldiers to put down an Indian uprising. The Osages allied themselves with the other tribes to fight the whites. The young Osage named Gra-to-moh-se, believing he had killed an American officer, leaned over him and grabbed his hair to scalp him. In those days officers wore perukes, the powdered wigs of the British courts. When the officer's white wig came off in the Indian's hand, Gra-to-moh-se screamed, amazed at how easily the white man's scalp had left his head. The scream awakened the wounded officer who also screamed, seeing that he was about to be scalped. The Indian thought he was witnessing a man rising from the dead. In the confusion, the American was able to run away, leaving the Indian amazed and still holding the white wig. From that day forward Iron Hawk was known as White Hair or Paw-hui-skah and he wore the white wig for the rest of his life, thinking it would protect him against death. ("The Deaths of Sybil Bolton" by Dennis McAuliffe, Jr., Random House, 1994; The Encyclopedia Americana, International Edition (Danbury, CT: Grolier, 1990, Vol. 24, 104; The New Encyclopedia Britannica, 15th Edition (Chicago: 1993, Vol. 10, Micropaedia, 313; and "History of the Osage People" by Louis Burns, 257.

[8] 1976 book, "Oil in Oklahoma" by Robert Gregory.

The streets of Pawhuska during the 1920's. (Details of a painting of the
Citizens National Bank by Bill Alsabrook of Tulsa.)

Details from a painting of Pawhuska's Duncan Hotel, the finest during the 1920's. The hotel was completely destroyed by fire in the late 1920's. (Paiting by Bill Alsobrook of Tulsa.)

Pawhuska's Bank of Commerce during the 1920's (Painting by Bill Alsabrook of Tulsa.)

Pawhuska's City Hall building which was originally built to serve as the Council House for the Osage Nation. It was purchased by the City of Pawhuska in 1907. (Painting by Bill Alsabrook of Tulsa.)

The Triangle Building in Pawhuska in the 1920's. (Painting by Bill Alsabrook of Tulsa.)

With beautiful modern houses, a camp in the backyard.

These auctions only gave successful bidders the right to drill for oil. There was no guarantee that they would find it and, if they did, they then had to pay royalties on what the well yielded.

The 1920 U.S. Census gave the population of Pawhuska as 6,414,[9] nearly triple what it had been ten years earlier, and by 1923 there was probably even more people there drawn like a magnet by the oil boom.

(The Osage Tribe's estimated population for the year 1807 was 6,200. In 1804, Lewis and Clark, who were sent on their expedition by President Thomas Jefferson, estimated there were 500 warriors in the Great Osage band, about half as many in the Little Osage band and about 600 in the Arkansas band. In 1843, the U.S. Indian Office furnished the figure of 4,102. In 1877, the U.S. Indian Office listed 3,001; in 1884, 1,547; in 1886, 1,582; and in 1906, 1,994. The 1910 census recorded 1,373, all but 28 in Oklahoma. The U.S. Indian Office report for 1923 listed 2,099 Osages. In 1930, 2,344 were reported and in 1937, 3,649.)

Not many of the Osage Indians lived in Pawhuska. They had a village of their own two miles from town, with a great circular meeting house in the center of the fenced-off community. In the Indian village the houses, with all modern conveniences, were small, but each Indian, in addition to his main house, had a summer house —

---

[9]The 1990 census gave the population of Pawhuska as 3,825.

a screened-in, but otherwise unwalled, frame structure where the family spent its summer days. They filled their homes with expensive furniture they often did not use. They bought brass beds and often slept on the floor or on blankets in the yard or summer house. Some of them bought solid silver knives and then ate with their fingers.

Most of the Osages had Mexican, Negro or white servants. These servants were supposed to till the land, care for the livestock, and perform all the menial tasks about the house, but they gave the least possible service for the largest obtainable wages, and were often a liability rather than an asset.

Most of the Indian women would not cook on stoves, but preferred camp fires on the ground. They also preferred to draw gourds of water instead of tapping the pump-filled mains. Surrounded with the comforts of civilization, many of them instinctively followed their old Indian ways and adhered to their old customs.

There were no street lights on the village roads. All the village houses seemed to have been recently painted and yellow seemed to be the color of preference. In some yards gasoline engines pumped water into back-yard tanks.

A Typical Osage Family

Bacon Rind, one of the wisest and most popular leaders of the tribe who had traveled to Washington with a delegation of other Osages to discuss the tribe's problems, was a member of the tribal council which urged that the federal government send the Department of Justice's Bureau of Investigation to solve the Osage murders. Bacon Rind lived in a typical two-story, yellow house, but he spent most of his time in his summerhouse. As most Osages, he was a large man. In 1923 he was about fifty-five years old with a deep and booming voice. He wore a big black felt hat, a brown shirt and two separate leather trouser legs hanging from thongs attached to a belt.

On the grass at the end of the wooden-floored summerhouse, Mrs. Bacon Rind, a large, black-haired woman dressed in a loose, clean, white gown, was cooking. She wore black silk stockings and patent-leather slippers, the latest fashion in Osage circles. She sat on a blanket spread on the grass. A healthy-looking, blond-haired white servant girl was setting the table in the summerhouse. On the fire, a kettle of grease boiled and on a board beside Mrs. Bacon Rind there were strips of rolled dough which she twisted into pretzel-like fig-

Bacon Rind, a popular, famous Osage leader at the time of the murders and a member of the Tribal Council which sought the FBI's assistance in solving the murders.

ures to make Indian bread. She dropped the dough into the boiling grease and it swelled until it resembles a doughnut large enough to fill a dinner plate. A long 20-seat wooden table dominated the summerhouse. There was one rocking-chair and a gaily painted oil stove.

Bacon Rind took his visitor to the front room, the company parlor of the house. "Come, see this," he bellowed.

On the wall across the room, he displayed a glass plaque of the American flag and the American eagle. At the bottom of the plaque there was a photograph of an American soldier.

"My son," bellowed Bacon Rind, tapping himself on the chest. "My son, George. Fought in Europe in Rainbow Division." He explained that he had held two feasts in honor of George, the first feast when word came that George had gotten into the fight. There was no news as to how George had fared, but the fact that he had been in battle upholding the warrior tradition of the tribe, was enough. Bacon Rind bought cattle and had them slaughtered for the feast and virtually stripped the Pawhuska stores bare, buying provisions for the celebration. There were dances in the roundhouse. Osage Indians came from many areas, and those who held grudges against each other or were from competing political or feuding factions exchanged peace gifts of horses, blankets, pipes, and other valuables. The feast raged for two days, in celebration of the fact that

George, the tribe's champion sharpshooter, fastest runner and best wrestler, had gotten his chance to kill America's enemies.

Bacon Rind gave an even more elaborate feast when George returned home. George had medals and a paper from Washington saying that he was a fine fighter. This second feast lasted much longer than the first and more was eaten, there was more dancing, more chanting, and an exchange of even more valuable peace presents.

"I got presents, too," Bacon Rind boasted. "Look!"

He opened a leather traveling bag and took out a magnificent

Chief Bacon Rind

feather headpiece and three ceremonial fans made of eagle feathers. The handles of these fans were covered with tiny beads and on each fan there was a beaded American flag.

Bacon Rind displayed another gift. He emptied a soft chamois-skin bag onto the sofa and what appeared to be dried apricots tumbled out. Bacon Rind admired a double handful.

"Mescal," he said. "Eat four, five! Then you come very close to God!" He raised his gaze toward heaven and held up a hand. "You put some in water and they get very large, like apple. Then you eat them slowly, like tobacco. Throw water away. Never drink mescal. Very bad."

The Osages did not consider mescal a narcotic, but believed it was a gift from God to bring them closer to Him. The effect of the mescal was very quick and strong, giving them a dreamy, happy feeling and they considered it a kind of sacred sacrament.

Bacon Rind[10] explained that he was going to talk about God in the meeting house the following Sunday. "It will be a mescal ceremony. Everyone will eat a little mescal and then he will talk about the Great Spirit. It will make everyone happy. Yes, yes!" he roared, raising a hand above his head. "We talk God, Sunday. That very good."

Before the Osages became rich, they could not afford the luxury of sending down into Mexico for the dried pods of the mescal plant. A bag of mescal such as Bacon Rind displayed would cost several hundred dollars in 1923.

In addition to mescal, alcohol was a problem among the Osages. The federal government tried to keep liquor away from all Indian reservations, but with little success. The Osage territory was very profitable for bootleggers.

Many Squander Their Money

Many of the Osages lived conservatively, invested their money wisely and used their wealth responsibly, such as for their children's education, but many squandered it and had little to show for the expenditures.

A large number of the Osages, taking advantage of their riches, spent their summers at Colorado Springs, Colorado, and other expensive resorts, enjoying the ultimate in luxuries.

---

[10]When Bacon Rind died, numerous mourners came from great distances to pay their respects at his funderal. Hundreds of cars formed a procession from Pawhuska to his burial spot on the top of a hill overlooking the Osage Village.

Unscrupulous white parasites, attracted to the area by the oil boom, preyed upon the wealthy Osages, selling them diamonds, jewelry, rare vases, fine rugs and tapestry and other things that they were not accustomed to owning. Many bought grand pianos (which were often left outside in the yard), phonographs and radios, all for exorbitant prices. Women's hosiery, which could be bought for $1 elsewhere, cost $5 a pair in Osage County. Shoes which cost $5 elsewhere, cost Osage women $25.

Many Osages found that leaving the management of their financial affairs to their creditors relieved them of much mental exertion. The creditors found this arrangement very profitable. The Osages received their income in quarterly payments. For some weeks preceding a payment they were often hard up for cash, having experienced no difficulty in disposing of their last installment. They applied to a bank for funds, or to one of the many loan sharks on the reservation. The Osage thumb marked a note and received a sum of money in return, often indifferent as to the relationship between the sum indicated on the note and the sum actually received.

At the many stores on the reservation, the Osages' credit was almost limitless. They bought freely, lavishly and kept no accounts. They could also borrow money at the store. On annuity payment day they took their checks to the trader and received without question whatever was given in exchange. If the balance proved to be insufficient to live extravagantly until next payment day, they ran up more credit. It did not occur to many Osages to audit their accounts.

In most of the cases of excessive indebtedness the obligations covered nothing of permanent value, such as the purchase of livestock or improvements on their land.

Marriage Swindles

Pretty Osage girls were wooed with flattery, smiles and lies by rough, swearing, illiterate men. The trusting girls, flattered to be courted by white men, would surrender to a short, passionate romance and then find themselves married to these rough characters or coming home with venereal diseases or unwanted babies. These swindlers got the Indian girl's oil money, spent it, stole from her and then deserted her. Unable to return to the tribe, she became an outcast, welcome neither by the Indians nor the whites.

A gray-haired doctor who had been in the Indian country for many years was the guardian for several Osage girls who had been victimized through such marriages. He said to a visitor, "They don't get a fair shake, these rich Osage girls. They marry some white rascal who's after their money and the girls often are left almost hopelessly diseased. It's a downright shame." He pointed out his window. "See that young rascal there? That villain ought to be run out of town. He married a fine Indian girl for her money and I had to take her to the hospital she was so diseased. We got a divorce for her. It's sad, but after an Indian girl has married a white man, few of the Osage men will marry her."

In May, 1923, Mary Elkins, one of the wealthiest Osages with 8 headrights, met Wilbur Corbet, a second-rate boxer. During a three-day drinking binge, she married Corbet in Kansas City. They traveled to Colorado Springs where she was arrested for drunkenness. Witnesses swore that she was so drunk during the wedding ceremony that she did not know what was happening. Meanwhile, Corbet kept Mary locked up in a drug- and alcohol-induced stupor while he spent her money as quickly as possible. Her guardian was able to prove that the marriage scheme had been planned by conspirators in Fairfax who hired Corbet to marry Mary and then, through him, bilk her out of her money. When the plot was exposed, Corbet accepted a $1,000 payment to agree to annulment of the phony marriage.

Osage men were also victimized through marriage plots devised by guardians and outlaws. Don Dickerson, a full-blooded Osage who lived in Fairfax, met a white woman, dated her for about one week and married her. Three days later, she left him, divorced him and received $100,000 alimony. The guardians and the crooks got a cut of the money. Up to the time oil was found in paying quantities, very few full-blooded Osages had married whites.

Many of the full-blooded Osages died young — many from the dissipation their sudden wealth made possible — and many from suspicious circumstances. Autopsies were seldom conducted and, when they were, accidental causes were usually ascribed to the deaths. Many of the estates of these deceased Osages were inherited in whole or part by whites.

Osages Loved Automobiles

In Pawhuska, large, high-priced automobiles crowded the curbstones. Very few four-cylinder or inexpensive were cars on the Osage County roads. Pierce-Arrows, the most expensive cars of the day, had replaced bow and arrows. It was reported at the time that there were more Pierce-Arrows in Osage County than any county in America. Almost daily, Osages drove into Tulsa in their great cars to make extravagant purchases. In more distant Oklahoma City, where they visited less often, hotel lobbies displayed magnificent oil paintings of prominent Osages.

In 1923 it was estimated that every eleventh person in the United States owned a car, but it was claimed that the Osages reversed that: nearly every Indian owned eleven cars.

One Osage woman, because of her large size, rode in a rocking chair in a purple hearse. Another Osage, while intoxicated, attempted to ford the Arkansas river in his car. When rescued in mid-river, he abandoned his car and afterwards made no effort to retrieve it. Few Osages washed their own cars or made any repairs on them. One observer wrote as follows:

"When an Indian's car ran into a tree or ran out of gas or got stuck in the mud, he would sometimes just leave it. The Osage were not impressed with the theory that what is damaged can sometimes be repaired. He'd just go buy a new one. That happened time and time again and of all the legends surrounding the Indians and their luxurious cars in the 1920's perhaps the most frequently mentioned: that they would get into some sort of difficulty with a car, leave it and go buy a new one. In fact, one Osage in one year had ten new cars. They loved them. And had the money to buy just about as many as they wanted."[11]

A large, expensive car pulled to the curb in Pawhuska. An unshaven young man, wearing a greasy golf cap, a well-paid chauffeur for a rich Indian family, was at the wheel. He brought the car to a stop, but he did not get out of the car to open the rear door as other chauffeurs do, but slouched back and began to roll a cigarette. A heavy-set Osage woman got out of the back seat. She wore a multi-colored blanket over her shoulders, and her shiny black hair was parted in the middle and brushed back above her ears. She wore a beaded necklace, silk stockings and stylish patent leather shoes. She carried a beaded handbag. A tall Osage man, dressed in typical Indian garb, followed fifteen feet behind her. His blue broadcloth trousers were edged with beads and a gaily colored blanket covered his shoulders. He followed his squaw through the entrance of a store.

Meanwhile, the chauffeur settled back in his seat to smoke. In Pawhuska a chauffeur did not even keep a car clean, much less wear a uniform. Mud and dust did not affect a car's speed.

Stores Attract Osage Buyers

Along the main streets there were many stores, all competing for the Indian's money. In any other town beaded moccasins and

---

[11]"Oil in Oklahoma" by Robert Gregory.

bags, blankets, necklaces of elks' teeth, skins and silver boxes would be lures for souvenir-seeking tourists, but inside the Pawhuska shops all the customers were Osage couples. When they saw things they wanted, they bought them, regardless of price. These rich Osages roamed the streets looking for ways to spend their money. It was not uncommon for the grocery bill of numerous Osages to amount to $500 to $1,000.[12]

A Congressional Committee examined several Osage accounts to consider the desirability of restricting Osage expenditures. Here are some of them. In one month one Indian woman spent $1,279 for food and clothing at one store. Another woman spent $743.55 in twenty-four days. A man and his wife spent $1,084.66 in one month. Another couple spent $1,336.42 in the same period. A young single woman spent $960.11 in twenty-six days. These sums were expended largely for foodstuffs alone! This list could be supplemented by the addition of literally hundreds of others. On one day a woman spent $12,000 for a fur coat, $3,000 for a diamond ring, $5,000 for a new car, $7,000 for new furniture (and $600 to ship it to California) and $12,800 for real estate in Florida — a total of more than $40,000[13] in one afternoon!

Up on the hill on Grandview Avenue overlooking the commercial area, the office of the U.S. Indian Agent was located where books recorded the money each Indian received — records for any merchant to see. Some merchants seemed to watch the Indians greedily as they passed along the street.

The Guardian System

Certificates of competency were issued to Indians who were deemed capable of handling their own financial affairs, and the recipients of these certificates could dispose of their headrights and property as they saw fit. Indians considered incompetent had to have a guardian appointed to guide them in their financial transactions. This spawned a system of fraud and corruption through which many of the Osages were swindled out of their land and headrights by guardians in conspiracy with merchants and outlaws.

Many ugly stories circulated about this controversial guardian system and the numerous ways swindlers tied in with the murder

---

[12]This would be approximately $25,000 to $50,000 per month in 1998 dollars.

[13]That would equivalent to over $3 million in 1998 dollars.

ring manipulated the guardian system to siphon off the Osages' money. Some guardians were honest, but many were not. Merchants wanted to be on friendly terms with guardians because an Indian had to trade at shops designated by the guardian and the guardian also fixed the amount an Indian could spend per month. Some guardians got kickbacks from storekeepers.

In automobile purchases, the Indian sometimes was prevented by his guardian from buying a low-priced car in favor of a more expensive one from a dealer designated by the guardian because the kickback was higher. In addition, money was often lent to the Indian at usurious interest rates to finance purchase of the car, even though the Indian might have had sufficient money to pay cash.

In one case an Osage was charged $6,000 for a car that was worth about half that much. One guardian bought a car for $200 and then sold it to his ward for $1250. Another guardian charged his ward $1200 per year to manage an annual income of $4,000.

Some guardians conspired to debauch the Indians. They furnished young Osage boys with prostitutes, got them to marry them, and then, in connivance with the guardians, the prostitutes would divorce the Indians, receive alimony, and share it with the guardians and the outlaws. The Indians were also furnished whiskey and narcotics to further corrupt them.

Osage G. Edward Tinker testified before Congress saying:

"The blackest chapter in this history of the State will be the Indian guardianship over these estates.... Men made a profession of it. Sometimes as many as 15 [Osages] have been under one man... Why should an Indian, any Osage Indian, have a guardian? This Department is there for the purpose of taking care of them, though I understand they are trying to shirk their duty by getting them under guardianship; but nonetheless, it is their duty to take care of them and not the courts of the county."[14]

One Osage was in debt $20,000 for mortgages held by his lawyer, despite the fact that he had inherited an estate of more than $90,000 that year and had been drawing payments averaging $7,000 to $12,000 annually for the previous five years. He was unable to account for $55,000 of his income.

Some folks in Pawhuska tried to justify the guardian system. One man commented, "These Indians don't want much, but they want it when they want it. Give 'em that, and they don't care what

---

[14]Testimony, Survey of Conditions of Indians in the United States, Hearings on S. Res. 79, 78th Congress, First Session, Part 41, Osage Indian Matters, Pawhuska, OK August 2 and 3, 1943, pp. 23018-23020.

becomes of the rest of their money. They're going to get a lot more next year anyhow."

"Have you got anything better to offer than the guardianship system?" a lawyer or judge would ask when someone pointed out the evils of the system. They related stories of Indians being cheated out of their money before the guardianship days. "One old lady who was getting about $10,000 a year was living like a dog in a dirty little hut on the outskirts of town. She got sick and the authorities investigated. They found that she signed over her checks to a certain man in this town who took all her money and then paid her little bills at the grocery store and the meat shop. We couldn't arrest the man, but we put the affairs of the woman into the hands of a guardian and she's rich and happy today."

"Some guardians may be bad," they claim. "but no guardians would be worse."

Whether these guardians should be appointed by the local judge or by the federal government was an issue that divided Pawhuska people.

Some federal government officials expressed the view that the federal government should appoint guardians. "Take it out of local politics," they said.

"Leave guardianships to the local judge," some in Pawhuska insisted. "If a judge by error appoints bad guardians, he is on the spot and can change them quickly. Or, if he is a bad judge, he can be kicked out at the next election."

"Do not have any guardians at all," the Indians themselves protested.

John Goodskin, a college graduate, had his own grievances about the guardian system.

"I have a diploma from Lawrence[15]," he complained to a visitor, "and they've put a guardian over me. I fought in France for this country in the World War, and yet I'm not allowed even to sign my own checks."

He added, "With my ample income I could see Europe and the rest of the world and get something out of life. But my guardian would want to go with me and hold the money strings. He's a little soul who doesn't know anything of the world. I don't know what chicanery he used to get control of me, but here I am, his ward. I've written to Washington, but I never get an answer. I'm a prisoner in

---

[15]University of Kansas

this place, and with all my money I can't get any good out of it."

"How can an Indian avoid being placed under a guardian?" the visitor asked.

"In the old days, before we had money, it was easy enough," he replied. "All you had to do was not get drunk. But now your good behavior has nothing at all to do with it. Your money draws 'em like flies and you're absolutely helpless. They have all the law and all the machinery on their side. They're scalping our souls."

He added, "Anyhow, I don't think Congress will let us have all the money that's due us. They're talking about keeping half of it back. They'll have some new law before long. And maybe, then, we'll be free men again."

Many Thought Wealth Hurt the Osages

Aunt Sophie Captain Chouteau, an 84-year-old woman who was frequently consulted by leaders of the tribe because of her intelligence and wisdom, was one of the few women ever made chief. She did not think that the wealth had been a blessing for the Osages. Aunt Sophie, whose hands were gnarled from years of hard work in her youth, said in flawless English, "We were poor once, but we were better off then! My heart cries for our young people, especially for our girls. Too much money is very bad." And then she added, "It hurts the old folks, too, even the wise men."

Fred Lookout, the great Osage chief who led his people for 29 years, agreed with Aunt Sophie's assessment when he said, "My people are not happy. Some day this oil will go and there will be no more fat checks every few months from the great white father. There'll be no more fine motor cars and new clothes. Then I know my people will be happier."

Osage Children Knew Only Luxury

Most of the Osage children attended the Boarding School at Pawhuska which was conducted for them by the federal government from Osage funds, but many went away to exclusive private schools.

The wardrobes of these children would make most other children and their parents gasp in amazement.

They had no recollection of the days of flour, beans and bacon handouts from the federal government which Aunt Sophie and their parents experienced when survival was an all-consuming pursuit. These young people knew only luxury and ease. Their clothes were the best obtainable — a girl's hat costing $90 was a mere trifle. The Osage young ladies were modern, very chic, and sophisticated. A stranger observing these Osage girls on the streets of Pawhuska wrote:

"One would think une tres jolie demoiselle of the Paris boulevards had inadvertently strayed into this little reservation town. The resemblance in type is amazing. There is the same glossy black hair, the same alluring dark eyes, the same white, colorless skin. The gown is Parisian, the hat is Parisian, the high heels are trippingly French. French, too, is their air of insouciance, the little mannerisms of a deep-rooted egotism, of these fortunate daughters of chance!"[16]

Wealth from Oil Increases

In 1906, when the original Foster lease expired, the production of oil was about 4,000,000 barrels. Oil then sold for 39 cents to 52 cents per barrel. In the fiscal year 1920 the production of oil was well over 17,000,000 barrels and sold for as high as $3.50 per barrel, netting the Indians in bonus payments and royalties over $16,000,000. Royalties from gas leases for the same period were slightly under one million dollars[17].

The average Osage income in 1923 was more than $10,000. An allotted family of husband, wife and two minor children received over $40,000. This represented undivided interests and did not include moneys which might have been paid to them as heirs of deceased allottees.

To give an additional idea of the enormous wealth of the Osages, they were paid a net revenue of $241,546,289.82 from the time oil was discovered on the reservation until June 30, 1931.

(In 1924 the Osages received and spent $18,000,000 oil money. In the four years following, the Burbank field alone paid them $76,000,000 in royalties and bonus money.)

When the Osage Tribe was forced to leave Kansas and settle in what is now Osage County, it was felt they had purchased a poor grave for the tribe. Some years later, however, the bonuses and royalties from the oil leases on each of the many 160 tracts within the reservation amounted to more than twice the purchase price of the entire reservation. For a period of eight years, beginning in 1920, the average annual income of each member of the Osage Tribe exceeded

---

[16]Estelle Aubrey Brown in the October, 1922, issue of *Travel* magazine.

[17]For approximate 1998 values, multiply by 80.

the original total purchase price paid for the entire reservation. The "poor grave" which the Osages had purchased made them the richest people in the world.

It had been considered at the time of allotment in 1906 that twenty-five years would be sufficient time in which to take out the oil and gas. However, it soon became apparent that the expiration of this period would find a large part of the reserve undeveloped. The Indians, with unprecedented foresight, began agitation for the extension of the mineral period beyond 1931 and Oklahoma took notice.

Some 425,000 acres of Osage land had been sold to white people. The deeds conveying these lands contained two contradictory clauses which formed the basis for litigation resulting in an investigation by the House Committee on Indian Affairs. Under one section of the Act of 1906, the Indians contended that the mineral rights of the land reverted to them, as the original allottees, at the expiration of the twenty-five years. The white purchasers contended that the rights reverted to them as the individual owners of that land. The white owners protested against the extension on both legal and ethical grounds. They displayed a new-found interest in the moral welfare of the Indians, claiming that the Osages' moral decay could be stopped only by not extending the Indians' mineral rights.

It was argued by others that, if the mineral rights were not renewed, Oklahoma would find on its hands hundreds of paupers who were accustomed to spending $1,000 per month just for food.

The House Committee's investigation resulted in the extension of the mineral period for fifteen years, but so thoroughly did the Indian establish his claim to incompetence and the need for supervision that the incomes of a certain class were limited to a quarterly stipend of $1,000 per each adult and $500 for each child. This class was composed of all those who were unable to secure a certificate of competency, most of whom were full-blooded.

Since the Osages had plenty of money, it was not necessary for them to work so play became their preoccupation. Their playfellows were white men and women, attracted to the Osage territory by this superabundance of loose money. It was a rough game. Many Osages lost their bank rolls month after month and year after year without complaining, but some of them appealed to the laws, and some got retribution. The jail at Pawhuska, the largest in Oklahoma, was filled with white men and women most of the time — renegades who invaded the area dedicated to acquiring the Osages' money.

Osage Indian dancers outside the Gray Horse dance hall.
Rituals of old have been retained by the tribe.

Old Tribal Traditions Were Maintained

In 1923 the Osages were still rendering at least lip service to their colorful heritage. Stomp dances were held several times a year when members of other tribes were invited to attend as guests. Gifts were exchanged between tribes and individuals. These stomp dances were the occasion for all-night and all-day feasts. The Indians, clad in picturesque costumes, danced in a circular formation to the rhythmic beat of the tom-tom under the stimulating influence of the dance, which began slowly, but soon became more enthusiastic and frantic. One person described the dance as "pawing the ground like a herd of wild steers." After the dance, they retired for further feasting while professional Indian dancers amused the assembled audience.

The tribe still maintained a tribal council and a chief, but now they were elected. The Principal Chief, Assistant Chief, and eight Tribal Councilmen — were elected every two years.[18]

Pawhuska, Not a Happy Town

Pawhuska was not a happy town in 1923. Wealth, greed and the

---

[18]The term was subsequently changed to four years.

horde of exploiting white lawbreakers placed a heavy curse on the Osages. The acquisition of wealth was a mixed blessing for the Tribe and the individual Indian. While bringing comfort, it also brought disease, immorality, human vultures and an appalling extravagance. The oil rush confronted the Osages with the same problem which historically plagued Indians — a concerted effort by the white man to acquire all that the Indian possessed.

One writer, commenting on the situation wrote[19]:

"Sensational writers of the time portrayed the Osages as guileless fools. There were a few guileless fools among the Osages, as there will be in any community of 4,000 people. A few were immoral, but the percentage of those gross or stupid certainly ran no higher than in any community of whites of similar size. Among the Osages there were men of great wisdom and sagacity — astute, perceiving men who used their wealth wisely and are today prosperous."

Some of the murders which were used as means to acquire the wealth of the Osages form the basis for our story.

[19]"Osage Oil" by Bill Burchardt, *The Chronicles of Oklahoma*, Vol. 41, Fall, 1963, page 264.

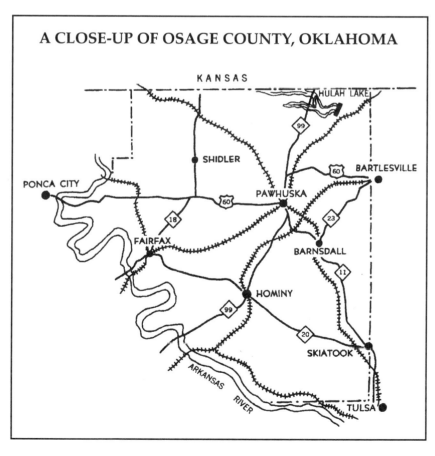

A CLOSE-UP OF OSAGE COUNTY, OKLAHOMA

KANSAS

HULAH LAKE

99

SHIDLER

60 BARTLESVILLE

PONCA CITY

60 PAWHUSKA

18

23

FAIRFAX

BARNSDALL

11

HOMINY

99

20

SKIATOOK

ARKANSAS RIVER

TULSA

OSAGE COUNTY — 1923

Osage County, geographically the largest county in the State of Oklahoma, is located between the meandering Arkansas River and the Kansas State line in the northeast corner of Oklahoma, comprising 2,298.6 square miles. It is more than twice as large as the entire State of Rhode Island and nearly 250 square miles larger than the State of Delaware. It is bound on the southwest by the Arkansas River and extends from Tulsa on the south to Ponca City on the north, a distance of approximately sixty miles. It is also sixty miles in width at its widest point. To give an additional idea of its immensity, Osage County at the time of the murders contained more than 1,800 public schools.

At the time of the Osage Indian murders, when Osage County was experiencing a boom in the exploration and development of the oil and gas fields, there were numerous towns and villages then which later went out of existence. Gray Horse (sometimes written as Grayhorse), an Indian community approximately six miles southeast of Fairfax, had at its crossroads, one store, which in the early days had been an Indian trading post, and four or five houses. The community is still known as Gray Horse.

Between 1900 and 1920, following the discovery of oil, the population of Osage County increased approximately 350 per cent. The majority of these new citizens were transient oil workers, "potlickers" (parasites who milked as much money from the rich Osages as they were able), criminals of every type and description, and tradesmen anxious to share in the exploitation of the Osages' wealth.

When the Osage Indian murders were being committed, Osage County and the surrounding territory contained very wild stretches of country, thickly wooded with timber unsuited for commercial purposes. This area, with its almost inaccessible canyons, afforded excellent concealment for the hideouts of the many notorious criminals who flocked to the territory from all parts of the country.

One of the U.S. government's representatives commented on the conditions in Osage County at the time, "There are a few men and women in Osage County as fine as may be found anywhere — but they are mighty few!"

The St. Louis Post-Dispatch in its Sunday, March 10, 1925, edition had the following to say concerning Osage County:

... There are only a few places remaining in the United States where

lawless men can make a stand, the Florida Everglades, the Bad Lands of South Dakota, the Tonto Basin in Arizona harbor fugitives from justice. But for wildness and wickedness, the Osage County of Oklahoma is the worst. Its population is recruited from three ranks — renegades who know no law; oil huskies who are indifferent to law; and Indians whose attitude toward law is a mixture of respect and ignorance, superstition and fear....

There are treacherous roads in the Osage wilds and trails that have led to many an ambush. If an Indian complains, reprisal is taken by the accused. He can hide in a ravine and pick his accuser off with a high-power rifle. He can use dynamite or poison. Having slain, the murderer can take to the hills. But this is usually unnecessary. He can walk in the streets of Pawhuska, brazenly confident that the terrified [Indian] will not appear as witness against him. "It ain't healthy to testify in Osage County...."

Osage County is dark and bloody ground .... When a murder is done in Oklahoma and the murderer flees, the newspapers report as a matter of course, "He has taken to the Osage Hills" When sheriffs cannot find their man they say: "He is hiding in the Osage Hills," as if that were sufficient explanation. Osage County is a refuge for every type of desperate, hunted man. In its woods and gullies, outlaws light their campfires and do not worry about the smoke. Killers, bank robbers, and absconders hold rendezvous in the Osage Hills.

"Don't go poking about up there," a visitor is warned at Guthrie, "It isn't safe country up there."

The <u>Literary Digest</u> for April 3, 1926, states in part:

...Whites camping on the rich trails, we read, comprise schemers, crooks, floaters, a backwash of the oil fields, uneducated rough men, many of whom are convicts, for the Osage County is a stomping place of the badmen, bandit card sharks, former cow-punchers now looking for an easy living, gamblers and roustabouts.

The criminal atmosphere of the Osage area is also well-illustrated by comments made to an FBI Agent by a convict in the Oklahoma State Penitentiary. He recalled that during the period of the Osage Indian murders he attended a gathering of thirty-two nationally known bank bandits and train robbers in the woods of Osage County where they were in hiding as fugitives from justice. During their time spent in that area, he said, they often engaged in pistol practice since skill in the use of pistols was absolutely essential in their profession.

Al Spencer, one-time criminal associate of Jesse James, used the area for a hideout for his notorious band of bank and train robbers. The man who was the mastermind behind the Osage Indian murders had tried unsuccessfully to hire Spencer to commit certain murders, but Spencer declined, stating that he had no compunction about robbing a train or blowing a safe and killing individuals in the course of such crimes, but he had not sunk so low as to murder helpless individuals for money. Other members of the Spencer gang, who had also been propositioned by the gang leader to murder Indians, later testified against him at his trial.

Prior to his death, the notorious Henry Grammer, former cattleman and rodeo performer, shared honors as boss of Osage County's criminal element with the King of the Osage Hills. Grammer monopolized the extremely lucrative Osage liquor traffic, both its manufacture and distribution. He reportedly kept certain woods surrounding his land illuminated by a privately owned power plant where a gang of criminal fugitives from all over the United States worked day and night making illegal liquor. Grammer was a protector and manipulator of law violators in the territory as well as a fence of stolen goods. Grammer was dead when the FBI began its investigation of the Osage Indian murders.

In recounting the story of Grammer's death, the April 3, 1926, issue of the Literary Digest stated:

... *Other things began to happen in that land of sudden mysterious death. The sinister tale had unfolded itself in startling chapters of daily news. There was Henry Grammer, champion rope thrower of the world. He had aroused the enmity of powerful interests in Oklahoma. And he knew more than he should know. One day he was out in his car driving when the steering gear became unmanageable. The car ran off a culvert and he was killed. Certain people in that section, it is said, are handy with tools so another mystery was added to the growing list.*

Others said Grammer was shot before the accident, but no autopsy was ever conducted.

Since Osage County was literally infested with ruthless outlaws, the lives of the investigating FBI Agents were constantly in jeopardy. These agents faced what was probably the greatest danger any Government Agents ever faced in the FBI's entire history.

THE INVESTIGATION

❧ Chapter 5 ❧

The Osage Tribal Council Meets

The Osage Tribal Council was in session.

Ne-kah-wah-she-tun-kah[20] (Man of Courage) was Principal Chief. Paul Red Eagle was Assistant Chief. The Tribal Council members were: George Aberthy, Bacon Rind, Andrew Bighouse, Arthur Bonnicastle, Samuel Kennedy, Francis Revard, Eves Tallchief and Wah-sho-shah.

The elders of the tribe sat morosely, their faces showing a mixture of fear and sorrow. A mysterious curse hung over the tribe, and they were assembled to find some possible means of dispelling it. Living in the open, on wild game, and holding their dances and councils of war, the Osage were truly men of strength, leaders among the first Americans. Confined to houses, wearing gorgeous adornments of wealth, riding in fast motor cars and drinking the white man's whiskey, have brought great changes to this once powerful tribe. It has been decidedly for the worse.

"In times gone by, when we fought the great wars, our name, 'Osage' meant 'enemy' to all the tribes of the Plains and the Woodlands," one elder said.[21]

"Yes," another said. "We were once a tribe of fighting people. We were warriors and hunters. Our deeds of bravery filled the pages of history. We lived in the open air and held our great dances and councils of war under open skies. Once we were feared; now we fear. Once we were envied for our fearlessness; now we are pitied. Once, we were men of strength, leaders among all Indians."

---

[20]Principal Chief Ne-kah-wah-she-tun-kah died on August 3, 1923 and was succeeded by Paul Red Eagle.

[21]The dialogue in this chapter is simulated.

The Osage Tribal Council adopted a resolution in March 1923, a plea for the FBI's help in solving the murders which plagued the tribe.

"Hmmm," another elder said, drawing on his pipe, "we have been ruined by too much money. Living in houses and wearing white man's clothes and riding in fancy cars instead of on our horses, and drinking the white man's whiskey have sapped our strength. Once we were eagles, now we are crows."

"True," another commented. "Once we were powerful, but now we are weak."

"We have become cowards," an old man complained.

"I am not a coward!" a younger man protested. "I am willing to fight, but you cannot fight what you cannot see. We are helpless."

"How can a warrior fight against the Evil Spirit?" another asked.

"Is it the Evil Spirit or the white man?" one asked.

"Maybe it is the same thing," a sage counselor observed. "Sometimes the Evil Spirit takes many different forms."

Bacon Rind said, "There are men amongst the whites who are honest men, but they are mighty scarce, mighty few."

An old man shook his head sadly, "When we had no money the white man left us alone. When the Osages were poor and had nothing, we were happy. Now, we are rich and have all the worldly pleasures any person could possibly want, but we do not have happiness."

The discovery of oil on Osage land had brought immense wealth to the tribe, but it also brought in its wake numerous unscrupulous white men who devised countless cunning strategies to swindle the Indians. The Osages were cheated in the sale of horses, cattle, automobiles, land, oil leases and in practically every way the mind of the white man could devise. Young Indians were introduced to whiskey, narcotics and general loose living. The spiritual tradition of the tribe was waning and in its place was an appalling immorality. When an Indian's stage of degradation reached its ebb, white men would have the Indian declared incompetent and have a guardian appointed. In many instances these guardians were prime movers in the swindling.

Now, the reign of terror was reaching its pinnacle: murder had come to the land of the Osage. The elders of the tribe looked from one of their brethren to the other, reading distress and sadness on the face of each. As the elders of the tribe observed, the warriors of old would have insisted on avenging the honor of the tribe, but you cannot retaliate against something inanimate, something you do not know and do not understand. Some truly believed that the Evil Spirit was responsible for the many deaths. Wiser men of the tribe said it was an organized gang of white men, headed by the mysterious King of the Osage Hills.

The discussion of the tribal leaders turned to the murders, dozens of which had been committed. It was difficult to account for many other deaths, supposedly from "natural causes," because those making that determination were often in league with the murderers. In some very suspicious deaths, doctors of questionable character would state "death from natural causes" or "death from alcoholism" when actually the death had been cleverly plotted. Members of the terror ring would get an Indian drunk, have a doctor examine him, pronounce him intoxicated, and give him an injection of morphine. After the doctor departed, the gang members would inject an enormous amount of additional morphine under the arm pit of the drunken Indian which would result in his death. Subsequently, the doctor's certificate would read "death from alcoholic poisoning."

The tribal leaders recounted the details of some of the murders.

☙ Chapter 6 ❧

Anna Brown

Fun-loving Anna Kile Brown (Wah-hrah-lum-pah), a 25-year-old wealthy, full-blood Osage, had been married to a white man, Ode Brown, an old-time squaw man and horse trader, but they had divorced. She was attractive, but was a very heavy drinker and was frequently intoxicated. It was rumored that she also used narcotics. Anna would get up at any time of night to join any party where whiskey and a good time were in prospect. She consorted promiscuously with many white men for whom she definitely had a preference. Anna was pregnant and there was considerable question as to who the father was. She claimed it was Bryan Burkhart, brother of her sister Mollie's husband, and she wanted him to marry her. She told others that Jim Moss was the father. It was rumored that Bill Hale, a wealthy businessperson-banker-rancher, was the father, but that he had made arrangements for Jim Moss to take the blame. It was also alleged that Anna had previously had an illegitimate child by Hale and that they had had a falling out because Anna would call Hale and his wife harassing them.

Anna was the youngest daughter of Lizzie Q and the sister of Mollie Kile (Mrs. Ernest) Burkhart and Rita[22] (Me-se-moie) (Mrs. W.E.) Smith. Another sister, Minnie (Wah-shah-she), who also had been married to Bill Smith, died in 1918. Anna owned one and one-sixth headrights in the wealth of the Osage Tribe which made her very rich.

On the morning of May 21, 1921, Anna Brown was at home talking with a neighbor when the telephone rang. Ernest Burkhart, husband of her sister Mollie, told her that her mother, Lizzie Q, who

---

[22]Her name was sometimes given as Reta or Retta.

Anna Brown, daughter of Lizzie Q. and sister of Mollie Burkhart and Rita Smith.
A kiss of death by a deserted creek.

lived with Ernest and Mollie, was very ill. He asked Anna to come visit her mother.

"Yes, of course, I'll come," Anna said.

She filled a small handbag with personal effects and called a taxi. When the taxicab arrived, Anna instructed the driver to take her to her sister Mollie's home in Gray Horse. En route, she asked the driver to drive by the local cemetery. At the cemetery, Anna left the car and walked slowly to her father's grave. When she returned to the car, she told the driver she was very unhappy with the condition of her father's grave and asked him to send a man out to the cemetery to take care of it. He agreed that he would.

When the taxicab arrived at the Burkhart home, Anna paid the driver and instructed him to return for her that evening.

Anna stayed at her sister's home all day visiting her mother, Lizzie Q. Anna, who was in a very grouchy mood, spent much of the day sulking in a summer house. The Burkhart men were away all day at horse races in Gray Horse.

The men returned that evening and, after supper, Anna left her sister's home with Ernest Burkhart and his brother, Bryan. Later that night, Anna made the rounds drinking at various roadhouses with other men and women. Well after midnight, the group left one of these taverns in two automobiles, heading toward Fairfax. About one mile northeast of Fairfax, at a fork in the road, one of the cars turned east away from Fairfax while the other car, in which Anna and another woman and two men were riding, turned west toward Fairfax.

They drove to a deserted area about three miles west of Fairfax, turned onto a trail off the main Pawhuska-to-Fairfax road, and parked at a lonely spot, a rocky ravine with trees bordering a small creek. The men helped Anna out of the car and supported her as they walked down into the hollow. The other woman stayed in the car while Anna walked with the two men toward the creek, about 40 steps from the car. Anna was very drunk and one of them walked with his arm around her waist, holding her up. They stopped a few feet from the creek, about 75 feet from the head of the canyon, and the men gave Anna another big drink of whiskey. Helplessly drunk, she sat down by the edge of the creek, laid her shawl on the ground and removed her shoes. She hiked up her blue, broadcloth skirt and dipped her feet in the cool water. Her head was spinning from intoxication and she passed out.

The two men returned to the car and drove away. When their woman companion asked where Anna was they told her that there was a group partying down in the hollow and Anna wanted to stay with them. They drove around for two or three hours and then took the other woman home.

They returned to the ravine where they had left Anna. While one of them was loving her, the other struck her on the head with the butt of a pistol. Anna screamed. While the first man held her up, the other shot her in the head. The loud report of the pistol echoed across the plains. Anna fell limp, the kiss of death still warm on her lips, as the blood seeped through her white shirt.

The two men ran to their car and, seconds later, it roared away, swallowed up by the stillness and darkness of night.

Anna lay on the ground, her life quickly slipping away as a forlorn train whistle mourned in the distance. She was 25 years old.

About a week later, about three miles west of Fairfax, about 300 yards south of the main Pawhuska-Fairfax road, near a trail used as a cutoff to Ralston and Gray Horse, some hunters found the swollen, badly decomposed body of Anna Brown. The body was about

Romantic scene in a ravine by the water's edge, where Anna Brown was murdered.

200 yards down a hollow (later to be called "Anna Brown gulch" by local folks) from where this cutoff road passes around the head of the small rocky creek.

An undertaker, F. S. Tureen, later took charge of the rotten and swollen body. While the body was being prepared for burial, the scalp slipped from the skull and a bullet hole was discovered in the back of the head. The doctors performed a crude and hasty autopsy. They bisected the cranium from front to rear and searched in the decayed brain mass for the bullet. These doctors, who were believed by many to be tied in with Osage County's gang of outlaws, said they found no bullet. They explained that, because of the condition and terrible odor of the body, a more thorough autopsy was not performed. For some reason, the body was cut up by the doctors and the flesh cleaved from her bones with a meat ax. It was prepared for burial by the undertaker who was also believed to be affiliated with the criminal gang.

An inquest was held which revealed no known enemies of Anna. The last person seen with Anna while she was alive was Bryan Burkhart, brother to Anna's brother-in-law, Ernest Burkhart. Bryan testified at the inquest that he had taken Anna from his brother Ernest's house to her home about 4:00 or 4:30 p.m. and did not see her again. Ernest corroborated this. The uncle of Ernest and Bryan, William K. Hale, posted Bryan's bond and he was released.

Local prosecutors admitted that they had no evidence against Bryan so the charges against him were dropped. An investigation of sorts was continued, but got nowhere. Bill Smith, husband of Anna's sister Rita (and widower of her deceased sister, Minnie) conducted a very active and thorough investigation of his own. He said he did not want his sister-in-law's murderers to go unpunished. Nonetheless, Anna Brown's murder remained a mystery.

Half of Anna's estate passed to her mother, Lizzie Q (Ne-kah-essey), who lived with Mollie and Ernest Burkhart. Lizzie Q died two months after Anna and her estate was divided between her two surviving daughters, Mollie Burkhart and Rita Smith.

ᵚ Chapter 7 ᵚ

Henry Roan

Henry Roan, also known as Henry Roan Horse, was Anna Brown's cousin and was a very likable and colorful full-blooded Osage who wore his hair down his back in plaits. He stood six feet tall and was a fine-looking specimen of Osage manhood. He lived with his wife and children in Fairfax, Oklahoma.

Henry had never drunk very much whiskey until he discovered that his wife was carrying on an affair with Roy Bunch, a white man. After that, Henry would go away from home on wild, drunken sprees for three or four weeks at a time. His friends said he seemed to go to pieces over his wife's infidelity. Twice he had attempted suicide. Because Henry was a drunkard and a spendthrift, he was made a ward of the federal government. He reportedly had tuberculosis and a venereal disease.

It was common knowledge that there was "bad blood" between Henry Roan and Roy Bunch and they were often overheard threatening each other. Bunch was Roan's only enemy.

On Wednesday or Thursday, January 24 or 25, 1923, Henry left his house with his little son and went to a garage. He returned later with an automobile mechanic and then left again with this mechanic, leaving his little boy at home.

On the road running from Fairfax to Burbank, Roan met with a man who got in Roan's car. This man had made friends with Roan through the Indian's love for whiskey and had taken him out drinking on several occasions. They drove to a desolate area where his companion told Roan they would get a drink of whiskey. When they got to a place out of sight of the road, the man shot Roan in the back of the head with a .45 caliber automatic pistol. The murderer then walked back to the top of the hill where he had met Roan and where he had left his own car.

Henry Roan, popular cousin of Anna Brown, Mollie Burkhart and Rita Smith. An unfaithful wife, a drunken spree, a ride in the country, and a bullet hole in the head.

When Henry did not return home at noon for dinner, his wife telephoned the garage.

"He left here an hour ago, Mary," she was told.

She then telephoned one of her husband's relatives at Hominy, Oklahoma, who told her that Henry had not been there. Several days passed, but Henry did not return home.

On Tuesday afternoon, February 6, 1923, an Indian boy discovered an abandoned automobile in a small canyon about five miles northwest of Fairfax, about 200 yards from the road. He hurried to Fairfax and told local law enforcement officers about the car. The officers, assuming it was a "whiskey car," rushed to the scene.

In the car, slouched over the front seat, was a dead Indian, his feet just off the floor pedals and his head with a cap under it, resting on the right side of the seat. There was a bullet hole in his head. They lifted his head to see his face.

"It's Henry Roan," one of them said.

The bullet had entered just back of the left ear and emerged over the right eye, shattering the windshield glass. Some pieces of glass were still lying on the hood of the car.

Deserted area where Henry Roan was killed.

"Looks like he's been dead for about ten days," one of the officers said, "since some time between January 26 and February 3 or 4, probably closer to January 26." He was 42.

A cold spell had frozen the body and it had just begun to thaw and decompose.

An inquest was held, but no evidence was developed.

Shortly after Henry Roan's murder, his widow, Mary Roan, married her lover, Roy Bunch.

William K. "Bill" Hale, a prominent, wealthy and influential citizen who was a pallbearer at Roan's funeral, told several people that Roy Bunch was responsible for Roan's death. Lending credence to this claim, many people had heard Bunch and Roan threaten to kill each other. Furthermore, it was common knowledge — to Henry Roan and many others — that Bunch and Roan's wife were carrying on a torrid sexual affair.

✎ Chapter 8 ✎

Bill Smith, Rita (Reta) Smith and their Servant, Nettie Brookshire

Bill Smith, Anna Brown's brother-in-law, continued his active investigation into the murders and apparently gathered much valuable data. He told several individuals that he knew who was responsible for the murders and knew the identity of their ring leader.

Fearing that the gang of murderers might dispose of him for the damaging information he had gathered, Bill Smith decided to move from his ranch house at Gray Horse to a house in the town of Fairfax where he and his wife felt they would be safer.

On the evening of March 9, 1923, shortly after they had moved to a new house, Bill Smith, his wife, Rita Kile Smith, and their white servant, 17-year-old Nettie Brookshire, were out late. Returning home about 2:00 a.m., March 10, they were very tired and immediately went to bed.

Outside, two men crouched in the darkness, watching the family enter the house.

After the lights went out, they waited about an hour, giving the occupants ample time to go to sleep. Shortly after 3:00 a.m. the two men stealthily approached the house. They huddled together by the side of the house, then quickly ran to an automobile parked nearby, and sped away.

The night watchman of the town of Fairfax saw a car speeding down the street, coming from the direction of Bill Smith's house. An insurance agent who was spending the night at a nearby hotel was awake at 3:00 a.m.. He glanced out the window and saw a flame flare up and then die down a few blocks away. "Someone's automobile must have caught fire," he thought as he sat on the side of his bed. In another hotel room, a man sitting in a chair also saw the

Rita Smith, wife of Bill Smith, daughter of Lizzie Q and sister of Anna Brown and Mollie Burkhart. Instant death in a fiery explosion.

same small fire.

Suddenly, a terrific explosion shattered the quiet night. The night watchman stood frozen to the spot. The man sitting in the chair in a hotel room was thrown over backwards onto the floor. The insurance agent sitting on the edge of his bed was thrust back onto the bed. Another man nearby, who was up with an ill family member, heard a deafening blast and the windows of his house were shattered.

The explosion awakened the entire town. All eyes focused on the fiery spectacle illuminating the sky.

"It's Bill Smith's house!" people shouted.

Citizens converged on the scene from all directions, hastily putting bathrobes over their night clothes. Bill Smith was dragged from the wreckage of his home and rushed to the hospital. His genitals had been blown away and he was close to death. His wife and their servant, Nettie Brookshire, were killed instantly. Pieces of their flesh were plastered on the walls of a house 300 feet away. Rita was 32 years old, having been born November 23, 1891.

Bill Smith, one of the strongest, most vocal opponents of the murder ring, died four days later on March 14, 1923, less than two months after Henry Roan's body had been found.

OUR SUMMER HOME IN HOT SPRINGS

Rita Smith and her 17-year-old servant, Nettie Brookshire, in happier times.

William and Rita Smith's comfortable home at 2:00 a.m....

And at 3:00 a.m., a grave of rubble. For Rita Smith and Nettie Brookshire,
a sleep that never ended.

Commenting on the destruction of the Smith home, one of the murderers commented, "We done a good job."

In the Smiths' garage, a hole six feet wide and 3½ feet deep. The explosion awakened the entire town. Body parts were found blocks away.

When he recovered consciousness, Bill Smith, whose genitals were blown away, said it felt as if he was burning to death. He died a few days after his wife and servant girl.

❧ Chapter 9 ☙

Other Murders

In addition to the murders of Anna Brown, Henry Roan and the Smith family, there were several other murders.

MARY LEWIS

In January, 1919, the body of Mary Lewis, an Osage, was found in a lake near Liberty, Texas. In August, 1918, witnesses saw her leave home with Blackie Middleton. Middleton and another man later showed up in Claremore, Oklahoma, with Mary Lewis' grandchild. They left the child in the care of local women and when these women contacted Mrs. Lewis' son, asking for sufficient money to take care of the child, the son contacted the police. Eventually, after an accomplice confessed to helping Middleton dispose of Mary Lewis' body, Middleton was arrested, convicted of first degree murder and sentenced to death. This is one of the few Osage murders which was solved.

CHARLES WHITEHORN

The body of Charles Whitehorn, a young Osage man, was found about May 22, 1921, in the woods on Dial Hill, a short distance from the north side of Pawhuska with two bullet holes in his forehead. He was last seen alive on May 19, when he left his home in a car with another man. The car was seen driving up Dial Hill. Later, the other man was observed returning alone to Whitehorn's home.

A local citizen who was hauling rock from Dial Hill to town reported that he heard three shots fired

Charles
Whitehorn

and a few minutes later he saw a tall, light complexioned man walking very fast away from the direction of the shots. The murder was never solved.

BARNEY McBRIDE
Barney McBride, an oil man whom Osage Tribesmen had consulted about their problems, volunteered to go to Washington, D.C. to intercede with the U.S. government to save the Osage Tribe from further murders. McBride never reached Washington. In August, 1922, his horribly butchered body was found stuffed in a culvert near Meadows, Maryland. The theory was that Osage County desperadoes had followed the oil man east and murdered him before he could meet with federal government officials.

JOE YELLOW HORSE
Joe Yellow Horse toppled over dead after frothing from the mouth from some strange poison in April, 1923.

ASA "ACE" KIRBY
On June 29, 1923, Asa "Ace" Kirby, a Osage County outlaw, died from shotgun blasts while attempting to burglarize a store. The owner had been tipped off that his store would be burglarized so he was waiting in the dark when Kirby climbed through a window.

GEORGE BIGHEART and W.W.VAUGHN
The same day Kirby died, George Bigheart died. George Bigheart, an Osage who had previously signed over management of his headright to William K. Hale went on a prolonged drinking binge. Hale and his nephew, Ernest Burkhart, took Bigheart from Gray Horse to Hominy to catch a train and took him to Oklahoma City's Wesley Hospital for treatment of his alcohol addiction. When Bigheart began to recover, he called his lawyer, W. W. Vaughn, and asked Vaughn to come to Oklahoma City to protect him. He apparently gave his lawyer important information about the mysterious murders. On June 29, 1923, before Vaughn could reach Oklahoma City, Bigheart died. An autopsy failed to show anything unusual, but the attending physician said he might have some important testimony to give if he were summoned before a Court of Inquiry. It was alleged that Bigheart had been given poisoned whiskey.
    There had reportedly been an argument at George Bigheart's

death bed over a deed which the Indian had supposedly made out to William K. Hale a few days earlier. W.W.Vaughn, Bigheart's attorney, claimed that the deed was fraudulent.

Vaughn told various people that he had sufficient evidence about the murders to put a certain party in the electric chair and that he knew the identity of the King of the Osage Hills. Vaughn also told someone else that he had learned that the "King" had given a certain attorney $5,000 to block investigation of the murders.

Shortly thereafter, Vaughn boarded a Midland Valley Railroad train en route to Pawhuska. He had asked the porter to awaken him when the train reached Pershing. When the porter went to Vaughn's berth he was not there. His mangled body was found the next morning by the side of the railroad tracks. He had been murdered and his body thrown from the train.

Vaughn had been a leader of the Osage County Bar and served as attorney for many members of the tribe. He was survived by a widow and ten children.

LIZZIE Q ALSO KNOWN AS LIZZIE KILE

Lizzie Q, mother of Anna Brown, Rita Smith and Mollie Burkhart, died on July 17, 1921, a few months after her daughter Anna's murder. She was 76 years old. It was said that she was poisoned, but, as usual, no autopsy was conducted. Lizzie Q had been married twice, the first time to an Osage named Bigheart by whom she had two daughters, Grace and Alice Bigheart. When this first husband died, Lizzie inherited his headright. Later she married Ote Q, another full-blooded Osage. This union produced four daughters, Minnie, Rita, Mollie and Anna. When her daughters, Grace and Alice Bigheart, died, Lizzie inherited their headrights. At the time of her death, Lizzie had four headrights. Minnie Smith had died on September 22, 1918, so, since both Minnie and Anna were deceased, Rita (Mrs. Bill Smith) and Mollie (Mrs. Ernest) Burkhart inherited Lizzie Q's estate.

ALFRED McKINLEY

Alfred McKinley was found suffering from a fractured skull and died before telling anyone who had struck him.

BILL STETSON

On February 28, 1922, Bill Stetson, famous Osage roper and World War I veteran, did not answer his door when someone knocked on it. He was dead in his bed. He died from drinking poisoned whiskey. It was said that a white man, Kelsey Morrison, had given him some denatured alcohol to drink. Later, Morrison, a member of the notorious band of outlaws led by the King of the Osage Hills, married Stetson's Osage widow. The coroner's report said the death was from "causes unknown."

MRS. BILL STETSON (LATER MRS. KELSIE MORRISON)
Morrison's new wife did not live long after the marriage and Morrison inherited her estate.

NINA SMITH
Nina Smith, Osage wife of a white man, was poisoned to death.

ANNA SANFORD
Anna Sanford, a full-blooded Osage Indian, died under suspicious circumstances. She had been married to a white man. She was suddenly taken ill at her home and died.

JOE BATES (Gray Horse)
Joe Bates, also known as Joe Grayhorse, an Osage Indian with a certificate of competency, died mysteriously and Bill Hale produced a deed in which Bates allegedly conveyed an undivided interest in certain tracts of land to Hale. Bates' heirs contested the conveyance, but other Indians shook their heads. Hale profited by the death of nearly every Indian in Osage County.

HENRY BENET AND HUGH GIBSON
Prior to his death, Henry Roan allegedly had passed information to his friend, Henry Benet, about the previous killings. Benet was going to Oklahoma City to relay the information to the Governor, but he was shot and killed two blocks from the State Capitol.

Before Benet died, he had shared the information with his friend, Hugh Gibson. When Benet was killed, Gibson left for Oklahoma City with the information. Gibson's body was found in an Oklahoma City alley.

HENRY GRAMMER
Henry Grammer, a notorious character who shared honors with the King of the Osage Hills as the boss of Osage County's criminal element, died in an automobile accident on June 14, 1923. While he was driving his car, the steering mechanism became unmanageable causing it to swerve off a culvert and Grammer was killed. It was

said that certain people, handy with tools, had tampered with Grammer's car because he knew too much. Others said he was shot before the accident.

At the time of his death, he had $15,000 in cash on his person, so robbery was not the motive behind his death. He was said to have been murdered by a notorious bandit who was with him at the time of the accident. In spite of the fact that he had a gaping wound under his left armpit, no investigation of the case was ever conducted. The death of Grammer was not mourned by the honest citizens of the territory.

Grammer, 42 years old, had been operating a large ranch on the western part of the reservation. He had been living on the Osage reservation since 1901 when he got a job as a cowboy on the Sylvester Soldani Ranch. He married an Osage woman in 1907 and bought a ranch. Grammer was survived by his wife and three children.

Grammer was one of the most famous men on the reservation. A few years before his death he had won the World Championship Roping Contest. Grammer performed in New York City's Madison Square Garden many times as a roping expert, as well as before some of the kings of Europe. While traveling with the 101 Ranch Wild West Show, he roped before King Edward and King George of England, King Leopold of Belgium, Emperor Wilhelm of Germany and other crowned heads of Europe.

A typical, old-time cowboy, Grammer was an expert horseman who kept a herd of well-trained roping horses. He always wore cowboy boots and spurs, and always had a lariat hooked over the horn of his saddle. Grammer also had a reputation as an expert gunslinger. He would draw quickly and shoot from the hip with uncanny accuracy. He was reported to have several notches on his gun, keeping score of the number of men he had killed. Grammer would reportedly let his opponent draw first, but it was always his gun which fired first. Knowing his reputation, most men, including hundreds of lawmen, avoided confrontation with him.

Glamour surrounded Henry Grammer and he lived in an atmosphere of mysticism, frequently in the limelight, similar to that experienced by border characters, and his career covered all that portion of the West from the Montana-Wyoming line to the land of the "Osage Hills"

On the streets of Pawhuska, Ponca City, Arkansas City, and many other western cities and towns he was a well-known, picturesque character. Grammer was a ranchman of considerable prominence who controlled an extensive acreage. No rodeo anywhere was complete without Grammer, and even at the age when other men had quit, Grammer was seemingly just as agile as ever, just as facile with the lasso, and just as good a horseman.

Grammer had monopolized the very profitable illegal liquor business in Osage County, both its manufacture and distribution. He reportedly kept certain woods surrounding his land illuminated by a privately owned power plant where a gang of criminal fugitives from all over the United States worked night and day making illegal liquor.

Grammer had also been a protector and manipulator of law violators in the territory, many of whom he hired, and was also well known as a fence of stolen goods.

Why was he killed? The talk in Osage County was that he had aroused the enmity of powerful interests and he knew too much.

"CURLEY" JOHNSON

"Curley" Johnson, a notorious bandit, gambler and bootlegger from the oil boom town of Whizbang, was killed under highly mysterious circumstances, apparently from drinking poisoned whiskey. He had been approached by other members of the murder ring at the instigation of the King of the Osage Hills and was asked to murder certain Indians. After Johnson's death, the rumor was common that the "King" had Johnson killed because he feared that he might "talk." The murderers later tried to fix the blame on him for one of the murders.

KENNETH ROGERS

Kenneth Rogers was murdered by an unknown gunman while he was reading by a window in his home.

STATE INVESTIGATOR CONVICTED

Following several murders, Pawhuska citizens petitioned state officials to investigate the deaths. In response, Governor Jack Walters appointed Herman Fox Davis, a special investigator, to check into the matter. Shortly thereafter, Davis was convicted of bribery and sent to prison. Walters later pardoned him.[23]

---

[23]"Osage Oil Boom," Chapter 8, page 111 et al, Oklahoma Heritage Association, Western Heritage Books, 1989.

✎ Chapter 10 ✎

The Tribal Elders Adopt a Resolution

As the tribal elders of the Osage Tribe in council session continued their discussion of the mysterious deaths, they related other outrages.[24]

"Not even the dead are safe," one said sadly. "They tried to blow up the grave of young Ruth Tallchief."

On the night of March 22, 1923, an attempt had been made to blow up the vault of the young Osage girl, apparently to steal diamonds and money believed to be entombed with her body. A bottle containing nitroglycerin was found near the vault.

The Osage elders shuddered as they remembered the many outrages. On the mind of each was the haunting thought: "Will I be next?"

The Indians and their white neighbors kept lights on in the front and rear of their homes all night, fearing that some violence might befall them at the hands of the ruthless murderers. Many were selling their homes and moving out of Osage County.

"The police are no help to us," one elder complained. "They are either tied in with the gang of criminals or they are hopelessly hamstrung by the politicians under the control of the King of the Osage Hills"

"The police don't like Indians," one said. "Remember John Stink."

The tribal elder referred to a very sad story which further embittered the Osages against the white man

John Stink (Ho-tah-moie or Roaring Thunder), a strong, robust man standing over six feet tall, was a plain, simple Osage. He was born about 1863, several years before the Osages left their Kansas

---

[24]The dialogue in this chapter is simulated.

reservation. John was a member of the Thunder Clan whose members have the right to burn cedar in tribal ceremonies and they can ask the Great Spirit (Wah-kah-tah) to make rain. John believed in the sun, earth and thunder as being deities comprising the Great Spirit, but he also had contact with the area's Catholic priests. His religious beliefs were related to his love of the outdoors and his deep affection for dogs.

One day John Stink fell ill with small pox or some other serious disease. He grew worse and worse. The medicine men of the tribe chanted their incantations, but John Stink continued to grow worse. Finally, he was taken outside the Indian village to die, the medicine men said their last words, and he was consigned to the great spirits. They believed that he died.[25]

But by some miracle John Stink did not die. He was deserted by his people and shunned by the whites. He finally was able to walk about. But he could not return to his own people, because to them he was dead. The greatest medicine men in the tribe had pronounced him dead and consigned him to the great spirits. So, the other Indians would not have anything to do with him and he became an outcast.[26]

John built himself a little tin hut out of oil and gasoline cans, and began to gather dogs around him. He loved his dogs, his only companions. John would buy steaks, cut them in strips and feed them to his dogs and all the strays which his generosity attracted.

Once a week John would go to Pawhuska to buy food and smok-

---

[25]Kenneth Jacob Jump, who has authored a pamphlet about John Stink, gives additional versions of this tale. In one, John during an illness lost consciousness and was believed to be dead. He was given a typical Osage funeral and stones were piled around him on a hillside. John revived and walked home to find his house and other possessions given away. Henceforth, John was shunned as a ghost. In another version, John got drunk, fell in a snow drift and froze. Later he was found frozen stiff and was believed to be dead. Again, he was interred in Osage fashion. He later thawed, sobered up, climbed out of the burial stone pile and went home. In a third version, John was found during a snow storm, apparently frozen to death. After being taken to his guardian's root cellar, he thawed out, got up and walked out, observed by the astounded people who thought him dead. Jump states, "As in most legends, the true facts have been distorted to make a more interesting story.... The truth is that many Indians and non Indians visited him often after this death-and-resurrection story got around. This proved people were not afraid of him and did not consider him a ghost."

[26]There are other reports that many people did, in fact, have dealings with John Stink up until the time of his death.

John Stink and one of his beloved dogs.

John Stink, famous Osage recluse.

ing tobacco. One hot August day he started on the two-mile walk to Pawhuska, with his dogs happily leaping and running about him. At the time, a mad-dog scare had broken out in Pawhuska and the constable was paid a bounty for each dog he killed. When the constable saw John Stink moving along the road with his pack of dogs, he approached him, firing his pistol at the dogs. Astounded and disbelieving, John begged the constable not to harm his pets and promised that he would immediately take them home, but the officer kept shooting the dogs. One after another, his dogs lay writhing in the dust and John Stink almost went mad. At last there was only one dog left and it ran frightened and cowering under the porch of a house. The constable got down on his knees, aimed his gun between the slats and shot the last dog. The dog was not quite dead. John Stink, now cursing the cruel whites, picked up the wounded dog and headed toward his little tin cabin, but the dog died in his arms.

Since that time, John Stink hated all white men and lived in solitude, a lonesome, bitter, rich Indian.

The case of Roy Tinker was another one which disturbed the elders. One quiet Sunday in Pawhuska, Roy Tinker was drunk and disturbing the quiet. He had been stopped for a traffic citation and, after signing the ticket, he began walking home. Hiram Stevens, the new police chief, came up to him as Roy started to walk across the street. Stevens called for Roy to stop. Roy either did not hear him or chose to ignore him. Stevens then shot Tinker in the back twice. The police chief loaded him in a taxi, took him to the Johnson funeral home and dumped him in the doorway to die and then left. Stevens was tried, but not convicted in the Osage version of justice when Indians were the victims.

The discussion of the tribal elders continued.

"What can we do?" one leader pleaded

"Perhaps we could offer rewards for solution of the murders," one suggested.

"When people are terrified for their lives, money will not influence them," one of the elders observed.

"Maybe we could plead with the Great White Father in Washington for help," one of the tribal councilmen suggested.

"How can we trust anyone from the government?" a younger man exclaimed. "It was the government which caused all our problems. It was the government which forced us from our reservation in Kansas where we were safe."

"How can we trust any white man?" another said sadly.

"We can't get help from law enforcement officers. We don't trust the government and we don't trust any white man, so what can we do?" one man pleaded.

"What choice do we have except to ask for help from the government in Washington?" a wise leader concluded.

Finally, after much heated discussion, the tribal elders decided to both offer a reward and send a plea to Washington for help. After consultation with one of the tribe's attorneys, the following resolution was adopted:

"Resolution Number 22

"WHEREAS several members of the Osage Tribe have been murdered during the last few months, and many other crimes committed against members of the Tribe,

"WHEREAS in no case have the criminals been apprehended and brought to justice, and,

"WHEREAS the Osage Tribal Council deems it essential for the preservation of the lives and property of the members of the Tribe that prompt and strenuous action be taken to capture and punish the criminals,

"NOW, THEREFORE, BE IT RESOLVED, that a reward of Five Thousand ($5,000.00) Dollars be offered for information leading to the arrest and conviction of the party or parties guilty of the murder of any member of the Osage Tribe, and,

"BE IT FURTHER RESOLVED, that a proper amount of money be appropriated to cover the expense of apprehending the parties guilty of crimes against members of the Osage Tribe, and,

"BE IT FURTHER RESOLVED, that the Honorable Secretary of the Interior be requested to obtain the services of the Department of Justice in capturing and prosecuting the murderers of the members of the Osage Tribe, and,

"BE IT FURTHER RESOLVED, that the Honorable Secretary of the Interior be authorized to ask for an appropriation from Congress of Osage Tribal funds to cover the provisions of this resolution.

"Done by the Osage Tribal Council duly assembled at Pawhuska, Oklahoma this ____ day of March, 1923.

/s/ Paul Red Eagle
Chairman and Assistant Principal Chief
ATTEST: /s/ Charles Brown
Secretary
/s/ Sam Barker
Interpreter."

❧ Chapter 11 ❧

The Bureau of Investigation Enters the Case

In Washington, D.C., an official of the FBI (then called the Bureau of Investigation), read a letter from the Commissioner of the Office of Indian Affairs of the U. S. Department of the Interior. Enclosed with the letter was a copy of the resolution adopted by the Osage Tribal Council and a copy of the letter from the President of the Fairfax, Oklahoma, Chamber of Commerce to the Superintendent of the Osage Agency, a field agency of the Department of the Interior. The FBI official scanned this letter:

"*March 13, 1923*

"*Dear Sir:*

"*Your special attention is hereby called to the number of deaths among members of the Osage Tribe of Indians residing in the Town and vicinity of Fairfax occurring during the past two years under conditions and circumstances suggesting willful murder.*

"*The citizens of our Town have become alarmed by the explosion effected in the house of W.E. and Retta Smith in the heart of the residence section of our Town on the night of March 9th, in which Retta Smith and her servant, Nettie Brookshire, were killed and W.E. Smith was seriously injured.*

"*It occurs to us that the resources of the Department of the Interior and of the Department of Justice ought to be available for the purpose of suppressing the continuous murder of the Osages, and of ferreting out the facts of these atrocious homicides.*

"*A vigorous investigation from these Departments of the Government might reveal the motive that is prompting these destructions of life and property, and a means whereby the future operations of these desperate characters might be thwarted.*

"*We appeal for your earnest and vigorous support in our efforts to*

bring the criminals to justice, and to forestall further destruction of life and property in our community.
Very respectfully,
/s/ L. R. Heflin"

Heflin, who was president of the Pawhuska Chamber of Commerce, circulated a petition which was signed by most of the local businesspersons urging the federal government to enter the case.

The FBI official picked up from his desk a newspaper article which had been clipped from the Brooklyn Times. He read:

"Osage Indians, Richest People, Will Receive New Oil Wealth

"Washington, March 21 (1923) — The Osage Indians, the wealthiest people per capita in the world, will receive more riches on April 5, the Interior Department announced today.

"Millions of dollars will accrue to the 2,100 Osage Indians from the public auction of oil and mineral rights on approximately 34,000 acres of tribal lands, to be held at Pawhuska, Oklahoma," the Department stated. The Indians will be paid a cash bonus and in addition will receive royalties on every barrel of oil taken from the ground.

"Last year the Department, through the sale of these oil leases, gave each of the Indians $10,000. Some of the families derived as much as $80,000. The present sale on April 5 is expected to bring a total bonus of something like $4,000,000 or $5,000,000 as a similar sale conducted in 1922 brought $7,000,000.

"The Osage Nation in Oklahoma holds the richest oil producing field in the United States. There is a wild scramble among oil men to purchase leases. Every member of the tribe is rich in his own right, with an annual revenue running above $10,000...."

The Government Agent sat for a moment digesting what he had read, then he called for an assistant. Thus, one of the most baffling manhunts in history was launched.

☜ Chapter 12 ☞

Federal Investigators with Special Talents Assigned to the Case

Special Agents, carefully selected for their knowledge of Indian and frontier life, were assigned to the Osage Indian murders case. It did not take long for them to realize the momentous task facing them. The obstacles seemed insurmountable.

The entire citizenry of Osage County was in such a state of panic and deep-rooted fear that most people claimed they knew nothing about the murders and were in a hurry to conclude the interviews with the G-men. "It is not safe to know too much," they said. "People who have information about the King of the Osage Hills do not live long."

Private detectives, many of whom were hired by the murderers themselves to frustrate the legitimate investigation, had spent many months on the cases, interviewing numerous persons many times. Other detectives talked too freely about the information they secured with the result that much of the information got back to the murderers. For this reason, many of those interviewed became unfriendly and reluctant to talk to any kind of investigator.

In addition, the fact that the Osage Tribal Council, businessmen, the City of Fairfax, the estates of murdered individuals and others had offered large rewards for solution of the murders had attracted numerous amateur detectives who further interfered with the FBI's work.

Many important witnesses had left the area, fearing that they would be the next victims of the murder gang. As an example, an Indian woman who lived next door to Anna Brown became such a "nervous wreck" as a result of the reign of terror in Osage County that she and her husband fled from the area. On the night of Henry Roan's murder a man returned home and fainted. When he was revived, he told his wife that he was with a cousin of Henry Roan and they were in a car going for some whiskey when they saw Henry Roan killed. They immediately drove away and came home. He said he was afraid that he, too, would be killed if he reported what he had seen. At the time of the FBI investigation, this man was dead, and Roan's cousin, who had also witnessed the slaying, had fled from the area, fearing death.

Many other witnesses had left the area as fugitives from justice. Law-abiding citizens were actually afraid to even talk with the federal Agents, worried that the murderers would see them. The people had lost confidence that anything would ever be done about the murders and they seemed anxious to forget about them and pass them off as unsolvable. The murders even ceased to be a topic of conversation in Osage County. It wasn't "healthy" to talk about them. Many prominent citizens told Agents that, even if they learned the truth, they would not believe it. The initial objective of FBI Agents was to rebuild the citizenry's confidence in law enforcement.

The Special Agents decided to concentrate on three of the numerous murders: Anna Brown, Henry Roan and the Smith family.

The general class of citizenry in the territory was very low. The rich oil fields had produced, not only an abundance of oil and wealth, but also graft, easy money, gambling, prostitution, illegal whiskey, and a horde of parasites bent on milking the Osage Indians of all they owned. The Osages themselves distrusted all white men, including the federal investigators.

Agents learned that the head of the outlaw ring employed spies to observe every move the Agents made and to get the public's reaction to their investigation. These spies made a checklist of those favorable to the "King" and those unfavorable.

Since this area abounded with criminals of every description, including crooked lawyers, politicians, law enforcement officers, doctors, etc., most of whom were affiliated with the gang of outlaws, Agents realized that information would have to come from the criminal element.

In order to accomplish this goal, the Agents conferred with the Special Agent in Charge of their Oklahoma City Office, and he in turn communicated with FBI officials in Washington. They decided to employ a special investigative technique.

As Special Agents continued interviewing persons who might

have information of value, one day a stranger came to town. An Indian. He said he was a medicine man and was searching for relatives who had moved to Oklahoma several years earlier.

A few days later another stranger rode into town, a rough-looking, typical cowboy who had the appearance of one who had known the life of a prison inmate. "A fugitive from justice," some thought. This suspicion seemed to be confirmed when they saw him in the company of some of the area's most notorious outlaws. "Another henchman for the King of the Osage Hills," citizens speculated.

Shortly thereafter, three more strangers came to town: an insurance salesman, a cattleman and an oil prospector. There was nothing unusual about an oil prospector, a cattleman or an insurance salesman in Osage County.

The presence of these individuals did not excite any suspicion, and these strangers seemed to melt into the population of Osage County. All were undercover FBI Agents.

Special Agents often worked for twenty-four consecutive hours or more to expedite certain phases of the investigation. (Even after the murders had been solved, they worked from early morning until after midnight and sometimes all night long to have the cases in satisfactory form for the next morning's session of court.)

The Agent who posed in the undercover capacity of an Indian medicine man was part Indian himself and had experience with cattle, horses, animal husbandry and farming. He was fairly familiar with the ranch business, and could easily pose as a cattleman, stock buyer, et cetera. Among his other interests were race horses and racing which proved helpful in some phases of the investigation. He was particularly qualified for undercover work among the rougher element in the West and Southwest. He made medicine, consisting mostly of sweetened water, and the Osages accepted him warmly. He gained their confidence and cooperation. He not only visited in their homes and attended their ceremonials, thereby gathering much valuable information about the murders, but he also served as medicine man in the inner circle and tribal councils, helping the Osages to make plans for the administration of their tribal government and in solving their problems.

The Agent who assumed the identity of an insurance salesman actually sold legitimate insurance policies, representing a national insurance company, and in so doing gained entrance to the homes of citizens. In this way he learned many details of the murder plots which the citizens, through fear, refused to give to the federal Agents who were working openly.

Agents working undercover often met late at night in dangerous places such as the woods which were used by Al Spencer as a hide-out for his notorious band of bank robbers, and Dead Man's Hill where many murders and robberies had been plotted and committed.

In the course of the investigation, Agents compiled an alphabetical list of residents of Fairfax, Oklahoma, and vicinity, assessing their possible connection with the gang of murderers.

Many people living in Fairfax and vicinity believed that, if the U.S. government was not successful in prosecuting the murderers, many citizens would move away to protect themselves, and others feared that they themselves would be killed for assisting the government investigators. Many said, "When the government takes the ring leader and his allies into custody, many people who now fear for their lives will come forward and tell all they know about these murders and the reign of terror."

(This proved to be true. One salient result of the trials convicting the murderers was to strengthen the confidence in federal law enforcement authorities and to indicate to the lawless element that, when the federal government takes up a matter, it follows it to a successful conclusion, irrespective of the many harassing obstacles placed in its way.)

False rumors and lies by the ring leader and henchmen caused Agents to make needless trips to California, New Mexico, old Mexico, Kansas, Colorado, Texas and Arizona, running down leads designed to frustrate the investigation.

❧ Chapter 13 ❧

Anna Brown's Autopsy Explained

The hunters who had found Anna Brown's body retold their story to Government Agents. They had not recognized the dead woman until her sisters, Mollie Burkhart and Rita Smith, came to the scene and identified the body.

A Fairfax undertaker, F. S. Tureen, said he had prepared the body for burial and arranged for the funeral that was paid for out of Anna Brown's estate. He had frozen the body with salt and ice at the very spot where it was found. When the scalp slipped from the skull as he lifted the body, he found a hole in the back of the head where the bullet had entered, but there was no exit hole. He said they had cut the skull in two. "As a matter of fact," the undertaker said, "I saved the part of the skull with the bullet hole in it." He departed and returned, bringing the portion of the skull to show the Agents.

The Agents noted that the bullet hole had been made by a .32 caliber bullet. One of the Agents inserted a pencil of the same diameter into the hole. The path of the bullet ranged downward at a fifty-degree angle through the body, indicating that Anna Brown probably had been sitting down when she was killed. The bullet entered the head about an inch below the crown and a half inch from the medial line on the left-hand side. The path of the bullet inclined slightly to the left so that it would have struck the floor of the brain cavity or become embedded in the brain. There was no indication that the bullet had passed through the brain to reach the floor of the cavity since there were no chips, marks, or fractures on the floor of the cavity. It appeared certain that the bullet had been fired from a gun of low velocity and lodged in the brain mass.

A physician told FBI Agents that he and his brother had performed the autopsy a few feet from where the body was found. They did not find the murder bullet, but did determine that it would have caused instantaneous death. They bisected the skull, spread the brains out on a board and probed through the brain mass with a small stick, looking for the bullet.

"It is quite possible," he admitted, "that we lost or overlooked the bullet, but the fact is we found no bullet. The condition of the corpse was so bad we didn't conduct a very thorough examination. She had been dead for five or six days."

"Why did you cut the body up into small pieces and cleave the flesh from the limbs with a meat ax?" an Agent asked.

"We were looking for the bullet.".

It appeared to the Agents that these doctors had favored the murderers in every way possible.

The housekeeper who had been with Anna when she left for Mollie Burkhart's house the Saturday morning of her death, said, "On that morning — May 21, 1921 — Anna Brown came to my house and woke me up at about 4:00 or 5:00 a.m.. Anna said that she had just gotten home from Pawhuska and was afraid to go into her house alone. She asked me to go with her, fix her breakfast, and clean her house. Anna was drinking — a common thing with Anna. She always drank a lot of whiskey and she had very loose morals with any man who had whiskey.

"I helped Anna bathe and dress and prepared her breakfast. Just before 8:00 a.m. Anna got a telephone call. She said it was Ernest Burkhart, her brother-in-law, who told her that her mother was very ill. He wanted Anna to come see her. Anna called a cab. Anna left, carrying a rather large handbag, a quart of corn whiskey, some quilts, and a bundle of clothes. She was wearing red shoes. I stayed at Anna's house after Anna left until about 10:00 a.m., making all of the beds, cleaning the rooms, washing the dishes — putting the house in clean and complete order. I left the windows open for fresh air.

"I never saw Anna alive again."

She said that the following Friday she heard that a murdered Indian woman's body had been found northeast of Fairfax. "I went there," she said, "viewed the body where it was found and saw that it was Anna Brown. Anna had no shoes on, and there were no shoes anywhere around, but Anna still wore the same skirt which she had worn that Saturday morning, a skirt which I had made for Anna myself.

"Later I went in Anna's house with Anna's sister, Rita Smith. The house was in the same condition in which I had left it the previous Saturday. No dishes had been used, the beds had not been slept in, and the windows were still raised. But I noticed a strange thing: laying on a table in the front room was the handbag which Anna had taken with her that morning and the quilts were laying over a chair in the front room. It looked like someone just came, put these articles there, and then immediately left again because the house was not disturbed in any way."

In the course of an interview with Bright Roddy, a storekeeper, Special Agents asked if Anna Brown had any enemies.

"Well, yes, you might say she did," Roddy said. "Rose Osage. Rose's father, Amos Osage, was on very friendly terms with Anna, if you know what I mean." He winked. The storekeeper consulted his records. On February 23, 1921, Amos Osage bought an alligator grip for $20, a blanket for $20, and four yards of silk for about $10.

"I gave this merchandise to Anna Brown," he said.

"You mean it was a gift from Amos Osage to Anna?" an Agent asked.

"Yes," the storekeeper replied. "Amos told certain people he was going to leave his wife and marry Anna Brown." Roddy continued, "On one occasion when Amos and Anna were in the store together, Rose Osage came to the door and asked if her father was there. When she was told that he was, she came into the store. Almost immediately, however, she left again. When someone asked Rose if she had found her father, she answered, 'Yes, but I don't want to talk to him when he's with that whore'."

Another source claimed that Rose Osage was jealous of Anna Brown because she suspected that Anna was romantically interested in Rose's husband, Jimmy Hicks, also known as Joe Allen.

Other witnesses reported seeing Rose Osage and Jimmy Hicks in an automobile on the night of Anna Brown's disappearance, very close to the spot where her body was later found. An examination of this car revealed bloodstains, and an Indian woman's red shoes were found in the back seat. Anna Brown was barefoot when her body was found. Rose had claimed that the shoes were her own.

Agents located another individual, one Frank Terrell, who said he felt Rose Osage and her husband Jimmy Hicks were responsible for Anna Brown's murder. He said, "Early on the morning when Anna was killed, Bill Trent and I drove into Fairfax and found Rose and her husband sleeping in a car about a quarter of a mile west of Trent's house. The car was headed toward Trent's house and was parked at a spot approximately a half mile from where Anna's body was later found."

A woman named Mrs. Johnson told Agents that Rose Osage had told her that she was afraid that she, Rose, was going to be arrested for the murder of Anna Brown. Mrs. Johnson said, "Iva, my little daughter, was walking down the street with Rose Osage when Rose told her that she had killed Anna Brown. Rose told Iva that they had knocked Anna over the head, then shot her, and took her out to Three-Mile Creek. Iva said that Rose threatened that, if Iva ever revealed this information, she would 'get her'."

The Federal Agents had a suspect in the murder of Anna Brown — Rose Osage.

❧ Chapter 14 ❧

Special Agents Interview Rose Osage

Agents interviewed Rose Osage, whose true name was Rose Osage Allen, and listened carefully to her story.

"On a Sunday morning, about a week before Anna Brown's body was found, Bill Trent and Frank Terrell passed the place where Joe Allen and I were sleeping in Fannie Lasley's car. This was about a quarter of a mile north of Bill Trent's house on Three-Mile Creek. It was after sunrise when they passed us.

"The day before, Saturday, Fannie Lasley, Jack Hale, my sister, Mary Osage, Joe Allen and I had all gone from Fairfax to Pawnee in Fannie's Studebaker sedan. We left Fairfax that afternoon before sundown and drove to Pawnee. At Pawnee, Fannie, Mary, and I went up to Mrs. Bennett's rooming house, and we stayed there for a few minutes. There was a street carnival at Pawnee at the time and Fannie stated that she was going to join it. She asked us to drive her car back to Fairfax, which we said we would do.

"Fannie stayed at a hotel at Pawnee that night, where we left her between 2:00 and 3:00 a.m. Joe Allen and I and Mary and Jack Hale then drove back to Fairfax where we let Mary out at the Smith-Williams Hotel where Mary and I had a room. Joe Allen and I then drove Jack Hale out to Bill Trent's place where Hale was staying at the time. We did not drive quite up to Trent's house, but stopped the car about a quarter of a mile north of the house. Hale got out and walked to Trent's while Joe and I stayed in the car until Bill Trent and Frank Terrell passed us after sunrise. It was not daylight when we let Jack Hale out. After Terrell and Trent passed us, Allen and I drove back to Fairfax, and I went up to the Smith-Williams Hotel.

"I did not see Anna Brown or anyone else that morning after we left Fairfax."

Rose said she had not been drinking that night and does not carry a gun.

When asked if she ever had any difficulties with Anna, she replied, "I never had a quarrel or fight with Anna Brown. The last time I saw Anna was five or six weeks before, in March, 1921, when the Donaldson boys were holding a roping contest at Burbank. In March, I think it was. On that occasion my husband and I got her out of a rooming house at Burbank where she was with some white men and drunk. We brought her back to her home in Fairfax."

(Kelsie Morrison had previously advised Special Agents that he had accused Rose Osage of killing Anna Brown and in reply Rose had allegedly yelled, "You don't know a God damned thing about it, Slim. I did not kill Anna. Jimmy Hicks killed her. The God damned son of a bitch jumped on me and Jimmy killed her.")

The Agents asked Rose about this incident. She vehemently denied that she had ever said such a thing.

"This was some time after Anna Brown was killed," she explained. "Kelsie Morrison and Joe White, who is my cousin, got Artie (Miss Artie Sawyer) and I to go riding. They got some whiskey and we all drank some. Kelsie kept asking who killed Anna Brown and I told him I did not know."

Rose said that later they went to Ed Cox's house and Kelsie threatened to choke her unless she told who killed Anna Brown.

"I told Artie to call the law," she continued, "but Kelsie and Joe White would not let her. They had the front door locked." Rose said she threw herself on the floor and screamed so someone would hear her. "Kelsie threatened to whip me to make me tell and I hit him with a spittoon, knocked him down, and kicked him. Bob Parker and Earl Gray came and arrested me.

"The next day Kelsie told me that he had not told the law that I had said that Jimmy killed Anna and that he did not believe we had killed Anna." Joe White, who was present at the time, in an interview with FBI Agents, corroborated Rose's story.

"I never learned anything as to who did kill Anna Brown," Rose insisted.

When questioned about the statement about Anna attributed to her by storekeeper Bright Roddy, she protested vehemently, "I positively never did make a remark in Bright Roddy's store, or anywhere else to the effect that I would not talk to Anna Brown or call her a whore. The Indians did say that Anna was getting money from Amos Osage, my father, but Anna and I never did have a quarrel of any kind."

When asked about the blood on the car, she explained, "Joe Allen told me that when they said they had found blood on Fannie Lasley's car that he remembered that Fannie had pinched her finger in the door which made it bleed."

Rose said that Mollie Burkhart told Rose's mother that she believed the man who killed Anna Brown was also the man who killed Henry Roan, Bill Smith, his wife, and Nettie Brookshire. Rose would not say so in plain words, but she implied that Mollie Burkhart had referred to the King of the Osage Hills

Rose Osage talked to Agents freely, frankly, and without any reluctance. She did not hesitate to answer any question fully. She rarely even stopped for a moment to consider her reply, and she answered with candor and unconcern. Many times she even volunteered information. Her whole demeanor was that of an entirely innocent person.

Agents then closely questioned Rose's husband, Joe Allen, alias Jim Hicks, an Indian with Kickapoo, Sao and Fox blood. He was 24 years old, stood 5'7", and weighed approximately 160 pounds. He also was very self-contained and answered the questions asked by the Agents readily and fully. He verified the story which his wife had told. He said the blood on the car came from a woman who had cut her hand. Recalling that Anna had been barefoot when found, Agents inquired about the Indian woman's shoes which were found in this car. He explained that these shoes belonged to his wife, as Rose had claimed.

An exhaustive investigation was then conducted to either prove Rose and her husband guilty or to establish their innocence.

Government Agents talked to Iva Johnson, the girl who had told her mother that Rose Osage had confessed to her that she had killed Anna Brown. They asked Iva, "Did Rose actually tell you that she had killed Anna Brown?"

"No, it was a lie," Iva admitted. "I just said that. I have never heard Rosie make such a statement. I made it up to have some fun out of my mother."

"Did Rose talk to you at all about Anna Brown's murder," the Agents asked the young girl.

"Yes," Iva replied, "Rosie said she didn't know a thing about it and didn't know why they suspected her."

Agents checked the spot where Rose Osage and Jimmy Hicks had been seen sleeping. Although this spot was only about one-half mile from the place where Anna Brown's body had been found, the actual driving distance between the two locations was one and one-half miles.

Additional investigation at Pawnee verified the fact that Rose and her husband were in that town on the Saturday night of Anna's disappearance; that Anna was not with them; and that they did not return to Fairfax until Sunday morning at about two o'clock when they took Jack Hale home. This accounted for their presence at the spot where they were found sleeping. The individuals who had accompanied them to Pawnee completely corroborated their story.

A thorough check of the activities of Rose Osage and her husband established their innocence and Agents crossed them off as suspects.

As often happens in murder cases, a man confined to the Kansas State Penitentiary for forgery confessed that he was one of the men who had been hired to murder Anna Brown. However, he was unable to pick Anna Brown's photograph from several shown to him, so he was not considered a suspect. No explanation can be given for this man's confession. Sometimes inmates will confess to crimes they did not commit because they want to go to a different prison, or because the association with a heinous crime enhances their reputation with their fellow inmates or because they get a thrill from the publicity their confession generates. It is possible, of course, that the real murderers contrived to have this man confess to throw the Agents off the trail.

⚙ Chapter 15 ⚙

Roy Bunch is Suspect in Roan Murder

Special Agents checked the spot where Henry Roan's body had been found in his automobile with a bullet hole in his head. This was in the restricted homestead allotment of Tom-Pah-Pe or Rose Little Star[27] which, the Agents reasoned, gave the U.S. government jurisdiction over the murder of Henry Roan.

The officers who had found Roan's body said that his feet had been just off the pedals and his head was resting on the right hand side of the front seat. The bullet went completely through his head and shattered the windshield. The broken glass was scattered for several feet behind the car along the tire tracks, convincing the Agents that Roan had been shot while he was driving and apparently while the car was still moving, probably by someone sitting in the back seat. Robbery was not the motive since money and valuables in Roan's possession were left untouched.

The wound had not bled very much, but some blood had dripped onto the inside panel of the right front door. Some blood had also dripped outside and had been blown and splattered back along the right side of the car, indicating either that a north wind had been blowing at the time of the murder or that the car had been moving when he was shot.

The undertaker who prepared Roan's body for burial told the investigators:

"Yes, I prepared the body for burial and arranged for the funeral. Very lovely funeral. Roan had lots of friends. Many prominent people were there, too, such as Bill Hale. In fact, Bill Hale rode in the front carriage in the funeral procession and served as a pallbearer. Very nice funeral."

---

[27]Part of the Smith 7 Ranch which was established in 1907.

Agents had a suspect from the very beginning for Roan's murder — Roy Bunch. Numerous people told them that Henry Roan and Roy Bunch were bitter enemies because of Bunch's affair with Roan's wife. Several people had heard them threaten to kill each other and Bunch had an obvious motive: he married Roan's widow on April 6, 1923, two months after Roan's death.

William K. Hale, a prominent local rancher and businessman, had told several people that Roy Bunch was responsible for the murder of Henry Roan because many people had heard them threaten to kill each other.

The operator of a pool hall reported:

"At the time Henry Roan was killed and prior to that time, I was operating a pool hall at Fairfax, Oklahoma. It was public talk prior to Roan's death that Roy Bunch was laying up with Roan's wife, and that there was likely to be a killing between Bunch and Roan. Some time before Roan was killed, Roy Bunch entered my pool hall hurriedly and went into the rear of the building and hid behind a partition. In a few seconds Henry Roan entered my place and, from his expression, he was mad and looking for somebody. He went toward the rear of my place with his hand in his coat pocket. He did not go back far enough to see Bunch behind the partition.

"Roan then walked out of my place, and after he had gone, Bunch came from behind the partition and asked me which way Roan went. I told him, 'Down the street.' Bunch said Roan was looking for him and intended to kill him and that he would have hard luck. Bunch then left.

"Bunch left the impression with me from his remarks that, if Roan had come back behind the partition where he was, that he would have been killed. I have seen Bunch with a small caliber automatic pistol on two occasions."

Agents decided to talk to Roan's widow, now Mrs. Roy Bunch.

"Before Henry Roan's death, covering about a year and a half," she admitted, "Roy Bunch and I were sweethearts. Henry Roan knew of this and during this period, and before, drank lots of whiskey and stayed away from home a great deal of time. Whenever Henry was away from home, Roy Bunch spent most of his time with me.

"Henry Roan was very mad about this," she continued, "and many times remarked to me that he was 'going to get himself a white man,' meaning Roy Bunch.

"At one time when Roy Bunch was working as a meat cutter for the Big Hill Trading Company, Henry Roan came home drinking and accused me of having Roy Bunch come to the house. I told Henry it was not the truth. Henry then said he was going to see somebody.

"I went with him. We went to the Big Hill Trading Company and found Roy Bunch there in the basement grinding sausage with his back to Henry Roan. Henry Roan then picked up a club and struck Roy Bunch across the back of his head. Roy Bunch fell to the floor.

"When he got up he said to Henry Roan, 'What does this mean? I haven't done anything to you.'

"Roy then told Henry to leave. I also pleaded with Henry to leave. Finally he did leave.

"This happened some time over a year before Henry Roan was murdered," the Indian woman continued. "After this happened, Henry Roan stayed home very closely for two or three weeks, and during this time I did not see Roy Bunch. Finally, Henry Roan left home and was gone for some time. As soon as Henry Roan left home, Roy Bunch came to my house and told me that Henry Roan was trying to get him, and that he, Roy Bunch, was going to beat him to it if he could."

She added that after that time Henry was away from home very often, sometimes for four or five weeks at a time, and while he was away she was always with Roy Bunch. She said Roy Bunch reiterated that Henry Roan was trying to kill him, but that he intended to beat him to it.

"Some little time after Henry Roan's body was found," Roan's widow continued, "Roy Bunch told me that they would probably mix him up, or try to stick him for killing Henry Roan on account of his going with me, and if they did, for me to swear that Henry Roan had threatened his life.

"Before Henry Roan was killed," she said, "Roy Bunch always carried an automatic pistol. I don't remember seeing Roy Bunch with this pistol after Henry Roan was killed."

Agents again interviewed the proprietor of the Fairfax pool hall for any additional information he might have concerning Roy Bunch.

"I have known Mr. Roy Bunch intimately for 12 years," he said. "He frequently visited my place of business for several months prior to the death of Henry Roan and at various times he stated to me that he loved Mary Roan, the wife of Henry Roan, and would marry her if he could get her.

"About ten days prior to the finding of Henry Roan's body, at about 12:30 a.m., I met Roy Bunch in front of the Ford garage in

Fairfax, Oklahoma. He stopped me and we entered into a conversation. Mr. Bunch asked me if I had ever heard Henry Roan make any threats against his (Bunch's) life. I stated to him that I had not. Mr. Bunch then asked me that, in case he had to kill Mr. Roan, would I swear that I had heard Mr. Roan make threats against his life. I told him that I would not. Mr. Bunch then stated that Mr. William Hale had told him that he would swear to having heard Roan make threats against his (Bunch's) life, and that he (Bunch) wanted to get someone else who would swear the same. Mr. Bunch cautioned me to say nothing about his having asked me to swear to such a statement.

"The morning of the day when Henry Roan's body was found, Mr. Bunch entered my place of business, apparently in a nervous condition, and handed me a .38 automatic revolver and asked me to keep it for him, saying at the time that he had heard that Henry Roan's body had been found, and that he did not want to be caught with a gun on him. He also stated at that time that there were not many guns in the country like the one which he had just handed me.

"Previous to that time, I had seen in Mr. Bunch's possession, a pearl handled, nickel-plated revolver and he told me Mary Roan had bought it for Henry Roan, but Mary had taken the gun away from Henry and gave it to him.

"To the best of my knowledge, Mr. Bunch called for and received the .38 automatic on the day following the discovery of Henry Roan's body or the next day."

Henry Cornett, a man with a very notorious reputation, stated that Bunch had come to him at Ponca City, Oklahoma, and told him he was expecting to be arrested at any moment for the murder of Henry Roan. Bunch told Cornett that he knew of his success at beating cases and wanted his help.

The investigating Agents compared notes. Clearly, many people thought that Roy Bunch had killed Henry Roan and he definitely had to be considered an obvious suspect, maybe too obvious, the Special Agents thought.

"It looks too easy," one of the Agents said. "It looks as if some people are making a deliberate effort to pin Henry Roan's murder on Roy Bunch."

"Yes," another Agent agreed. "Something else bothers me about Bunch as the perpetrator. The murderer was apparently riding in the back seat of Roan's car when the shot was fired. Does it seem reasonable that Roan would allow Bunch — his bitter enemy — to be riding out in the country with him, let alone sitting behind him in the back seat of his car?"

"No," the other investigator agreed. "It doesn't ring true."

"But we have to consider Bunch a suspect until we prove otherwise," another commented.

❦ Chapter 16 ❦

Special Agents Review the Smith Massacre.

A chemist from one of the Oklahoma universities, who was called in to conduct an examination of the Smith premises after the explosion, said he reached the conclusion that a large quantity of TNT or nitroglycerin had been placed under the building near the garage door at a point where a hole was blown in the six-inch concrete floor six feet wide and three and one-half feet deep. This concrete floor was blown to bits. The house had apparently been soaked on one or more sides with some flammable substance since it had been seen blazing up once or twice a few seconds before the explosion.

Agents learned from a representative of the Osage Torpedo Company that on March 7 or 8, a day or two before the Smith explosion, the company's magazine, located in an isolated spot northwest of Denoya, Oklahoma, had been burglarized and ten quarts of nitroglycerin stolen.

Bill Smith, who had been very actively investigating the murder of Anna Brown and Henry Roan, had told various individuals that he knew the identity of the mastermind who was causing the murders. Several persons told Government Agents that Bill Smith had confided to them that he was afraid that the King of the Osage Hills was going to have him killed. For this reason, he moved from his ranch house to a house in Fairfax. These individuals said Smith had only lived in this house one or two days when the explosion occurred. Others said the explosion occurred the very day he had moved into this house.

The night watchman of the City of Fairfax told Agents that, a few minutes prior to the explosion, he had been at a hotel four blocks from the Smith home. As he entered the lobby, he saw a car drive west about two blocks from the Smith home. He said there was nothing unusual about a car being on the streets at that hour of the morning, so he thought nothing of it. He said that, as he went into the hotel lobby and sat down, the explosion occurred almost instantly.

One man told government Agents that he had been at the scene of Smith's home immediately after the explosion. He said he saw Ernest Burkhart there. Most people who were there had bathrobes on over their night clothes, but Ernest Burkhart had a bathrobe on over his trousers. One of the firefighters who had been at the scene verified this information and said he had conversed with Burkhart. He said he told Ernest Burkhart that the explosion was a terrible thing. Burkhart replied that it was "some fire." This firefighter told Agents he had remarked that the one responsible for this should be thrown in the fire and burned. He said Burkhart made no reply to this but wheeled around and immediately left.

Another man, who resided two doors south of W.E. Smith, reported, "On the night of the explosion I was up practically all night because of illness in my family. At approximately 2:00 a.m. I heard a car pass my house. This car drove to the end of the block south of my home and stopped to let a man out. This man walked north on this block toward the Smith house. I paid no particular attention at the time, thinking someone was bringing one of my neighbors home. Fifteen or twenty minutes prior to the explosion, I heard a car pass my house going south at a high rate of speed. The explosion broke the window glass in my house and particles of debris fell in my yard and on my house."

Several persons saw a car racing from the scene of the explosion, but none of them had recognized the occupants. One of these witnesses stated that this automobile had two regular headlights and a spotlight on the windshield.

Agents found through their investigation that Kelsie Morrison, a notorious criminal in the area, owned an automobile with a spotlight on the windshield. Furthermore, a man who worked at the Pawnee, Oklahoma, light plant saw an automobile similar to Morrison's pass through Pawnee at about 4:00 a.m., March 10, 1923, the morning of the Smith explosion.

The government investigators also learned that two or three days prior to the explosion, when Kelsie Morrison was arranging to buy his automobile, he told the car dealer that he had to go to Pawhuska to get some money from Bill Hale. The investigation disclosed that Hale was surety on notes for Morrison totaling approximately $2,000, but this really did not indicate much because Hale, one of the wealthiest men in Osage County, often lent large sums of money to various individuals. Hale had been in Campbell, Texas, at a cattleman's convention with Henry Grammer at the time of the Smith explosion.

Agents interviewed the proprietor of a store, inquiring about Kelsie Morrison. He said Morrison, who had a vicious temper, had some difficulty with an attorney, as a result of which Morrison broke the lawyer's nose. "Later," the shopkeeper said, "Morrison came into my store and wanted me to take a check for $50. He told me the check was no good, but it would be some time. Said his mother, father and brother were dead and he might as well be dead. Wanted to buy a shotgun. Said he was going to have to kill a man."

"Let's find out where Morrrison was on the evening of March 9 and the early morning of March 10, when the Smith home was blown up," an Agent said.

Morrison had an alibi. He claimed that he had been in Oklahoma City registered at a hotel and was not anywhere near Osage County on March 9 or 10.

Subsequent investigation revealed that a Kelsie Morrison had in fact been registered at that hotel on those dates. However, Agents also located a witness who had seen Morrison in Osage County on the evening of March 9, 1923.

"Are you certain it was March 9?" Agents asked.

"Yes," he said, "I'm sure of the date. It was between 11:00 and 12:00 p.m. I saw Kelsie Morrison and another man in a cafe in Osage County. Morrison was very talkative — more so than usual — and said they had just driven from Oklahoma City and got on the wrong road driving into or near the town of Stillwater. Morrison went to the icebox, raised the lid, and asked me whether I had any cold milk. The other individual with him might have been Asa Kirby, but I'm not sure."

Another man insisted that Morrison had not been in Oklahoma City on March 9-10, as he claimed, but had arranged with another man to register at an Oklahoma City hotel under Morrison's name to provide him an alibi. The Government Agents also considered it interesting that, in months following the Smith massacre, Morrison exhibited large sums of cash while previously he had been trying to borrow $50 from the shopkeeper. Another man told Agents that he had held stakes in a poker game on one occasion when Morrison played two out of three best hands and lost a large sum of money.

"Why would Morrison lie and create a phony alibi?" an Agent asked rhetorically.

"I can think of a very good reason," another Agent offered.

"Could it be that Kelsie Morrison is the King of the Osage Hills?" one FBI Agent speculated.

"Naw," his partner disagreed, "He's not big enough for that. A hireling, perhaps. A trigger man. But not the big boss."

Kelsie Morrison was listed as a suspect in the Smith murders.

John Maye, a convict in Kansas State Penitentiary at Lansing, Kansas, gave FBI Agents a great deal of valuable data concerning the Smith massacre.

"Asa Kirby and myself operated a rooming house at Webb City for about four months, from January to April, 1924," Maye said, "About two weeks before Bill Smith's house was blown up, John Ramsey came to the rooming house ... and had a private conference with Asa Kirby. The following morning Asa took me out into the country near Webb City in his car and told me we could get $2000 to kill a man and his squaw, meaning Bill Smith and his wife.

"A few days later Kirby came to our rooming house at Webb City with a roll of fuse about 100 feet long and some dynamite caps, and told me we would get ready to go over to Fairfax and do the job, meaning blow up Bill Smith's house and kill Smith and his wife. Kirby asked me if I knew where a nitro magazine was located near Webb City, and I told him I did not.

"Kirby then said John Ramsey had told him that there was a magazine on the road to Kaw City.

"The next day Kirby and myself went to Henry Grammer's and Kirby looked for a magazine but could not find it. We drove on to Henry Grammer's and had a talk there.

"The next day John Ramsey came to our house at Webb City, and Ramsey and Kirby had a talk. Ramsey drove away in his Ford car and Kirby followed him in his own car.

"Kirby returned to our house later and told me John Ramsey had showed him where a nitro magazine was. The next evening Kirby came home with a new five-gallon oil can and left the can there until dark.

"After dark, Asa came and got the oil can, wrapped it with an old quilt, put the can in his car and drove away. This was between 8 and 9 p.m. the night before Bill Smith's house was blown up.

"Kirby returned home after midnight the same night, and the next morning Kirby told me he had taken the stuff, meaning nitroglycerin, over there and left it and was going back that night as he wanted to be sure Smith and wife were at home.

"The night Smith's house was blown up Asa Kirby left our house in Webb City about dark.

"Kirby woke me when he came in the following morning.

"About 11:00 a.m. the same day, when Kirby got up, he told me that it was a dandy job, that they heard her explode when they were about seven or eight miles away."

The inmate stated that one of the outlaws came to their house later and, in his presence, said that they 'done a good job.' Maye continued, "They said that they had killed two of them, Smith's wife and a servant girl, and blowed Smith's privates off. They said Smith was in the hospital and would be gone in a day or two.

"Two days later Kirby and myself went to Grammer's to get some whiskey and while at Grammer's Asa Kirby and Grammer went down to Grammer's barn and had a long talk. When Kirby came back to where I was he said he'd be ready to go as soon as Grammer gave him some money. Kirby walked to Grammer's back door and Grammer handed Kirby a big roll of money."

If Maye was telling the truth — and the Agents had no reason to think he was not — Asa Kirby was one of the Smith murderers.

❧ Chapter 17 ❧

False Leads — A Young Man Provides New Information

Special Agents spent a great deal of time pursuing leads which proved unproductive. One day they were approached by a 19-year-old man. "I know all about who killed Henry Roan and the Smiths," he announced, "and why."

"We're listening," one of the Agents said, skeptically.

"In 1923, I had some business with a man named Duffield and two other guys named Blackie and Curley. Duffield lived at Fairfax and was in jail at Pawhuska on a whiskey charge in late 1922 and early 1923."

"What did this Blackie look like?" an Agent asked.

"Blackie was about 25 years old, dark-complexioned and had dark eyes. Really dark eyes. The upper lid of one of his eyes was grown to the eyeball."

One of the agents made a mental note: from that description, Blackie could not be identical with Blackie Thompson, a notorious man whose name had cropped up during the investigation.

"How about Curley?" one of the Agents prompted.

"Curley was young, sort of blond, slight build."

This Curley could not be identical with Curley Johnson, another man of bad reputation in the area, because Johnson was about 45 years old.

"These guys were all bootleggers in Osage County," the young man continued. "but they had left the area. Folks say they're near Oklahoma City."

One of the Agents asked, "What makes you think they had something to do with the murders?"

"Well, about six or eight months earlier Duffield told me that he had killed Henry Roan because Roan and Duffield had been partners in bootlegging whiskey and Roan cheated him. He told me that, while Duffield was in jail at Pawhuska, Roan sold their partnership's Buick roadster and collected some money which was due them, but he refused to split it with Duffield when Duffield got out of jail. Duffield told me that he had seen Roan in his car north of Fairfax and went up and spoke to him. When Roan looked away Duffield said he shot him and Roan fell over backwards over the back seat. Duffield told me he had killed Bill Smith for revenge. He told me that Smith and a Mr. Bennett had ordered two quarts of whiskey. When Duffield and Curley brought the whiskey to Gray Horse, Smith and Bennett had some police officers there to trap them, but Duffield and Curley broke one bottle of whiskey and threw the other away. Curley also told me that Duffield had killed Henry Roan and blew up the Smith residence."

The young man was very excited when telling the above story and volunteered that, if his expenses were paid, he would find these three men, gain their confidence and get them to tell all of the facts. He stated he would work to recover the rewards which had been offered in the case.

Agents thoroughly checked out the information furnished by this young man and found it to be entirely false. Although the young man himself sincerely believed the story to be true and sincerely wanted to help the Agents, the information Duffield, "Curley" and "Blackie" had furnished him proved to be no more than boastful lies.

☞ Chapter 18 ☜

Undercover Agents Gather Information

One of the undercover Agents struck up a conversation with an old man in Fairfax, Oklahoma, one of the few people who did not mind talking with strangers.

The old fellow said he was 84 years old and had come from Canada at an early age and settled in Osage County, taking contracts to dig water wells for the Osage Indians. He said he knew all of the Indians who had been murdered, mentioning Anna Brown, Henry Roan, and the Bill Smith family. "Smith was the fellow who got blown up and killed in his house at Fairfax with his wife and a servant girl." He said, "Smith's wife and Anna Brown were sisters and they were related somehow to Henry Roan. Folks think a rich ranchman was the mastermind behind all three murders." He did not mention the rancher's name.

The old man told the stranger that those murders were being investigated by the federal government detectives. Then, turning to the stranger, the old man cautiously asked, "You a detective?"

"That's a good one: me a detective!" the undercover FBI agent chuckled.

"I guess I've said too much already," the old-timer said. "My son-in-law has told me not to talk for the bunch may bump me off if I did."

At a filling station on the Fairfax-Pawhuska road, one of the other undercover Agents talked to the woman who serviced his automobile.

"You thinking of locating in this area?" she asked.

"Well, I'm looking around for a location," he said.

She mentioned that the ranch across the road from the filling station belonged to a man named Bill Hale. She said Hale was not a very good neighbor. "He controls everything around here," she said. "One time Bill Hale owed us an account of $50. We offered Hale $10 for an old house that stood in his pasture across the road from our filling station. Hale told us he'd let it rot before he'd take $10. Finally, he agreed to take $25 for it. We all agreed on the price and we moved it over to the filling station.

"Later we sent Hale a bill for the balance of $25 he owed us on his account. He then sent us a bill for $250, claiming that we owed him that amount for things we had bought from him at various times. My brother and I, who operate the filling station together, didn't owe Hale five cents, but Hale did owe us. That's just the kind of man Hale is."

She pointed to an area nearby where she said an Osage woman had been murdered.

"It's generally felt by folks in the area that Hale had her murdered. She said there was also an Indian man killed whose body was found in a pasture near Fairfax. She added that there was also a house blown up in Fairfax killing a man, his wife and a servant girl.

She told the stranger that Hale controlled about 30,000 acres of land near their filling station and that some time earlier he had the grass on this land insured for one dollar per acre. Hale then had his cowboys go around at night and set fire to this grass, and every acre which was insured was burned off. Hale then collected the $30,000 insurance.

At this point in the conversation another car drove into the filling station and the stranger had to leave to let the other car drive in.

Two of the other undercover agents stopped for the night at the Jones Hotel in Ralston and engaged the proprietor in conversation. He said he had lived in the Osage country for about thirty-two years and had been running the hotel since his stepfather's death about two years earlier. In a general conversation about investments and so forth, he commented that the country in the vicinity of Fairfax and Ralston was owned and controlled by a gang of men, the leader of which was a man named Bill Hale. He said hijackers, bootleggers and other criminals marry Indian women to obtain the royalties and other income from their oil and lands.

One man told an undercover agent that a friend had told him that he overheard the murder of Anna Brown being planned. He said the guilty party was a very wealthy rancher who lived at Fairfax. (He mentioned no name.) He said other wealthy men related to this man were also involved. He said these men were very desperate and dangerous, especially the rancher, who was highly influential. He said these men would surely kill anyone who they feared might inform on them.

✇ Chapter 19 ✇

Federal Agents Rendezvous

The federal Agents, joined by their undercover colleagues, conferred in a deserted area on the outskirts of Pawhuska and compared information gathered in their respective investigations. The cowboy rode to the rendezvous on horseback. The insurance man and the oil man came separately by car to protect their undercover status.

"This guy Bill Hale's name keeps popping up."[28] one began.

"Yeah, I keep hearing it too," another Agent said, "but the strange thing is he had been very outspoken against the lawlessness and reign of terror. He's even offering a $100,000 reward to help solve the murders."

"Some say he's a very gentle, polite person," a third reported. "Has a lot of influential friends and some low-life friends also. He claims to be a good friend of the Osages."

"He's made a lot of money here," one pointed out.

"He drifted here from Texas an uneducated, uncouth cowpuncher," the Agent posing as the Texas cowboy said. "He first arrived here on the reservation about 1900. He was a cowboy hired to drive a herd of cattle from Texas to Kansas. They paused here to fatten up the trail-worn cattle and Hale decided he liked it here. On the return trip, he decided to stay instead of going back to Texas. He sent for his wife to join him and talked his nephews into coming here too. He and his wife lived in a tent when they first got here. Hale hired himself out to an Osage family and lived with them illegally in the Gray Horse Osage settlement."

---

[28]The dialogue is simulated.

One federal investigator shook his head. "What surpirses me," he said. "is a lot of people say he's very kind and generous, especially with old folks, kids and handicapped people."

"Yeah," one of his fellow Agents added, "one day he saw a little boy he thought was depressed, so he told one of his underlings to buy the kid a pony to cheer him up!"

"He can afford it," the undercover insurance man said. "He's one of the wealthiest men in Osage County."

"With all the good things you hear about him, you hear a lot of bad stuff too," the undercover medicine man commented.

"He's made a lot of money in some underhanded deals," the Agent in charge of the investigation reminded them. "Reputedly, he has no scruples and has an insatiable hunger for money and power."

"Yeah," the insurance man said. "Folks say he's money crazy and women crazy."

"People also say," the undercover cattleman said, "that, if he's mixed up in anything, you can bet his nephews, the Burkhart boys, his sister's sons, are also involved. He's sort of a foster father to them."

"Is he married?" the Agent in charge asked.

"Yeah. Has one daughter. Willie. Good looking young lady," he was informed.

"These nephews... did you get their names?"

"Yeah. Ernest and Roy Burkhart. He has another nephew named Duke Burkhart, but Duke is in the cattle business and apparently doesn't get mixed up in the shady deals."

"Hale's now a big rancher and farmer," the cattleman said.

"They say Hale's become a multimillionaire through his dealings with the Indians," the medicine man observed. "They say that, one way or the other, he makes money on every Osage that dies."

"Yeah," an Agent agreed. "One of his own relatives told me that Hale profits from the death of every Indian in Osage County by filing various false claims against their estates and by stealing their cattle."

"He owns a stable of fine horses and controls a bank in Fairfax, Oklahoma," the cattleman reported. "Also owns an interest in the Big Hill Trading Company and the Big Hill Undertakers."

"If he is mixed up in these murders, it's very convenient that he's in the undertaker business," one of them joked.

"Strangely enough, lots of prominent people hold him in the highest respect," the Agent posing as the oil man said. "He controls many of the land transactions, oil interests and other business deals. He's also very influential politically, both on the state and local levels."

"Right," the Agent in charge summed up. "Apparently he completely dominates Osage County — its business, its politics, and, according to many, its illegal activities. He supposedly brags that he'll never stand trial for anything because of his influence."

"I personally heard him boast that he controls everything from the road overseer all the way to the top," the undercover insurance man said. "Says he's too smart to catch cold. He also controls most of the chiefs of police in the County and other law enforcement officials."

"Then we'd better be very careful what information we share with local law enforcement people," the man in charge of the investigation warned.

"Hale employs a variety of reckless characters," the undercover cowboy said. "Ex-convicts or fugitives from justice and killers for hire. He makes their bond and hires lawyers for them when they're arrested. That's how he recruits them. He gets them out of jail and then puts them to work."

"The word is Hale gets guardians appointed for some of the Indians, then he conspires with the guardians to swindle the Indians in selling them horses, cattle, automobiles and so forth. In some cases he serves as guardian himself," one Agent said.

"A white woman, described as a 'sporting woman', was a close friend and neighbor of Hale," the pseudo cowboy said. "He got her to marry a wealthy Osage Indian to get his money. It apparently is common practice for Hale and his outlaw associates to get an Indian married to a prostitute and then have her divorce him and get a sizable alimony, a share of which Hale and his fellow outlaws get."

"Well, I think we should concentrate our efforts on this guy Hale and his nephews," the man in charge said.

"Yeah," the oil man agreed, "that's what I think. It won't be easy, though, because he either has people in his hip pocket or they're terrified of him."

"Let's meet back here in a few days to compare notes," the Agent in charge of the case instructed.

Although they did not know it at the time, the federal investigators were on the right track: William K. ("Bill") Hale was the King of the Osage Hills, the powerful, unscrupulous puppeteer who pulled the strings for Osage County's criminal element.

✒ Chapter 20 ✒

Bill Hale, King of the Osage Hills

William King Hale, with aliases Bill Hale and "King," a man whose desire for riches and power was said to be devoid of scruple, had drifted into Osage County from Texas as an uneducated and uncouth cowpuncher.

Born and raised in Greenville, Texas, Hale settled in Osage County in the early days. He worked for a while as a cowboy, living in a tent. He later established himself as an important cattle owner and a man of political and financial influence. He managed to gain control of 45,000 acres of select Osage grazing land by means of leases and acquiring outright ownership of 5,000 acres, and became immensely wealthy through his dealings with the Osage Indians, eventually becoming a multimillionaire. He owned a stable of fine horses, controlled a bank in Fairfax, Oklahoma, and owned an interest in a store, the Big Hill Trading Company, as well as the Big Hill Undertakers. He owned a home in Fairfax, Oklahoma, and a ranch house near Gray Horse, Oklahoma, in the center of his immense holdings.

Hale was said to have been a virtual foster father to his Burkhart nephews, sons of his sister. He completely dominated them and their properties.

Hale was of medium stature, standing 5 feet 8 or 9 inches and weighed approximately 165 pounds, but he had a prepossessing figure and a domineering personality. He was very self-confident and affected a military air, carrying his shoulders back and his chest out. He was a very neat dresser with black hair, gray eyes and a ruddy complexion. His eye sight was poor, requiring him to wear thick glasses and he also had a slight hearing impediment. He listed his occupation as stockman and farmer. At the time the FBI's investigation began, he was in his late forties. Hale had the reputation of

William King Hale, King of the Osage Hills

having a very high opinion of himself.

His method of building up power and prestige was to bring various individuals under obligation to him by gifts or favors. Consequently, he had a tremendous following in the vicinity, composed not only of the riffraff element, but of many good, substantial citizens as well. He had in his employ from time to time a number of reckless characters, many of whom were ex-convicts or fugitives from justice and known as killers-for-a-price. For the past twenty years he had completely dominated Osage County.

Hale had a commission as deputy sheriff and, although he did not serve process papers as other deputies did, it permitted him to carry a gun and gave him easy access to the jail and its inmates. He was always interested in the welfare of the prisoners and frequently posted their bond and secured lawyers for them. Then he recruited them for his gang.

One of his closest friends was the mayor of Fairfax, Oklahoma, reputed head of the local Ku Klux Klan who served as a lookout for Hale and continually furnished him information and assisted him in all of his various questionable deals. He also served as guardian for Mollie Burkhart, Osage wife of Hale's nephew, Ernest.

Agents learned that Hale had "set up" numerous crimes in his manipulation of Oklahoma criminals. In one instance Hale paid a bribe to enable a man to secure a pardon. Later Hale told this man that large sums of money were being moved out of the state to avoid taxation. He said some of this money had already been moved, but he would give this criminal advance information as to when more of it would be moved.

Hale was once intimate with a rich widow in Osage County who had no faith in banks and kept very large sums of money at her home in the country. She had an 18-year-old daughter with whom Hale was having sexual relations while borrowing the widow's money. When the widow learned of this, she and Hale had a falling out, and the widow hired a big, tough Negro to work for her. Hale proposed to a certain criminal (who also had been a sheriff) that he go to the widow's place, kill the Negro and rob the widow.

Hale tried to get this same man to steal diamonds from a Mr. Fred Denoya of Osage County. Shortly after this proposition was made, Ernest Burkhart arranged with Blackie Thompson, Jim Parker and a criminal named Anderson to rob Fred Denoya and his wife of their diamonds. Burkhart told them to then take the diamonds to Bill Hale, who would buy them. This trio did rob Denoya and his

Bill Hale's Big Hill Trading Company in Fairfax, now a furniture store.

wife and, pursuant to Ernest's request, they took the gems to Hale, who evidently knew all about the deal suggested by Ernest.

Thompson approached Hale and simply said, "I have that Denoya stuff. Do you want it?"

Hale answered, "Yes, how much do you want?"

Thompson replied, "A thousand dollars."

Hale said, "The most I will give you is $650."

Thompson refused to sell them at that price since they were supposed to be worth about $3,000.

Hale brought Fred Denoya to this same criminal (the former sheriff) whom he had propositioned to do the job in the first place and asked for his assistance in recovering the diamonds for Denoya.

Hale and the Burkharts bragged that they were not at all worried that they would ever be convicted of any crime or be made to serve time for the murders because of their wealth and Hale's influence with state authorities.

Hale told an acquaintance that he was not afraid of the government investigating the cases since he felt they were too slow to get anything. Hale was also of the opinion that the government had no jurisdiction over the murder of Henry Roan, as the government claimed, and he did legal research on cases of a similar nature which had been adjudicated in New Mexico. He thought these cases would be valid precedents to deny the U.S. government jurisdiction in the case.

Hale had no known arrests.

Agents talked to a man in Los Angeles, California, who had formerly resided in Osage County, who stated that Bill Hale had always been a political power in Osage County and had, therefore, always held a commission as a deputy sheriff, thus empowering him to carry a gun. He stated that, in his opinion, Bill Hale did not actually commit the murders, since Hale was a coward, but had procured someone else to commit them. He said Hale had been the head of a gang of criminals, cattle thieves, robbers et cetera, for many years, and had dealt with young Indian boys, selling them cattle and then beating them out of the cattle.

Ernest Burkhart and his wife, Mollie, had Joe Bigheart, Grace Bigheart's son, and his wife, Bertha, adopt the youngest child of Ernest and Mollie. (Grace Bigheart was Mollie's half sister.) This child was a baby girl named "Anna" after Anna Brown. She said that, following this adoption, Joe Bigheart died and this adopted Burkhart child inherited half of his estate, approximately $75,000. Bertha and Joe Bigheart had no other children so the child stood to inherit half of Bertha Bigheart's estate at her death, approximately $150,000[29]

Mrs. John Bigheart, Grace Bigheart's daughter-in-law, informed one of the Agents that a rumor was circulating at Fairfax that the Hale-Burkhart faction was planning to kill Mrs. Joe (Bertha) Bigheart and then kill her parents so that the adopted Burkhart daughter would inherit all of Bertha's estate.

---

[29]Equivalent to approximately $11.8 million in 1998 dollars.

❧ Chapter 21 ❧

Ernest Burkhart

Ernest Burkhart with aliases, Earnest Burkhart and "Burkie" was born on September 11, 1892, in Greenville, Texas. He had come to Oklahoma when he was a young boy and lived his whole life under the influence of his uncle, Bill Hale. He was 5 feet 8 inches tall, weighed 150 pounds, and was of medium build. He had dark-brown hair, blue eyes, and a ruddy complexion. Described as very nervous, "money mad," a miser and an avid poker player, Ernest was weak-willed and would not hesitate to do anything which his uncle asked him to do. He had been a taxi driver in Fairfax until he married Mollie, wealthy daughter of Lizzie Q, and allegedly did not work from that day forward. He and his wife had two children, James William and Elizabeth Ernestine. He had enlisted in the United States Army on June 27, 1918, and was honorably discharged on July 9, 1919.

In July, 1921, Burkhart had smuggled two fine steel saws and some nitric acid to certain inmates of the Pawhuska Jail. This acid, which one of the prisoners kept in a cup made from soap, was used to soften the steel bars, after which the bars were sawed, making a hole through which about twelve prisoners escaped. However, the convict who had preserved the acid in the soap cup and who had done all the work sawing the bars was too large to exit through the hole. He stripped and soaped his body, but to no avail. He was still unable to escape.

In 1920, Ernest Burkhart told Blackie Thompson that he wanted Bill Smith and his wife killed. He explained why: "My wife and Mrs. Smith are sisters. Their mother, Lizzie Q, is old and very ill and liable to die at any time. If the old woman dies first, Smith's wife will inherit part of her estate, but if Mrs. Smith dies first, the old woman's

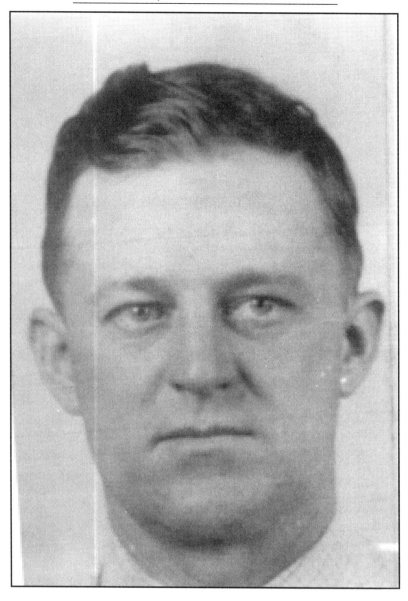

Ernest Burkhart
(October 4, 1926.)

wealth, or most of it, will pass at her death to my wife, Mollie." As compensation for this deed, Burkhart said the perpetrators could rob the Smiths of their diamonds and a roll of $300-$400 which Smith usually carried. In addition, he and his uncle, Bill Hale, would pay them $1,000 and give them a Buick automobile.

(In collusion with Burkhart, Thompson had once stolen Burkhart's Buick automobile so the latter could collect the insurance money. Police officers had caught Thompson with this car which Ernest had reported as stolen. Ernest had prevailed upon Thompson to plead guilty and take all the blame, promising that, if he did, Ernest would get him out of prison in four or five months. Thompson received a five-year sentence on his guilty plea and was sent to McAlester Prison in November, 1920. He was paroled on March 7, 1922, without the help of Ernest Burkhart.)

Thompson had returned to Osage County and pulled off additional jobs with Ernest Burkhart and others, including several diamond robberies.

Again, Ernest tried to induce Thompson to kill Bill Smith and his wife, but later, Burkhart told him that others had been hired to blow up the Smith home.

Mollie Burkhart, wife of Ernest Burkhart, daughter of Lizzie Q and sister of Anna Brown and Rita Smith. She was the innocent conduit in the murderers' quest for their victims' headrights. Her dibilitating sickness, apparently from slow poisoning, was cured when FBI Agents removed her from Osage County.

❧ Chapter 22 ❧

FBI Agents Meet in Desolate Area

Investigating Special Agents would send secret signals to each other that a meeting should be held to compare notes. The medicine man, the insurance salesman, the cowboy and the oil prospector mingled undercover with local people and gathered a wealth of important evidence which they shared with their colleagues who were working openly.

The Indians told the undercover medicine man many things about the murders which they would not tell the other Agents. Likewise, the insurance salesman learned many things while ostensibly selling insurance. The cowboy established a close association with the employees and friends of the Bill Hale, gaining the confidence of the criminal element in Osage County, so much so that they often discussed the murders with him casually, unwittingly contributing valuable information for the investigation.

The Agent posing as an insurance man even contacted Bill Hale himself and almost succeeded in selling him an insurance policy. He originally met Hale at a hotel in Fairfax, Oklahoma, and after that time saw him on several occasions. The Agent found that Hale was very talkative about his cattle deals and his boyhood days, relating how he had run away from home to become a cowboy. Hale was very nervous and complained to the Agent that he had stomach trouble and was having trouble sleeping. He remarked that he had sold all of his cattle interests, retaining only 250 head of cattle and about seventy-five tons of cottonseed cake. He said he did not know exactly what he was going to do but felt he needed a long rest. The Agent learned that Hale had already earned $75,000 that year (1925) from his cattle dealings and other interests. Hale was very friendly to this undercover Agent and introduced him to several prominent citizens of Fairfax. The Agent learned that Hale, apparently because of the investigation, was conducting a propaganda campaign to win as many friends as he could by giving away numerous presents to various individuals, buying them suits of clothes, co-signing notes for them, giving ponies to children, and being exceedingly kind to old people and those suffering from afflictions.

This undercover federal Agent ascertained that Hale had ordered a new suit of clothes and an overcoat from a tailor to whom he remarked that he was going to take a trip to Florida. Hale's eighteen-year-old daughter, Willie, had commented that the family had everything packed and were prepared to leave at a moment's notice. Hale told others in the presence of the undercover Agent that he was too slick and keen to catch cold and he was tired of two-bit crooks riding on his reputation.

At their rendezvous, the undercover Special Agents exchanged information and furnished leads for the Agents working openly to follow. The sum of the data gathered by the Agents indicated that there was a definite relationship between the murders of Anna Brown, Henry Roan, and Bill Smith, his wife and their servant girl, and probably many of the other murders.

William K. Hale, the Agents learned, produced a $25,000 insurance policy on the life of Henry Roan after the Indian's death. Hale claimed Roan owed him that much for various cattle deals.

Bill Smith and Hale had been on very unfriendly terms. Smith alleged that Hale owed him $6,000 and Hale had refused to pay. At the time of his sudden death, Smith had a suit pending against Hale for this debt.

The Agents developed a rationale for the murders: it appeared to be a plot to centralize the wealth of Lizzie Q's family through Mollie Burkhart into the hands of her husband, nephew of William K. Hale.

Lizzie Q, also known as Lizzie Kile and Lizzie Kyle, was a full-blooded Osage squaw who was born in 1849. She married Jimmy Ne-kah-e-sey who died on March 18, 1913. They had four daughters: Mollie who was born in 1887; Minnie born in 1890; Rita in 1891; and Anna born in 1896.

Lizzie held three headrights in the Osage Tribe while her daughters held one and one-sixth headright each. Her property interests as an Osage woman were estimated at $330,000.[30]

---

[30]Approximately $27 million in 1998 dollars.

Some time about 1912, Minnie Kile married William E. (Bill) Smith, a white man. When Minnie died in September, 1918, half of her estate went to her mother, Lizzie Q, and the other half to her husband. Smith had previously been married to another woman and had a daughter named Ella Rogers by that prior marriage. After Minnie's death,[31] Smith married Minnie's sister Rita in 1920.

Mollie married Ernest Burkhart and was the first means of drawing to Hale the assets of Lizzie Q's family.

Anna Brown left an estate of approximately $100,000[32] half of which, under Oklahoma law, went to her mother, Lizzie Q. The remainder was divided between Mollie Burkhart and Rita Kile Smith, Anna's sisters, and Grace Bigheart, a half-sister.

At the time of Anna's death, Lizzie Q was ill. She died July 27, 1921, at age 72, two months after Anna's murder, while living at the home of Mollie and Ernest Burkhart. Her estate approximated $200,000, in addition to the $50,000 which she inherited from Anna. She left a will devising tracts of real estate to her daughters, Rita Smith and Mollie Burkhart. She also left certain tracts of land to her granddaughter, Elizabeth Ernestine Burkhart, and her, grandson, James William Burkhart. She devised her homeplace at Gray Horse to her granddaughter and grandson to be held by them jointly. As to her rights in Osage Indian lands and government funds, she devised 1/3 to Rita Smith, 1/3 to Nellie Burkhart, 1/6 to Elizabeth Ernestine Burkhart and 1/6 to James William Burkhart. This will contained a residual clause dividing the remainder of her estate between Rita Smith and Mollie Burkhart. This will, made while she was living at Ernest Burkhart's home, revoked all previous wills.

When Rita and Bill Smith were murdered in March, 1923, this left Mrs. Ernest Burkhart the only surviving member of Lizzie Q's family. The murder of the Smiths was calculated to further enrich the Hale-Burkhart faction by approximately $150,000 since Mollie was Rita's only surviving sibling.

However, the Smiths had been worried that they might be murdered, so, without anyone's knowledge, they had an attorney draw a joint will by which the survivor of the two was to inherit the entire estate of the other or, in the event of the simultaneous demise of both, one half was to pass to Ella Rogers, Smith's daughter by a previous marriage, and the other half to Grace Bigheart, Rita's half

---

[31]Minnie died September 22, 1918.

[32]Approximately $8 million in 1998 dollars.

sister, less $5.00 which they bequeathed to Mollie Burkhart. The making of this will was not common knowledge at the time of the explosion which resulted in the Smiths' death. Since Smith died four days after his wife's death, her wealth passed to him. He, in turn, left it to his daughter who resided in Arkansas. If this will had not existed, Mollie Burkhart would have inherited their entire estate which, of course, was the intention of the murder ring.

Bill Smith was said to have been absolutely fearless and Bill Hale avoided meeting him whenever possible. Prior to their death, Smith and his wife were both very outspoken in their belief that Hale and his nephews were responsible for the murders. In addition to the rich inheritance which the murderers felt was at stake, Hale had two other reasons for wanting Smith killed: Cutting off Smith's relentless investigation of the murders and the $6,000 debt Hale owed him.

After much contentious litigation, the court probated the Smiths' joint will, giving Ella Rogers one-half; Mollie Burkhart, one-sixth; Grace Bigheart's estate, one-sixth; and John Bigheart, Jr., one-sixth.

The identity of the King of the Osage Hills, the mastermind behind the murders, was no longer a mind-boggling mystery. It seemed unbelievable: Hale was a multimillionaire rancher, a prominent man in the community, a deputy sheriff and, seemingly, the friend of everyone.

One of the FBI men wondered, "What does Hale's middle initial "K" stand for?"

"What else?" another Agent responded. "King."

❧ Chapter 23 ❧

Bryan Burkhart

Bryan Bradford Burkhart, alias Byron Burkhart, and his brothers were sons of Bill Hale's sister. Hale practically raised these boys from the time they were small children and completely dominated them.

(A third brother, Horace Burkhart, was apparently not involved in the extensive criminal operations of his uncle and brothers. He lived on a ranch ten or twelve miles northeast of Fairfax, and he and his uncle owned some steers in partnership, but Horace very seldom came to town and did not associate very much with his brothers even when he did visit Fairfax. He did not take part in the poker games and bootlegging activities of his brothers. However, he, too, would do what-

Bryan Burkhart, whom Anna Brown wanted to marry, but his designs on her were for murder, not marriage. (Photo taken October 23, 1922.)

ever his uncle Bill Hale told him to do.)

Bryan Burkhart was born in Greenville, Texas, on February 21, 1899. He had a medium build, his height being 5 feet 11 inches and his weight 163 pounds. He had black hair, hazel eyes, and a fair complexion. He listed his occupation as stock raiser, but in 1943 he applied for a job as a slab helper.

Some time after Anna Brown's murder, Bryan married an Osage squaw.

Bryan was somewhat younger than Ernest and was said to be an entirely different type of person. He was more reserved and had an inclination to keep things to himself.

He had been arrested for the murder of Anna Brown shortly after it occurred, but his uncle, Bill Hale, furnished bond and he was released.

☙ Chapter 24 ❧

The Henry Roan Probe is Broadened

Not satisfied that Roy Bunch had been the murderer of Henry Roan, Agents pursued the theory that, since Roan was shot in the back of the head, he was probably killed by a friend, someone he trusted.

Agents again talked to Roan's widow, now Roy Bunch's wife.

"Soon after Henry Roan's body was found," she said, "Roy told me that Bill Hale offered him money to leave Fairfax. Roy said it was a good thing he didn't take it because, if he had left, it would have made things look bad for him."

Agents decided to interview Roy Bunch.

Bunch said he knew that people were saying that he had killed Henry Roan, but it was not true. He was innocent. Bunch said that some time in the latter part of 1922 Bill Hale came to him and told him that Roan was likely to kill Bunch at any time because of Bunch's relationship with Roan's wife. Hale advised Bunch that he carried an insurance policy on Roan's life and, if Roan were killed before a certain date, he would not be able to collect on the policy. He suggested that Bunch leave town and stay away until after this date and Hale would give him the money with which to leave. Hale said Bunch could return later and, if he killed Roan, Hale would get him out of it.

Bunch also said that, after Roan's death, the body was taken to the Hunsaker Undertakers, Bill Hale came to Bunch and tried to get him to use his influence with Roan's widow to have the body transferred to the Big Hill Undertakers, one of Hale's business interests.

Agents located an individual who stated that some time prior to the murder of Henry Roan, he had overheard a conversation between Bill Hale and Henry Grammer, then deceased, in which they plotted Roan's murder. Their plans were to have Roan killed on the ranch of a man named Cornett to leave the impression that Cornett committed the murder. Affiliates of the Hale-Grammer gang repeatedly circulated rumors that Cornett and Roan were bitter enemies and that Roan was going to kill Cornett. They circulated a general line of propaganda to impress the public of the animosity between Cornett and Roan.

Information was furnished by a very prominent rancher and stockman, a close associate of the Hale-Grammer gang, that some time in 1922, Hale told him that he had lent money to quite a few Osage Indians and did not see how he was going to make them pay. "I said to Hale: 'Don't give me any of that bunk about your lending Indians money.' Hale then told me that he had insured the life of Henry Roan for $25,000. He asked me if I could get some outlaw along the Mexican border to come up to Osage County and kill Roan.

"I then asked Hale why he didn't get some of his Oklahoma outlaws to do the job. Hale replied that the Oklahoma outlaws were mostly bootleggers and would not come up from behind.

"I then suggested to Hale that a member of the Little Italy Gang in Kansas City, Missouri, might do the job. Later, I put Hale and Henry Grammer in touch with W. J. Emery, a Kansas City hoodlum."

When Agents interviewed W. J. Emery, who was then serving a 35-year sentence in the State Penitentiary at McAlester, Oklahoma, for payroll robbery, he told them that Henry Grammer used to bring his car into the garage in Kansas City where Emery worked and leave it there loaded with whiskey which Grammer would later haul back to Osage County.

"Not long before the murder of Henry Roan of Osage County," the inmate said, "Henry Grammer was in Kansas City and told me a big rancher there named Bill Hale had a big job he wanted done.

"In the year 1922 I saw Grammer frequently. He was coming to Kansas City and getting whiskey for his business in Oklahoma. Grammer and I got well-acquainted, and in 1922

Grammer approached me and asked me if I knew any high-powered men he could get to pull a job in Oklahoma. I told him I did, but joked with him about what had become of the Oklahoma outlaws, and he said he did not want to deal with them on this job. Grammer told me to look up some high-powered men and he would see me when he came back to Kansas City next time."

Emery told Agents that he did line up several notorious criminals who expressed interest in the job, but they were curious to know what kind of job it was — bank robbery, payroll heist, or what.

"Grammer mentioned twice about wanting to get some high-powered men for a job in Oklahoma," the prisoner continued, "The third time he mentioned it, he introduced me to Bill Hale in my paint store in Kansas City. This was September, 1922. Grammer and Hale came in a Cadillac sedan. Grammer asked me what success I had in getting any men and I told him we could go meet the two men I had in view. Grammer then told me in Hale's presence, 'This is the man who wants to talk to them,' indicating Hale. Hale asked me when we could see these men." Emery said on that day and on later occasions he put Hale and Grammer in touch with several criminals.

He continued , "Hale asked me if I knew these men and could guarantee them to stand hitched. I told Hale they were high-powered men with bad reputations and that was what I understood he wanted, but I would not guarantee anything."

The convict said that many of the criminals whom he introduced to Hale and Grammer actually made a trip to Osage County to "look the job over," but none of them could come to an agreement with Hale and Grammer, complaining that there was not enough money in it. After his trip to Osage County, one of these criminals had stated, "They wanted a whole regiment bumped off and $1,000 a head was not enough."

Emery said, "Grammer again came to see me in early December, 1922. He asked me if I did any high-powered work. He also asked me if I would take a load of whiskey from Kansas City to his place in Osage County. I told him I would.

"I did go from Kansas City to Grammer's place about January 5, 1923, and found Bill Hale there. Hale and Grammer asked me if I had ever done that kind of a job. I asked them, 'What kind of a job?' They answered, 'Putting a fellow out of the way.' I told them that I never had, and they told me to think it over. I told them that I would.

"I went back to Kansas City and returned to Grammer's place about January 12, 1923. He told me not to bother any more about that job because they had arranged with another fellow to do it.

"Not very long thereafter," the payroll robber continued, "I learned of the murder of Henry Roan, an Osage Indian, and I believed — and I still believe — that was the job Hale had in mind for me to do or to get done."

Later Emery stated to Agents, "I know Bill Hale well now and I hope he is acquitted, though I believe he's guilty."

The Agents asked if he would be willing to testify as to what he had told them. He replied that he would not. He said he did not want to testify and, even if he was subpoenaed, he would not testify since it would make it hard for him in the prison if he did.

"I'm a member of the prison's band — the drummer," he explained, "and have been for years. I have it as easy as it is possible to have it in prison. Have a nice bed to sleep on, am first class, and am doing my time the shortest way. When a prisoner here squeals or talks against some other man being prosecuted, the rest, or many of them, make life miserable for him. It would be impossible for me to testify and then come back here and do my time the easy, shortest way, as I would be sure to have trouble with some of the others doing time here."

Agents found out from another source that a short time before Roan's death Hale had approached a man in Pawhuska and asked him if he thought Al Spencer would kill a man for money. This man said he did not know and arranged a meeting between Spencer and Hale.

FBI Agents, through this investigation, had two "dead" leads to follow — Al Spencer and Henry Grammer were both dead. Grammer, who had shared honors with Hale as boss of the criminal element of Osage County, had died in an automobile accident prior to the FBI's investigation. As was pointed out previously, at the time of his death he had been carrying $15,000 in cash so robbery was not the motive. He had a gaping wound under his left armpit and it was rumored that he was killed by a criminal who had been with him at the time of the accident, but no investigation of Grammer's death was ever conducted.

One man told the Agents that, while he was attending an inauguration in Oklahoma City in January, 1923, he overheard a conversation between Bill Hale and Henry Grammer. Hale told Grammer that he was ready for a man to do that "Indian job." Grammer replied that he would send "John to do it."

Agents wondered, "Who is John?"

◈ Chapter 25 ◈

Evidence Mounts in The Henry Roan Case

The FBI men located a waiter who stated that he had been employed at a cafe during late 1922 and early 1923. While he was working there, Henry Roan came into the cafe on several occasions with a man named John Ramsey. He said that some time in January, 1923, just prior to Roan's murder, Ramsey and Roan came in to eat and sat next to the coffee urn.

"Ramsey was very nervous," the waiter said, "and could hardly hold the cup in his hand. I called Ramsey's attention to his drinking so much and told him he had better cut it out."

He said he felt that John Ramsey was working for Bill Hale because he often came into the cafe with Hale's men.

The Agents located other individuals who also said they had frequently seen Roan and Ramsey together shortly before Roan's death. Roan and Ramsey were said to have gone on drinking sprees together.

John Ramsey, a 40-year-old western criminal and a member of the notorious Henry Grammer gang, had been born in Eureka, Kansas. He stood 5 feet 8 inches tall and was of medium build, weighing 150-160 pounds. His hair was black and his eyes were described as gray or slate blue. His complexion was described variously as ruddy and sallow. He bore a red-and-blue tattoo on his right forearm with the initials "J.N.R." He was stoop shouldered and walked with a slight limp. He had a fifth grade education. His parents were deceased. Married, he was the father of six children ranging from small children to adults. His various legitimate jobs included cowboy, carpenter and farrier. He farmed a 160-acre farm in Fairfax. During this time Ramsey was reportedly in very poor health. His brother said of him, "He never has been in very good health. He takes medicine practically all the time."

Investigation reflected that John Ramsey went to Ripley, Oklahoma, shortly after the Roan murder and paid off several outstanding debts.

A short time before Henry Roan was killed, Bill Hale and John Ramsey were playing pool in a pool hall in Fairfax. Hale put up his cue stick and told Ramsey to meet him outside. While Hale went out the front door, Ramsey went out the back door and they met a short distance away where Hale gave Ramsey some money.

John Ramsey told another individual that Bill Hale had bought him an automobile for a job he had done for him. He also said that he would have plenty of money to install an electricity-generating system at his home when Hale finished paying him for the job.

Dewey Selph, a prisoner confined at the Federal Penitentiary at Leavenworth, Kansas, told Agents that he had met Bill Hale at Fairfax, Oklahoma, a short time before Henry Roan was murdered. Hale told Selph that he held a $25,000 insurance policy on Roan's life and would like to get him out of the way. He later told Selph that he would give him $500 to "bump Roan off." "I told Hale that I had never killed anyone. Hale told me to forget what he had said since he had someone else he thought would do the job. Selph said a short time thereafter he again met Hale who told him he had arranged with John Ramsey to do the job." Selph was reluctant to testify, but he said, if he were called upon to do so, he would testify truthfully since he did not believe in protecting anyone guilty of murder.

One man informed Agents, "Some time late in the Fall of 1922 John Ramsey came to my ranch and began doing repair work for me. He helped to build a garage and make other improvements. I assisted Ramsey financially in a small way for his services since Ramsey at the time was in serious financial straits.

"Some time after Christmas Ramsey came to me and said that his family needed some money. He asked me to lend him $100 which I did. Some time around the middle of January, 1923, Ramsey disappeared from the ranch for a few days and, when he returned, he was driving a new Ford roadster. Becoming suspicious, I asked Ramsey where he got the car. He said he bought it and paid cash for it.

"After that time, Ramsey spent very little time at my ranch, claiming to be sick and not feeling well enough to work. Ramsey would return to the ranch late at night and appeared to be rather restless and worried. Some time in the early part of February, 1923, he came to me and told me he expected to have a bankroll soon and wanted to rent my ranch. I told him that I didn't want to rent my place, but suggested that he see another individual who did want to rent his ranch. Ramsey then left, leaving his personal belongings at my ranch.

While rolling a cigarette, John Ramsey was asked if he had killed Henry Roan. "Hell, yes," he cried, tossing the cigarette to the ground, "I killed him!"

"Two or three months later he returned to get his belongings. I asked him where he was then living and what he was doing. He replied that he was down near Fairfax on a ranch which Bill Hale helped him get.

Matt Williams of Pawhuska also stated that he had been propositioned by Bill Hale to kill Henry Roan, but said that Hale later told him he had gotten John Ramsey to do the job.

Another man made a statement to the effect that he had overheard a conversation between Ramsey and Hale prior to Roan's murder during which Ramsey stated, "We're ready to go. Everything is ready to go."

"Be sure and don't fail," Hale had answered.

Agents heard of another of John Ramsey's conversations through a confidential source they had developed. "I was visiting Ramsey's home one Sunday afternoon," the source reported, "and Ramsey was showing me his farm. After a pause in the conversation, I watched Ramsey roll a cigarette, then I asked him point-blank, 'John, did you kill Henry Roan?'

"'Hell, yes,' Ramsey replied quickly, tearing the cigarette in two and hurling it to the ground, 'I killed him.'

"Then I asked Ramsey if Bill Hale had anything to do with the killing.

"'Hell, yes,' Ramsey said, 'He knew all about it, but he's a man that won't talk.'

"We then went into Ramsey's house for dinner. Ramsey was so nervous, he could hardly feed himself and spilled water on his lap while eating."

Ramsey made friends with Roan through Roan's fondness for whiskey and took him out on several occasions, ostensibly to furnish him liquor but in reality to murder him. Upon each occasion Ramsey lost his nerve, but on January 26, 1923, he persuaded Roan to drive to the bottom of a canyon. Here, out of sight of the nearby road, he shot Roan through the back of the head with a .45 caliber pistol which he had obtained from Henry Grammer's arsenal. Surprisingly, at the time Ramsey killed Roan, he did not even know his name, but merely had him pointed out to him as the Indian Hale wanted to have killed.

Hale later expressed anger that Ramsey had shot Roan in the back of the head since it had been planned to make it appear that Roan committed suicide.

Hale was a self-appointed pallbearer at Roan's funeral. Ramsey became very emotional upon viewing the body, pretending to be deeply affected.

As it turned out, the murder of Roan was the only one over which the U.S. government had jurisdiction since this murder occurred on a restricted government allotment.

John Ramsey, trigger man and father of six, who murdered Henry Roan.
(Photo taken January, 1926, at the Tulsa County Jail.)

⚜ Chapter 26 ⚜

Insurance Company Settles With Hale on Roan Insurance Policy

Shortly after Roan's death, when Bill Hale presented for payment a $25,000 insurance policy on the life of Henry Roan, the insurance company refused to pay on the grounds of fraud and misrepresentation. Consequently, Hale filed suit in federal court and, since it is usually less costly to settle than to litigate, the insurance company settled out of court for $2,000.

Government Agents located an agent for the Mutual Life Insurance Company of New York who resided in Tulsa. He stated that in 1921 he asked Bill Hale for the names of Indians on whose lives he might be able to write life insurance policies. He told Hale he had been talking to Henry Roan, but he did not know whether or not Roan could get a policy.

Hale said, "You couldn't get a policy on that drunkard." But then Hale added, "If you could get a policy on Roan, I would pay you an extra premium." Hale was advised that he would have to be a creditor of Roan's before he could get a policy on Roan's life. Hale replied that Roan owed him between ten and twelve thousand dollars. (Court records disclosed that Roan had petitioned the District Court of Osage County for the appointment of a guardian and at that time he owed Hale $6,000, the balance due on a house in Fairfax. There was no evidence of any other indebtedness of Roan to Hale.)

The application for a policy on Roan's life was rejected by the Mutual Life Insurance Company. Hale later called this same insurance man via long-distance telephone and said, "That fellow has got that policy. I want you to come up and pass on the policy before I accept it." After examining the policy, he told Hale that the answers to the questions in the application were falsely stated and that he knew Henry Roan had been previously turned down. Nonetheless, the policy — from the Capital Life Insurance Company of Denver, Colorado — was issued for $25,000 payable to Hale as beneficiary.

The doctor who had examined Henry Roan in connection with both this insurance policy and the previous one which had been rejected told Agents that Hale was present at the time of the examination. He had asked Hale who the beneficiary was.

"By God, I am," Hale replied.

The doctor then asked Hale if he was going to kill that Indian for the money.

Without hesitation, Hale answered, "Hell, yes!"

Hale also made statements to various persons that he intended to get someone to kill Roan after the one-year suicide clause in the policy expired. Subsequently, he hired John Ramsey to commit this murder.

✺ Chapter 27 ✺

The Smith Case

A woman who had been the night nurse at the hospital attending Bill Smith when he died told the investigators that Smith never made any statements to her regarding who might be responsible for the explosion of his home, but during his sleep he muttered several times, "They got Rita and now it looks like they've got me." She said he was always afraid that he might mention names while he was asleep and, upon awakening, he would immediately ask her if he had mentioned any names. Upon being told that he had not, he would seem relieved. It was her understanding that Smith had made a dying statement, but she had not been present when it was made. Only Dr. Shoun and some attorneys whom she did not know were present. They had asked her to leave the room.

Some time after Bill Smith's death, she was asked by Dr. Shoun to go to the home of Bryan Burkhart as nurse for Bryan who was ill. She at first refused to go, but finally agreed to take the case for one day until they could obtain another nurse. During the day she was there, she said, Bill Hale, Bryan's uncle, visited him and she was asked to leave the room so they could talk. She went out on the porch. Bill Hale asked her if Bill Smith had made a dying statement. "If he did," she replied, "I would not be telling it." She said Hale seemed anxious to secure any information she had about Smith's death.

Agents questioned Dr. Shoun and the attorneys referred to by the nurse. Dr. Shoun said that, when Smith first regained consciousness after the explosion and was able to talk, he inquired about his wife and asked what damage had been done to his home. "Smith's first thought was that he was being burned to death."

"Did he make a dying statement?" an Agent asked.

"Dying statement? Oh, yes," the doctor replied. "He said the only enemies he had in the world were Bill Hale and Ernest Burkhart."

Many of the law enforcement officers in Osage County were unscrupulous and a number of them were directly affiliated with the King of the Osage Hills and his gang of outlaws. One notable exception, however, was Sheriff Harve Freas who rendered much valuable assistance to the FBI Agents. Freas, a big, upstanding, typical western sheriff was very active and aggressive, even though he weighed over 300 pounds. He told Agents that a few days before the explosion, William Smith had dropped by Freas' office and said he was going to sue Bill Hale for a sum of money which Hale owed him and refused to pay. Smith told Freas, "I've heard a rumor that Hale is going to murder me."

Freas also remarked that two or three days before the explosion Bill Hale also came to see him and advised him that he owed Bill Smith several thousand dollars for which Smith was going to sue him. Hale had said, "If you want to serve process on me you can just call me on the phone. Before leaving, Hale said to Freas, "You know I cannot afford to be sued. Smith is a God damned son of a bitch for suing me."

A check of the court docket showed that Smith actually had filed suit against Hale on September 25, 1920, based on an indebtedness of $6,000 which Hale had allegedly borrowed from Smith. At the time of this loan, Smith and Hale were said to be on very friendly terms. The loan was unsecured and supposedly for a short period time, but when Smith asked for repayment, Hale continually put him off. After repeated requests and repeated refusals to pay, Smith filed suit.

In answer to this suit, Hale claimed that in March and April, 1916, he had lent Smith $2,500 in cash and at another time $3,000 in cash and at a third time such an amount that, together with interest, the total would be $6,000. He claimed the $6,000 check which Smith had given him was in payment for these loans from Hale to Smith.

This suit would have come to trial in April, 1923, but a month earlier Smith was killed.

At the time of the explosion at Smith's home, Bill Hale was in Campbell, Texas. On March 9, 1923, the day before the Smith massacre, one of Hale's intimate friends and business associates sent him a telegram from Fairfax, Oklahoma, which stated, "DEAL STANDS GOOD. I WILL GO IN THE MORNING."

Agents believed that this message alluded to the Smith explosion and they followed leads along that line.

On the day before the Smith home was blown up, Bill Smith had told a man that he expected to be murdered at any time. Smith explained that he had just met Bill Hale on the road near Fairfax and Hale drew his six-shooter on him and said, "You God damned son of a bitch, if I hear you talking about these Indian murders I'll send you to hell."

A woman, who had seen Ernest Burkhart at a dance some time after the Smith explosion, reported that Burkhart, while drunk, told her that he knew all about the explosion. He said he was afraid for his wife and, if it wasn't for the kids, he believed the parties who had done the other job would do the same thing to them. He did not mention the identity of the individual responsible for the murders.

"I met Ernest the following day," she said, "and I told him he shouldn't get so drunk because he talked too much when he got drunk. I tried to make him believe that he had told me a lot more than he actually had. He said, 'I don't know what I told you, but whatever it was, forget about it.' "

☞ Chapter 28 ☜

Associate of Hale Furnishes Information

Special Agents located Matt Williams, a former close associate of the Hale faction, and he furnished a wealth of valuable information about the murders.

"Three or four days after Anna Brown was found dead," Williams said, "Kelsie Morrison saw me at Pawhuska and told me that Bill Hale had him do the worst job he had ever pulled, and that Hale had promised him $5,000, but had paid him only $200 and now refused to pay him the balance."

Williams said that Morrison told him "that the job was a terrible one, that while Bryan Burkhart was loving Anna Brown, he, Morrison, knocked her in the head from behind with a pistol, and she hollered so loud and showed so much life that he, Morrison, and Bryan Burkhart carried her from the car to where she was found murdered, and laid her down and she still had some life, and he, Morrison, shot her in the back of the head. Morrison further stated to me that Katherine Cole Morrison (his wife and a full-blooded Osage whose Indian name was Gra-to-me-tsa-he) was with them on the party for a while and that they had let her out of the car before Anna Brown was killed. Morrison also told me that, if Hale did not pay him in full for killing Anna Brown, he was going to kill Bill Hale.

"A few days later, Hale came to my room at Ralston about 3:00 a.m. and told me he was afraid that damned son of a bitch Kelsie Morrison was going to squeak about the Anna Brown killing, and asked me if I could help him to keep Morrison's mouth shut. I then told Hale I thought, if he would pay Morrison, it would be all right. Hale then asked me to see Morrison, and use my influence in keeping his mouth shut. I told Hale I didn't think Morrison could afford to holler.

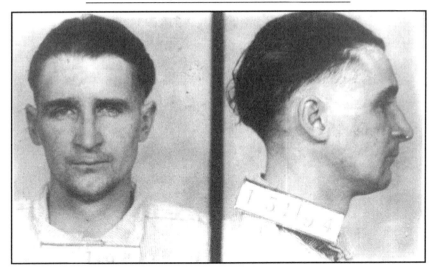

Kelsie Morrison, June 2, 1925. For a life a crime, life in prison and
a bloody death in a Fairfax, Oklahoma, gun battle.

"I later saw Morrison, and told him what Hale had said to me.
Morrison said Hale had given him some more money and, if he did
not pay him the balance, he would bump him off, too.

"I asked Hale why he had Anna Brown bumped off, and he said,
'So Ernest Burkhart's wife would get the Anna Brown estate'."

Other investigation proved that Morrison, at the behest of Hale,
had been the trigger man in the Anna Brown murder.

Kelsie Morrison, with aliases, Kelsey Morrison, Kelsie Lloyd
Morrison, Lloyd Miller, and "Slim" was a neat-appearing squaw
man[33] with a very bad reputation in the Osage Territory. Morrison,
approximately 6 feet one inch tall and about 160 pounds, had light-
brown hair, a rather light and sallow complexion, and small gray-
ish-blue eyes with a narrow space between them. He had a prominent scar over his right eye which extended from under the edge of
his eyebrow into the eyebrow for an inch or more. His face was thin,
but he had a well-formed nose and a rather full under lip. He had
the habit of frequently sniffing his nose and working his mouth and
nose like a rabbit, especially when he was excited. He had a very
noticeable cleft in his chin, and one of his upper front teeth was
crowned with gold. His hands were extraordinarily large. The second finger of his right hand had a bullet scar at the middle joint
which was considerably enlarged. He also had scars on the back off

---

[33]A white man married to an Indian woman.

his right hand from an automobile accident. Morrison was very loquacious and smoked a great many cigarettes.

At one time Kelsie Morrison suggested to a certain man that he should marry an Osage squaw and "bump her off" for her wealth as Morrison himself had done. Morrison gave this man a detailed account of how he had killed Billy Stetson, an Osage husband of an Osage woman, by giving him denatured alcohol and then married Stetson's widow. The bride did not live very long after their marriage and Morrison inherited her estate.

Later, Morrison married another Osage woman named Katherine Cole and disposed of Stetson's widow's estate to Bill Hale.

Katherine knew of Morrison's implication in the murder of Anna Brown, but he had threatened that he would kill her if she revealed this information.

An attorney told one of the Agents about another of Kelsie Morrison's alleged schemes. Kelsie's deceased wife had two children by Stetson. Morrison asked this lawyer if, in the event he, Morrison, were to adopt these two children and they were to die, would he inherit their estates. These children, being Osages, possessed headrights.

This lawyer explained that this question actually indicated that Morrison wanted to know whether he could adopt these children, murder them and then inherit their estates.

When Morrison fled from the area to avoid serving a federal sentence for bootlegging, he took the two Stetson children with him. A state warrant was issued charging him with the kidnapping of these children.

Morrison told FBI Agents that he was certain no convictions for the Osage Indian murders would ever be had in the state courts of Osage County. He said that he knew practically every state judge, officer and official in Osage County and practically all of its prominent and wealthy men; that he had drunk, gambled or been drunk with nearly every one of them. He said he knew that money would buy the protection or acquittal of any man for any crime in Osage County. He mentioned in detail two cases of deliberate murder where this was done, and claimed that he knew the sheriff's and attorney's offices at Pawhuska could both be "bought."

✺ Chapter 29 ✺

Witnesses Give Evidence in Brown, Smith and Roan Cases

Matt Williams told the Special Agents:

"*In January, 1923, Bill Hale met me at Ralston, Oklahoma, and told me that he had got some insurance company from Denver, Colorado, to insure Henry Roan's life for $25,000 in his, Hale's, favor; that the insurance company at Pawhuska had failed to write the insurance, but he, Hale, had got by with the Denver insurance company. Hale asked me what I thought about John Ramsey, if he was all right. Hale told me that he had arranged with Ramsey to bump Roan off, and collect the $25,000 insurance. I asked Hale how he expected to get by with that kind of stuff. Hale said he had let Roan have some cattle, and he could make it appear that the insurance was for security on the cattle deal, and would be for insurance on the cattle trade, and that he could get by with it all right. I then told Hale that I thought Ramsey would do as he agreed to do, and in a short time Roan was found dead, shot in the back of the head, near Fairfax, Oklahoma.*

"*Three days after Roan's body was found, I met John Ramsey at Mike Folly's Hotel at Fairfax, Oklahoma, and Ramsey told me about killing Henry Roan, where he was found shot and that he, Ramsey, had done what Hale had told him to do. Ramsey said he had told Roan to meet him out there alone to get some whiskey, and when Roan met him, Ramsey opened the side door of the car and shot Roan in the back of the head while Roan was still in the car. Ramsey said that Hale had promised him $5,000, but that Hale had only paid him $500 and given him a Ford car. Ramsey asked me to help him prevail upon Hale to pay the balance of the money due Ramsey for killing Roan.*

"*Hale told me that he told Ramsey he'd pay him the balance when he collected the insurance money, and that was the agreement he had had with*

Ramsey for killing Henry Roan."

Williams said he would have furnished this information sooner but "I was afraid of the consequences to a man if he volunteered this information."

"You were afraid that, if you told all you know, you'd have been bumped off like the others?" Agents asked him.

"Yes," he answered, "and I would, too. It looks bad for me... for a man who knows these things, but there is just a lot of people like me who knows these things, and is afraid to tell them."

Following the interview with FBI Agents, Williams was questioned by one of the Government's prosecuting attorneys:

"You have lived in and around Osage County for how many years?" the Government attorney asked.

"35 years."

"You formerly lived at Ralston, Oklahoma?"

"Yes."

"You know W.K. Hale?"

"Yes."

"Since you have known Hale where has he been living?"

"Fairfax, Oklahoma."

"What has been his occupation?"

"Cattle man, stock man, farming."

"Did you know W.E. Smith?"

"Yes."

"And his wife, Rita Smith?"

"Yes."

"Were you well-acquainted with them?"

"Yes."

"How long had you known them before their death?"

"I knew Bill Smith for 30 years, and Rita I have known ever since she was born. She was Lizzie Q's girl."

"Did you know anything about the controversy between W.K. Hale and Bill Smith over money?"

"Yes."

"Just state what you know about that matter."

"Hale informed me that William Smith had loaned him $6000, and gave him a draft on the Nat Cook Bank."

"That is in Ralston?"

"No, Fairfax. He said he took that draft from that bank and deposited it in the First National Bank of Fairfax. Bill Smith gave him a check for it."

"Bill Smith?"

"Yes. Nat Cook's records show that."

"When was it he told you that?"

"Let me see, — that was — well, I remember the time. I met him and Louis in the road. Hale at that time was going to Pawnee and he gave me $200 and we went down to the Jay & Jay Drug Store."

"Where is that?"

"Pawnee, — and he cashed a check for W.E. Hale, and Cecil gave me the $200."

"What was the $200 for?"

"Just borrowed."

"You go on and tell anything further you know about the controversy between Hale and Smith over this $6,000."

"Then Bill Smith's wife, Rita — Bill Smith had met W.K. Hale at the Spurrier Garage, Fairfax, Oklahoma — "

"That is Spurgeon, isn't it?"

"Yes, Bill Spurgeon. And Smith demanded this $6,000. In consideration of the same, W.K. Hale had purported to sell a bunch of cattle in the Creek County to W.E. Smith."

"Was that false or true.?"

"That is right."

"But did he sell the cattle to Smith?"

"No, he went down and showed Rita the cattle. That was just a frame-up between Smith and Hale."

"A frame-up to keep Mrs. Smith from knowing he had loaned Hale the $6,000?"

"No, she knew it, but that was supposed to be in payment. They went to the Creek County, Hale, Smith and his wife, and they showed the squaw these cattle in the Creek County. Then, after that, Hale come to my room over the First National Bank."

"What time of the day or night was that?"

"Three o'clock in the morning."

"Over the First National Bank in what town?"

"Ralston. He called me out. Sleeping with me that night was Everett Goodson. He called me out and says to me, 'Matt, I think you made the best witness I ever seen in that Jess Smith case'."

"That is, Hale said that to you?"

"Yes, he said, 'I want you, accompanied by John Morris and Louis Oller, to go to Pawhuska tomorrow morning and swear the following: That Bill Smith had told you that I paid him this money in full in cash at different times and places; that he, W.E. Smith, had spent this money for whiskey and on women; that is the only reason he couldn't acknowledge the

debt paid in full, because it would bust him up with his wife, Rita.' And he solicited my testimony to swear to that, that he received the money in full from W.K. Hale, but the only reason he couldn't acknowledge same was because it would be at the expense of losing his squaw."

"Was anyone present when he told you that?"

"No, we was out. Everett was sleeping in the room."

"All right, go on."

"I said, 'Bill, this Smith is an uncle of my former wife, and I am just about to get back again with Rose. While I would like to accommodate you, I don't care to have anything to do with it for the reason stated."

"Rose was your former wife?"

"Yes."

"Now, was the case tried at that time?"

"A continuance was granted. Hale had the case put off."

"Did he talk to you about it afterwards again?"

"Yes."

"Tell where and what he said and when."

"Well, he said afterwards, said they practically settled the case, because Rita was the only one who was crowding him and she was blowed up now and couldn't testify."

"Was that before or after the Smith home was blown up."

"After, about ten days after. Another time, Bill Smith come to my home at Ralston, previous to this time, and said, 'If Hale don't settle up with me I am going to inform on him for the murder of Anna Brown.' I told Smith at the time, 'Bill, you are taking a long shot, because Hale has already asked me about this thing, and you better move off that creek over there, because he will get you there sure.' He at the time told me he was going to move to Fairfax."

"Smith did?"

"Yes."

"Now, after that, did you tell Hale what Smith said about informing on him with reference to the Anna Brown killing?"

"Yes."

"Just state what he said."

"I said, 'Bill was over here and told me he was going to tell on you, Hale, in connection with the killing of Anna Brown.' After this murder that morning they come to his house on the Gray Horse Creek and informed him of the act being committed."

"Who had done that?"

"Kelsie Morrison and Bryan Burkhart. They went to Bill Smith's house that morning."

"Go on and tell what you told Bill Hale."

"I told Bill Hale, I said, 'Bill Smith's been over here and made that assertion,' and I said, 'Bill, he is going to inform on you.' He said, 'I will put him away, because it ought to have been done years ago.' He asked me at that time of some man that would put Bill Smith away, and I told him Blackie Thompson may do that for him. He said he didn't know whether Blackie would do that or not, and wanted me to get in conversation and ask how he could get in touch with Al Spencer. I told him Al Spencer came to see my friend, Ed Snyder, living on Main Street, Pawhuska, Oklahoma, and probably Ed Snyder could arrange a meeting between him, W.K. Hale, and Al Spencer, but, if Al wouldn't pull that deal, I thought John Ramsey would. I think that was about three months before the Smiths was killed."

"Now, you say you suggested to him at that time that maybe John Ramsey would do it?"

"Yes."

"What did he say with reference to that?"

"He said Ramsey was kind of a chuckle-headed boy and he didn't know whether he could trust him or not."

"After the house was blown up, did he talk to you about Ramsey?"

"Yes."

"State what he said."

"That was when he told me, 'As far as we are concerned, she will never be able to testify any more. She was really the only one I was afraid of'."

"What did he say about Ramsey blowing the house up?"

"He said the deal was pulled off according to schedule."

"Did he say through Ramsey?"

"No, I don't believe he did. That was the time I phoned for him and he gave me $38."

"Did you have any further talk about it at any other time — about the blowing up of the Smith home or about Ramsey?"

"No, I believe that was the last conversation I had with him."

"Where was it you had that?"

"Over at Ralston in the middle of the street between the First National Bank and that little restaurant, about 5:00 in the afternoon. I phoned his wife and told her to tell Bill to come to me and he came down to see what I wanted. But he at numerous and other times for the last two years had mentioned about killing Bill Smith, with the equity that he may have in his estate. In the first place, Bill arranged for me to marry Mollie, Ernie Burkhart's wife. He said, 'You can marry Mollie and change from one to the other and finally wind up with the estate.' I had been going with Mollie and they moved a house down there on the creek for Mollie and I to get

married in. That is the first proposition Bill and I started out with in this deal."

"Well, now, suppose we go to the Anna Brown murder. What is the information you have on that matter?"

"Well, that is awful strong."

"Tell the whole thing just as you know it. Who was in it and all about where you first got your information."

"I think it was on the 21st day of May, my birthday. About eight o'clock in the evening, Bryan Burkhart and Anna Brown, driving a Buick car, come to Ralston, Oklahoma, come up to my room and purchased two quarts of whiskey; Bryan Burkhart paying for same, $15. He told me at that time he was going to meet Kelsie Morrison at the end of the bridge. I said, 'What are you going to do, Bryan?' He said, 'I'm going to do some work for Uncle Billy tonight.'"

"Who was Uncle Billy?"

"Hale. He said he had made arrangements with Shorty Wheeler to bring them some more whiskey at the Salt Creek bridge about nine or ten o'clock. I let Wheeler have my car, a Maxwell roadster. He got there just as they was killing Anna Brown. He heard her scream. Bryan Burkhart was holding her in his arms, Kelsie Morrison beating her over the head with a six-shooter from behind. They carried her to the bank of the creek. She still showed life and they shot her in the back of the head. After that Kelsie Morrison came to my place — my sister lived out here,— and he was living with Bill Stetson's widow and told me, 'Matt, that was the most brutal deal ever I pulled off.' After that Shorty Wheeler was released or escaped from jail somehow and was purported to go to Ernest Burkhart's house to receive expense money to get out of the country and has never been seen or heard of since…I remember it plain because it was my birthday."

"Who told you about how they killed Anna Brown?"

"Shorty Wheeler and Kelsie Morrison both."

"Did you ever talk to W.K. Hale about the Anna Brown murder?"

"All he ever said to me was, 'One by one they are going.'"

"With reference to the Henry Roan murder. Had anyone talked to you about that prior to the time Henry Roan was killed?"

"Hale."

"What did he tell you?"

"Well, he come up about the insurance on that Indian for $25,000 to Hale, and he asked me at that time and suggested bumping him off on the creek. I said, 'Bill, how you going to get off with stuff like that?' He said, 'Because I sold him some cattle, and the insurance was for the equity for

what he owed me for the cattle, because,' he said, 'If Henry lives he would pay me, but if he dies the insurance will make it.'"

"What was it he said about bumping him off?"

"He said in the first place he would not need no more cattle. He said the insurance would cover that up. I said, "How you going to bump him, Bill?' and he said, 'Down on the creek some time.' I said, 'Bill, if you do that, you better bump him off in town someplace, because if you bump him off on an Indian allotment, the United States will assume jurisdiction.'"

"What did he say to that?'

"He said, 'No, Matt, you are wrong. I talked to John F. Tillman, and Tillman tells me the United States has no jurisdiction whatever in Osage County any longer.' Hale told me several times that he had everything squared in Osage County from the Road Overseer to the top and he was exempt from prosecution for the murders."

"Did he tell you anything about any plans he had further than bumping him off on the creek some time?"

"Yes, he told me he had Ramsey to do that."

"Now, did he tell you what, if anything, he was paying Ramsey?"

"He said he was giving him $5000."

"How was he going to pay him?"

"He was going to pay him $500 in money, a Ford car, and the rest when he collected the insurance."

"After Henry Roan was killed did you talk to Hale any about it?"

"Yes."

"Where?"

"I talked to him over there — Where was it I talked to him about that? — I forget whether it was in Fairfax or Ralston, but I remember the conversation."

"What was it?"

"John Ramsey told me that he would only give him $200."

"John Ramsey told you?"

"Yes, He owed him $200 and asked me to see Hale and tell Hale he better settle up. I went and told Bill and said, 'Ramsey is liable to yelp, and you better give him the other $300.' He told me he would."

"He told you he would?"

"Yes, I afterwards seen Ramsey and he told me that he had."

"Did you ever talk to Ernest Burkhart about any of these matters?"

"No, only just in a general way. I talked to Ernest once about his connection with Hale."

"With Hale?"

"Yes."

"What did he say?"

"He said it would be his wife next and then he would be the next one. He said he was afraid of Hale and afraid to antagonize him in any way in the world."

After furnishing this information, Williams seemed relieved and stated, *"I believe the day is past when a man will just get shot down by doing right."*

"Do you also feel that it is a matter of your putting yourself right before the people by telling the truth?" he was asked.

"That is the only motive I have. I feel I owe that to the nation and tribe and people like you who is interested. I am skeptical, you know. I haven't got confidence in every man. It looks bad to a court or jury," he concluded, *"when a man like me knows this and didn't come out, but you know conditions here and the power Hale had. I wouldn't have been here to tell this story if Hale had known that."*

Later, Matt Williams wrote a letter to the Agents requesting protection:

"In view of the fact that I do not feel that it would be safe for me to remain in Osage County, and also feeling that any man who willingly testifies in this case is in danger of loosing [sic] his life if it is known, I would feel grateful to you men if both or either of you could accompany me until after the trial of the case of State versus Hale & Ramsey.

"Yours truly.

"Matt. H. Williams."

The FBI granted his request.

❧ Chapter 30 ❧

Al Spencer Associate Adds Details

Running down the Al Spencer angle, FBI agents interviewed Dick Gregg, an inmate of the Kansas State Prison who was serving a 10- to 21-year sentence for bank robbery.

"In the late part of 1922, in July or August," Gregg stated, *"Al Spencer told me that Bill Hale of Fairfax, Oklahoma, wanted two men killed at or near Fairfax. A couple of days later Al Spencer and myself met Fred Rowe of Pawhuska, Oklahoma, in a Ford roadster on Pawhuska and Pershing paved road about three or four miles east of Pawhuska. Max Billings, who was with Spencer and myself when we met Rowe, asked Rowe where we were supposed to meet Bill Hale. Rowe told us to follow him and he would take us to Hale. We drove to a spring about two or three miles northeast of Fairfax, Oklahoma, and met with Bill Hale in one of his pastures. Hale asked Al Spencer what he thought of the proposition. Spencer then said he didn't care about the proposition; it was the money he wanted.*

"Hale then said he would pay $5,000. Spencer then asked Hale whom he wanted killed. Hale said, 'Bill Smith and his wife'.

"Al Spencer then turned to the man who had originally approached him about the matter and accused him of lying to him, telling him it was two men who were to be killed. Hale said he didn't recall whether or not he had said it was two men, but it didn't make any difference, he would pay $5,000 for the job.

"Spencer told Hale he might be cold-blooded, but he wouldn't kill a woman for money. Hale took Spencer to one side away from us and talked to him for about 30 minutes. When they came back to where we were, Spencer told Hale we'd come back in a week or ten days.

"Hale gave Spencer a note telling him to go to Hale's ranch and give it to a ranchhand. But we didn't go there. We went back to Okesa,

Oklahoma. I didn't see Bill Hale again until January, 1923, when my father, John Gregg, Lee Clining and myself met Hale on his ranch near the same place we had first met him.

"Hale told me the same offer of $5,000 still stood good for the job, and he still wanted Bill Smith's house blowed up and he didn't care how it was done just so it was done. Hale said that he'd get the soup for me to do the job. Hale claimed that he had given $5,000 to Fred Rowe who was instructed to give it to the person who killed Smith and his wife. After I talked to Hale and told him I would do the job, he said he wanted to talk to Clining. Hale, Clining and myself then had a talk. Hale told Clining we, — Hale and myself — had come to an understanding about the job. Clining told Hale that any arrangements made by me was all right with him. We, — Clining and myself — then left Hale with the understanding that Hale would go to Wichita, Kansas, to establish an alibi and Clining and myself was to blow up Bill Smith's house the following night.

"The following day," the bank robber continued, *"Clining and myself drove to the Bill Smith home which Hale had pointed out to us. We arrived at Smith's home about dark and called at the front door on the pretext that we were interested in buying Smith's house.*

"We were met at the door by Bill Smith who invited us into the house. We talked with Mr. Smith and a farmhand who lived nearby and worked on Smith's farm. There was also a boy about 14 or 15-years old, Smith's wife, a girl and an old lady. They were all at Smith's house at the time.

"After looking the house over and talking with Mr. Smith for thirty or forty minutes and seeing several people there, Clining and myself decided not to do the job as there was too many people there, some of them women. Clining remarked, 'We don't want to massacre the whole country just to kill two people'."

When Agents interviewed W. L. Clingan, alias Clining, of Ficher, Oklahoma, he corroborated everything Dick Gregg had told them and added:

"Hale said for us to go look the Smith house over and, when we got ready to blow the Smith home up, to let him know the day before so he could be away, that he would go to Ponca City or Wichita or some other place where he could register at some prominent hotel for an alibi. Hale pointed out Bill Smith's home to Dick Gregg and myself and told us to do a good job and put them out of the way."

Clingan said he and Gregg had looked the Smith home over

but "after seeing women and children there" they refused to do the job. "We did not want to kill several innocent women and children," he explained. "Hale said for us shoot them, kill Smith and wife, or kill them any way we wanted to, just so we got them out of the way."

☜ Chapter 31 ☞

Inmate Gives Statement About Anna Brown Case

Agents talked to B. B. Crane, an inmate of the county jail at La Junta, Colorado, who told the following story:

"*Several days before Anna Brown was found murdered, I was at Ernest Burkhart's home at Gray Horse. I recall that Dewey Selph, Clarence Bailey, Kelsie Morrison, Ernest Burkhart and several others were there. We were all drinking and we played Indian stud poker. I was very drunk while we were playing poker. I don't remember the time of night when Ernest Burkhart, Kelsie Morrison and Dewey Selph went into another room and talked. Then Dewey Selph came back and called me to one side and told me that Ernest Burkhart wanted Anna Brown bumped off and asked me what I thought of it. He said our time would be made worthwhile. I told Dewey that kind of money wouldn't be any good to us. Dewey did not say any more and we went back to the poker game.*

"*Later on, the game broke up, and Dewey Selph said to me, 'Come on.' He and I, Kelsie Morrison, Ernest Burkhart and Clarence Bailey, went out and got in Ernest Burkhart's Buick car. Ernest Burkhart drove us to Pawhuska and stopped west of town near a bridge. When the car stopped Kelsie Morrison got out of the car, and walked away. I was drinking and paid no attention to what was said before Kelsie left the car.*

"*Kelsie was gone some time and came back in a car and in this car I remember seeing Anna Brown and another woman that I paid no attention to, and I can't say who she was. I don't remember what was said, but Kelsie stopped his car and then drove off and Ernest Burkhart followed.*

"*Ernest drove on to his home at Gray Horse. We got there some time about morning. We all got out and I laid down and went to sleep. Later, Dewey Selph woke me up and Dewey, Clarence, Bailey, Ernest Burkhart and myself drove to Fairfax in Ernest's Buick and ate breakfast. I recall we all went to Gray Horse and saw some races.*

"After the races, some time in the evening, I remember that Dewey, myself, Kelsie Morrison, Ernest Burkhart and Clarence Bailey went to Ernest's home and ate supper. This was late in the evening.

"Some time after supper, Ernest Burkhart, Clarence Bailey, Dewey Selph and I, in Ernest Burkhart's car, left Ernest's house. Kelsie Morrison was not with us when we left. When we got in Gray Horse, which is a short distance from Ernest Burkhart's house, I saw Kelsie Morrison, Anna Brown and another man and woman, that I don't remember, sitting in a car in front of some store. Ernest Burkhart stopped his car near Kelsie's car and I paid no attention to what was said, but we then drove on and Kelsie with Anna Brown and the other two, followed us. We drove down to Fairfax. We stopped at Fairfax and Kelsie Morrison, Anna Brown and the others drove up and stopped. Ernest Burkhart and Dewey Selph got out of our car and walked over towards Kelsie's car. Clarence Bailey and I remained in our car and I went to sleep.

"The next thing I remember I woke up and our car was in front of the hotel at Ralston and Kelsie Morrison's car with Anna Brown and the other two were at Ralston. We all got out of our car and went into the hotel. Clarence and I set down in the lobby of the hotel and all the others left us and went somewhere in the hotel, except the man and woman, whom I don't remember, that was riding in Kelsie's car. They stayed in Kelsie's car.

"In a little while Clarence and I wanted a drink and was afraid to drink in the lobby as we went out and got in Ernest's car and drank some whiskey, and I went to sleep.

"Some time later, I don't know what time, but around daylight, Ernest and Dewey came and got in the car and drove to Fairfax.

"I did not see Kelsie and Anna Brown again. At Fairfax Dewey Selph took me to a hotel and put me to bed. When I woke up, I ate and later saw Dewey, who was sitting in front of the place where I slept. I told Dewey that I believed I would go to Denoya and see Albert Sturnson. I left Fairfax in a bus going to Denoya. The next day I came back to Fairfax and met Dewey and the next day I went to Ponca City. In about four or five days later I saw in the paper where they had found Anna Brown murdered."

Agents interviewed Dewey Selph who corroborated what Crane had said and added several details. At the time of the interview Selph was being detained in Osage County Jail for violating his parole from the State of Arkansas. He said that on the night before Anna Brown disappeared, he Selph, Blackie Gore,

Kelsie Morrison, Bob Crane, Clarence Bailey, Bryan and Ernest Burkhart were all at Ernest Burkhart's home near Gray Horse, Oklahoma, playing poker and Ernest Burkhart would give $2500 'to get shut' of Anna Brown and $2500 after she was done away with.

Selph continued, *"After Ernest Burkhart made this statement, Blackie Gore, Kelsie Morrison and Ernest Burkhart went into another room and stayed about twenty-five minutes then returned to a room where we all were and Morrison said he, Morrison, had seen Anna Brown at Pawhuska, Oklahoma, that day and she was drinking. Kelsie Morrison, Blackie Gore, Bailey, Crain and myself went to Ralston, Oklahoma, in Ernest Burkhart's car where we met Morrison, Gore and Anna Brown about 4:00 a.m. Anna Brown stopped at the Jones Hotel for few minutes and Ernest Burkhart, Bailey, Crane and myself left them there at Ralston in front of the Jones Hotel and went to Ernest's home. We went to horse races at Gray Horse that day and returned to Burkhart's home the same day about 4:00 p.m. and Anna Brown was at Burkhart's home at that time in the summer kitchen drinking and didn't eat supper with us.*

"About 5:30 p.m. the same day — the day she disappeared — Bryan Burkhart and Anna Brown left Ernest Burkhart's home in a Ford car and drove away toward Fairfax. We then, all of us got in Ernest Burkhart's car and started for Fairfax. A short way out of Fairfax we met Bill Hale and his daughter. They turned around, back to Fairfax where we all got out of the car. The women and children went into a picture show where they were showing a Mutt and Jeff comedy and us men talked for a few minutes. Ernest, Crane, Bailey and myself went to the pool hall and later went to Ralston in Burkhart's car and got Morrison and Blackie Gore. All of us then went to Ernest's home in his Buick car. Crane, Bailey and myself then remained at Burkhart's home and Ernest took Kelsie Morrison and Blackie Gore in his Buick and drove away. I did not see Ernest Burkhart until next morning at Fairfax and did not see Kelsie Morrison or Blackie Gore for several days.

"Before Bryan Burkhart left Ernest Burkhart's house with Anna Brown, he loaded a .38 Colt automatic revolver in the presence of Crane, Bailey and myself. Katherine Cole, now wife of Kelsie Morrison, was with Anna Brown at Ralston when we picked Gore and Morrison up, but I do not know what become of her after that time."

G-men then located Katherine Cole, wife of Kelsie Morrison, who shed additional light on the mystery of Anna Brown's death.

"About eight or eight-thirty on the night Anna Brown was killed,

Kelsie Morrison came to my house in Fairfax and told me to get my clothes on, that we were going on a party. I asked him who was going, and he said that they had a squaw out there for Bryan Burkhart, and that they, Kelsie and I were going.

"When we got out to the car in front of the house, Bryan Burkhart and Anna Brown were sitting in it...."

"Later in the evening we drove to a place on what I think is the old Gray Horse road, and stopped under a tree near a ravine. When the car stopped, Kelsie walked around to the left side of the car, and Bryan got out on the left side. They went to the left back door and Kelsie reached in and caught Anna by the arm. They both reached in and helped her out of the car, Bryan being on the right side and Kelsie on the left side. They walked her away from the car, going towards the ravine. I looked out and back from the right side of the car and cleared my throat as if to speak, and Kelsie looked back at me and said, 'God damned son of a bitch, keep your mouth shut! Keep quiet!'

"They then walked on with Anna Brown, and I did not again look out of the car. I stayed in the car alone for about twenty-five or thirty minutes until they returned.

"Anna Brown was not with them and I never saw her alive again.

"I told Kelsie that I wanted to go home, and they drove on to my house in Fairfax. When they got to my house, Bryan remained in the car and Kelsie went into the house with me. When we got into the house Kelsie said he was going to town. I started to ask Kelsie some question, and he turned to me and cursed me and told me to keep my mouth shut. Kelsie then got a suit of clothes and left my house, going to the car, and told me he was through with me, that he was going to quit. He and Bryan Burkhart drove off north. I heard the car turn and go back towards town.

"The following day about 3:30 or 4:00 o'clock in the afternoon Kelsie came back to the house. I had a Buick car and Kelsie had sold it, and I asked him about the money which he got for it. He said he got $100 for it, but later I found out that he got $450 for it. Kelsie showed me a paper that said he had $2,700 in the bank, and left me under the impression that it was a deposit slip. I think this deposit was in the Fairfax National Bank, for Kelsie does all his banking there.

"Kelsie said that his mother, who had been visiting us about three weeks before this time, had given him the money. I knew Kelsie was not telling the truth when he said his mother gave him this money because she would have said something to me about it if she had. When Kelsie came to the house, he had the same suit on that he wore the night we were out with Anna Brown and Bryan Burkhart. The buttons on his shirt were torn off.

"I believe that Kelsie filed suit against me for divorce at Pawhuska the same day he came to the house….

"While at the house, Kelsie seemed to be very nervous, and cursed me and said he would stomp me to death if I didn't keep my mouth shut. Kelsie asked me to go with him and his brother for a ride in his Hudson. We went out west of Fairfax about two miles where there were a bunch of men, whom I think were shooting dice. We were there about thirty or forty minutes. Then we drove back to Fairfax, and I got out of the car and walked up to my mother's house.

"Anna Brown's body was found, about a week or ten days after we were riding with her in Bryan Burkhart's car. It was reported in Fairfax that they had found a dead Indian woman, but they didn't know whether it was an Osage or a Kaw. As the body was found, I hired a taxi and Margaret Walters and I went out to the place.

"When we got there the body was already in the box, and I didn't get to see it, but when I noticed that the body was found at the same place where Kelsie and Bryan Burkhart had assisted Anna Brown out of the car that night when we drove out the Gray Horse road, I knew it was Anna Brown's body they had found.

"I never mentioned to anyone that it was Anna Brown, or that we had been out riding with her. Kelsie Morrison had threatened me several times that, if I did not keep my mouth shut, he'd kill me and I was afraid to say anything about it.

"I would have told about this, but I didn't have any confidence in the officers of Osage County, and I knew that, if I told them, that Kelsie Morrison would soon learn about it, and would either kill me or have someone else kill me."

Agents reviewed the testimony taken at the inquest following Anna Brown's murder, paying particular attention to the testimony given by Bryan Burkhart.

Bryan Burkhart was questioned by an Assistant County Attorney on May 28, 1921.

"State your name."

"Bryan Burkhart."

"Do you live in Fairfax?"

"Yes."

"Do you know Anna Brown?"

"Yes."

"When did you see her last?"

"Saturday afternoon."

"A week ago?"

"Yes, sir."

"Where was she?"

"She was at Gray Horse. I brought her to town Saturday afternoon."

"What business are you engaged in?"

"Well, not anything now. I drive a car."

"You have a car of your own?"

"Yes, sir."

"What kind of a car is it that you drive?"

"A Ford."

"When you brought her back, where did you go?"

"Come to town."

"When was this?"

"Last Saturday, about 4 or 4:30."

"You haven't seen her since then?"

"No, sir."

"Heard anything about her, or talked to anyone that knew anything about her?"

"No, sir."

"What did the fellows about town say about her?"

"Don't know."

"Talked to any certain one?"

"Just overheard, just heard everyone talking about it and everybody wondering."

"Did you know that she was absent from her home for the past week?"

"Yes, sir."

"Who told you?"

"Her mother and sister."

"Did they ask you where she was?"

"No."

"Did you ask them where she was?"

"No."

"The afternoon you took her to her house who was there?"

"I didn't get out."

"She got out?"

"Yes, sir."

"Positive you haven't seen her since then?"

"Yes, sir."

"Heard any talk around town, anything special as to who was guilty?"

"No, sir."

"No one guessing at it?"

"No, sir."

"Did you get out there where the body was found?"

"Yes, sir."

"Did you see some automobile tracks there?"

"Yes, saw some; but there was lots of cars out there."

"Bryan, was she intoxicated that day?"

"Yes, she was."

"She had been at Gray Horse all day?"

"Yes, sir."

"Had any whiskey with her?"

"Didn't see any."

"She was still drunk that evening?"

"Yes, sir."

"What did she talk about?"

"Didn't talk much. She didn't say anything much to me. Wanted to know where I could get some booze. I told her I don't know, didn't think I could find any."

"Did she say she was going to try and get some?"

"She didn't say."

"What else did she say?"

"Said she was going to have a party that day."

"Where?"

"At her house."

"Did she say who she was going to have there?"

"No, sir, didn't say a word about who was going to be there."

"Did you go?"

"No, sir."

"Did she invite you?"

"No, sir."

"Saturday evening as you brought her back, did she have a small satchel with her?"

"I believe she did, I am not sure, I think she had it with her."

"Did you hear her say anything about her friends in Burbank?"

"No, sir."

"Ever hear her mention any of them?"

"No, sir."

"Did you notice how she was dressed?"

"Well, I think she was in her stocking feet, might have been moccasins."

"Didn't she have any shoes on?"

"I don't think she had shoes."
"You ought to remember whether she was in stocking feet."
"I think she was in her stocking feet."
Various individuals told Agents that Bryan Burkhart was extremely nervous and uneasy while giving this testimony.
Agents then studied the testimony which Ernest Burkhart had given at the inquest.
"State your name."
"Ernest Burkhart."
"Mr. Burkhart, are you related in any form to Anna Brown?"
"Yes, sir."
"What relation?"
"Brother-in-law."
"Did you marry her sister?"
"Yes, sir."
"Where do you live?"
"Gray Horse."
"And she lived in Fairfax?"
"Yes, in Fairfax."
"How often did you see her?"
"Sometimes every day and again a couple or three weeks, just off and on, a week at a time and sometimes a couple of weeks."
"Did she have any other person living with her?"
"She had a girl from Pawnee. She stayed with her, but I don't know how long."
"When did you see Anna Brown last?"
"A week ago."
"Did she have anyone living with her at that time?"
"She had a girl with her some time ago, a week or so ago."
"Did you go about her place since last Saturday?"
"Been there twice."
"Was there anyone there?"
"No one. The house was locked."
"Did you make any inquiries about Anna?"
"Yes, her neighbor."
"Did she know anything about her?"
"She seen her on that Saturday morning. She came and fixed breakfast for her."
"Did you know who Anna chummed with during her lifetime, who her friends were?"
"She had several."

"Who are they?"

"Well, I heard her speak of several and have seen her with some, there is Jim Moss and Wayne McFay and several others, and said she had a keen fellow in Burbank."

"What was the nature of the conversation about the gentlemen she spoke of?"

"She told me one time that she was going to get married."

"Who to?"

"Jim Moss."

"When did she say she was going to get married?"

"Some time in June, I think."

"Did you ever see her with Jim Moss?"

"Yes, sir."

"How often? When?"

"About a month ago, or something like that."

"Did you ever hear her speak of any enemies?"

"Not that I remember of."

"What girls did she chum with or speak about?"

"Well, there was Pearl McKinley."

"Did you ever see her with any other girl?"

"Rose Osage."

"Mr. Burkhart, were you in any way alarmed at her absence from home?"

"I asked the neighbor lady and she said she fixed her breakfast for her on the morning before her disappearance, but she didn't know anything about her."

"She couldn't give you any information as to when she went away, or where or who with."

"No, sir."

"Mr. Burkhart, have you any information whatever that you could give this jury as to how Anna Brown met her death?"

"No, sir, I couldn't."

"I ask for information. I am not asking for positive information."

"No, I don't know of enemies she had or anyone that disliked her."

"Who did she speak of when she got drunk or who did she drink with?"

"Just anybody. I have been told that she has been drunk with Charley West."

"Have you heard anything since the discovery that she was dead as to how she died?"

"No, only what the conversation was out there."

"Or heard who she was with Saturday or Sunday night?"
"No, sir."
"Did Anna Brown wear a diamond ring?"
"Three of them that looked like diamonds, but they weren't. She had a good diamond at one time. I think she sold it about a year ago."
"Did they have the appearance of good quality stone?"
"I don't know much about them if she hadn't told me."
"Did she carry any money with her?"
"Yes, seen her with quite a bit sometimes."

Agents located a private detective who was employed by Bryan and Ernest Burkhart in June, 1921, to cover up Bryan's part in the Anna Brown murder. It was this detective's job to "fix" witnesses who had information which might incriminate Burkhart. Burkhart told him that he, Burkhart, had testified in the inquest that he had taken Anna home at about 4:30 p.m. on May 21, but that he had been recognized by a woman who lived near Anna's home when he was taking Anna home about 3:00 a.m. and he was desirous of finding some way to get around this woman's testimony.

This detective also learned that Bill Hale had furnished Bryan with the .38 caliber gun which was used to kill Anna. All of the details of the murder were said to have been worked out by Hale and Bryan in a whiskey joint west of Ralston on that Saturday night.

The woman who lived near Anna and who had reportedly seen Bryan at Anna's home early on the morning of her murder was interviewed by FBI Agents. She stated that in the early morning hours of May 22, 1921, she was waiting for her husband to return home. About 3:00 a.m. she heard voices talking on the road south of her house and she saw a car. She heard a man's voice remark, "For God's sake, Anna, stop your foolishness and come get in this car."

This car then drove on and stopped in front of Anna Brown's house. This woman stated the porch light was on at Anna Brown's house and she observed a man and woman walk up on Anna Brown's porch. When they came under the porch light she could plainly see that the man was Bryan Burkhart and the woman was Anna Brown. She said she paid no further attention and, when she last saw them, they were still on the porch.

Another witness said he saw Bryan Burkhart drive into Gray Horse in Ernest Burkhart's Buick just after daylight on Sunday morning, May 22, 1921. He said he stopped and spoke to Bryan. Subsequently, Bryan asked him not to mention this meeting to anyone.

Agents interviewed the taxicab driver who had driven Anna to Gray Horse early that Saturday morning. He said that she was drunk when he took her. She offered him a drink of whiskey, but he declined. Anna told him not to drive through Gray Horse but to go around the town to the home of Ernest Burkhart where her mother was staying. On the way, she told him that she was pregnant and that Jim Moss was the father. Agents had learned from a different source that the rumor was that Bill Hale was actually the father, but had arranged with Jim Moss to accept the responsibility. Anna also told others that Bryan Burkhart was the father.

A domestic who was employed at Ernest Burkhart's home reported that some time on the morning of May 21, Anna Brown came to Ernest Burkhart's home. She had been drinking and had a bottle of whiskey with her. She seemed despondent and spent the greater portion of the day in a summer house drinking whiskey. She remained at Ernest Burkhart's home all day.

The servant said, "Anna Brown told me that she was jealous of Bryan Burkhart and that she would kill any woman she caught flirting with him. On this same day Bryan told me that Anna Brown had threatened to kill him unless he married her, but that he was going to beat her to it. Some time about 7:00 or 7:30 p.m. on the evening of May 21, Bryan Burkhart, Ernest Burkhart and Anna Brown left Ernest's home in two cars, a Ford and a Buick, the latter being Ernest's car."

Another woman who had been visiting at the Ernest Burkhart home on May 21, 1921, also had a conversation with Anna Brown. She told the FBI investigators that Anna had told her that she was pregnant by Bryan Burkhart and that Bryan Burkhart had to do something about it.

"Anna asked me if I would come to work for her at her home," the woman said "and an arrangement was worked out for me to begin work the following day. Anna said she would send for me the following morning.

"Anna didn't send for me the following morning and, in the afternoon of May 22, Duke Burkhart, brother of Bryan and Ernest, came to my house and asked me to go to work for Mrs. Ernest Burkhart. I told Duke that I had promised to work for Anna. Duke Burkhart told me that Anna Brown was gone. At the time I supposed this to mean that Anna had gone away on a spree, so I went with Duke to the home of Ernest Burkhart where I worked for the next four weeks. I was working there when Anna Brown's remains were found."

Three men were located who stated that after sundown but before dark at about 8:00 p.m. or 8:15 p.m., Saturday, May 21, they were all in a group talking in front of a hotel in Ralston about nine miles south of Fairfax and Gray Horse when a Buick touring car drove up from the east (the direction of Fairfax and Gray Horse Road). The car drove up to the curb within three or four feet of where they were standing. Bryan Burkhart and Anna Brown were sitting in the front seat. No one else was in the car. Anna spoke to one of the men, calling him by name, and he spoke to her. She said she was hungry and asked where they could get something to eat. He pointed to a restaurant about a block away. She thanked him and they drove off. The Buick pulled to the curb at this restaurant. Bryan Burkhart got out and went into the restaurant and came out later with something in a paper bag. He got in the car and drove out of town. All of these men had known both Bryan and Anna personally and well for many years and were positive of their identity. The assertions of these men contradicted Bryan Burkhart's sworn testimony at the inquest that he had not seen Anna after 4:00 or 4:30 Saturday afternoon.

Another man stated that he met Bryan at a whiskey joint west of Ralston on the night of May 21, 1921, and that they had formed a party. They had stayed at this establishment drinking until about 10:00 p.m. when they got into Ernest's Buick and departed while Anna Brown, Edith Davis, George James, and Bill Hale drove in another direction with the agreement that they would all meet later at Paul Johns' roadhouse at Shotgun Corners three miles northeast of Burbank. Later, James and the two women did arrive at Paul Johns' roadhouse about 11:00 p.m.. Hale left them somewhere in the meantime. At about 11:30 p.m. a man named Bridges and Bryan arrived at this roadhouse where the party reunited. They stayed until after midnight drinking. About 12:30 p.m. the party left this roadhouse with Bryan and another man taking Anna Brown in Ernest's Buick with James and Edith Davis going in their car. They drove about one mile toward Fairfax with the Buick in the lead to Shorty Morgan's whiskey joint two miles east of Burbank. Here they stopped and Shorty Morgan sold them some whiskey in soft drink bottles. They did not get out of their cars, but drove on toward Fairfax. About one mile northeast of Fairfax where there is a fork in the road, James and Edith Davis turned east away from Fairfax and Bryan and Anna turned west toward Fairfax.

Paul Johns, who saw Bryan and Anna together at his roadhouse on May 21, stated afterwards that he knew that Bryan had killed Anna, that Bryan had made a mistake in letting several people see them together that night.

Bryan was the last person known to have seen Anna alive. He had been arrested on the basis of evidence collected by local officers, but a trial was never held because these officers supposedly were afraid to trust the decision of the magistrate before whom the warrant had been issued.

The FBI's investigation revealed that Bryan had held Anna Brown while Kelsie Morrison shot her. He was arrested on April 29, 1926. He turned state's evidence in state court, however, and was never convicted.

☜ Chapter 32 ☞

State Prisoner Confuses the Issues

The federal Agents felt they were making progress in the solution of the murders, but something happened which did not fit into the pattern which they saw evolving. Burt Lawson, an inmate of the Oklahoma State Penitentiary at McAlester, Oklahoma, confessed to blowing up the Smith residence. His confession, though lengthy and detailed, did not fit into the general puzzle which the Agents had pieced together.

"The definite date I have forgotten," Lawson said, *"but as nearly as I can recall, I was in the employment of W.E. ("Bill") Smith as a foreman on his farm and ranch, located near Gray Horse, covering a period from some time in 1918 up to some time in 1921. While in the employ of Smith, I lived in his ranch house with my family. Some time around the early part of 1921, I discovered an intimacy between my wife and Bill Smith, which finally developed in breaking up my family and caused me to leave the employment of Smith.*

"After leaving the employ of Smith, I then moved with my family to a place about three and one-half miles southeast of Hominy, Oklahoma. Some time, as near as I can recall, in July, 1922, Ernest Burkhart came to my house, which was a two-room house, a combination kitchen and a bedroom and dining room. My wife and my mother-in-law, Mrs. S. J. Case, were at the house at the time and in the kitchen. This was about two o'clock in the afternoon. Ernest came into the bedroom and sat down and, after talking a few minutes, turned to me and said, 'Burt, I've got a proposition I want to make to you.'

"I remarked, 'What is it Ernest?'

"Ernest said, 'I want you to blow up and kill Bill Smith and his wife. He is the dirtiest-principled man in Oklahoma and he wrecked your home and you have good reasons for killing him, and, if you will blow him and

his wife up with nitroglycerin, I will pay you $5000 cash.'

"Ernest then said that Bill Smith's wife and his, Ernest's, wife were sisters; that if he could get rid of Bill Smith and Smith's wife, that his, Ernest's, wife would fall heir to all their property, which would then make him worth around two million dollars. I turned to Ernest Burkhart and said, 'Ernest, I don't know anything about using nitroglycerin and I would be liable to get my hand blown off, and I just did not want to do anything like that anyhow.'

"Burkhart then said, 'The reason I mentioned it to you was because I know you was solid and would not talk; that you had been working for old man Herrod for six years and knew everything on him and never told anything on him.'

"I then told Ernest that I just did not want to do it and would not do it. Ernest then got up and started to go and, as he walked out of the house, my wife came in from the kitchen and said to me, 'What is it of his durn business of our family affairs.'

"In the next two or three days, possibly four days, W.E. (Bill) Hale came to my house between eight and nine o'clock in the morning. My wife, my mother-in-law, Mrs. S. J. Case, and my sister, Mrs. Bessie C. Lacy, were in the kitchen. There was a curtain between the bedroom and the kitchen. Bill Hale sat down in my front room and began talking about things generally, and then turned to me and said, 'Burt, I've got a proposition I want to put to you.'

"I said, 'What is it, Mr. Hale?'

"He said, 'Burt, I'll give you $5000 cash, and it won't be a check, if you will blow up Bill Smith and his wife. The reason I want him blown up is that I borrowed $10,000 from Smith and he is crowding me for the money and I can't raise the money at the present time, and, if I don't pay it, he will foreclose on me and cause me a lot of trouble, and if I have Smith out of the way, I won't have to pay him this money. You can use nitroglycerin with a fuse and I will fix the nitro and the fuse and all you will have to do is place it under the corner of his house and touch it off. The fuse burns only so many feet to the minute, and I will cut the fuse long enough to give you plenty time to get away.'

"Hale then pulled from his pocket a piece of white fuse about three feet long and said, 'I'll show you how to use it.' He then took his pocketknife and cut off a piece about six inches long, then spread the ends open. Then he took a match from his pocket and lighted the end of the short piece of fuse, then placed the ends of the short piece and long piece about an inch apart and said, 'You see, the spark will fly from the short piece to the long piece, which will be a more sure shot of setting it off than by using a match.'

"About that time my wife and her sister, Mrs. Bessie C. Lacy, came into the room and my wife remarked, 'What in the world is he doing?' meaning Bill Hale.

"Bill Hale answered and said, 'I'm teaching Burt how to be a mechanic.'

"By that time the short piece had burned down close to Hale's fingers and Hale threw it on the floor. My mother-in-law, who was in the kitchen, put her head in the door and said, 'I smell rubber burning.' She looked around and saw the piece of fuse burning on the floor, and remarked, 'What are you trying to do, blow up this place?'

"Bill Hale remarked, 'No, I'm just pranking with Burt.'

"My mother-in-law went back to the kitchen, and my wife and sister left the room.

"I then turned to Hale and said, 'Hale, I can't afford to do that and I'm not going to do it.'

"Hale then said, 'Well, Burt, I'll see you later.' Hale then left my house.

"About two weeks later, as near as I can remember, after Bill Hale left my house, I was driving to Fairfax, Oklahoma, in my car and when I got near Salt Creek Bridge — which is about a mile out of Fairfax — I met Kelsie Morrison in a car driving towards Gray Horse. As we passed, Kelsie called to me to stop. I had got a little past him and backed my car up to him. Kelsie got out of his car and came around to me and said, 'Burt, I got a good deal on and I want you to help me to pull the job. There will be good money in it, $5,000 apiece. The reasons I came to you is I know that Hale and Ernest Burkhart had been to you, and that you are solid and will not tell anything. The job is to blow up Bill Smith and his wife, and we can do it and do a good job and there will be no danger.'

"I asked Kelsie who was going to pay the money, and he said, 'Bill Hale and Ernest Burkhart will pay half each of $5,000.'

"I told Kelsie that, if I had wanted to do it, I would have taken the first offer made to me by Hale and Ernest Burkhart.

"Kelsie said, 'Well, I know that they offered you $5,000.' We then parted.

"A few days after I talked with Kelsie Morrison, I was in Fairfax and met Bryan Burkhart near the first blacksmith shop on the south side of town. Bryan said to me, 'Burt, why didn't you take up that proposition that Kelsie offered to you to help blow up Bill Smith and wife? That would have been easy money for you.'

"I told Bryan that the proposition did not look good to me; that if I wanted the electric chair I would have taken the proposition, but I do not want anything to do with it.

"He said, 'I know that Bill Hale, Ernest and Kelsie had talked to you about it, and I know that you are all right.' This was all that man said

about it.

"Some time in August, as I recall, the latter part of August, 1922, I met Roy Bunch at Fairfax near a white church, which is about one block west of the Smith-Williams Hotel. I had know Roy Bunch for a long time, and we got into a conversation about making money.

"Bunch said, 'Burt, do you want to make some easy money?'

"I said, 'It depends on how you want me to make it.'

"Bunch said, 'Henry Roan is a good friend of yours and you know him well, and he'll go anywhere with you. I'll give you $1,000 if you will let me put some strychnine in some whiskey and you give the whiskey to Roan and kill him. I've got Roan and his wife separated and we're on bad terms, and I'm going to have his wife if I have to kill him myself.'

"I told Roy that I liked Henry Roan, and would not hurt a hair on Henry's head, and would not have anything to do with it; that if he wanted to kill him, that was his business and for him to hop to it.

"A short time thereafter I was arrested in September, 1922, as I remember, and put in jail at Pawhuska, charged with murder, and I remained in jail until April 4, 1923, at which time I was released after the jury found me not guilty of the charge of murder.

"I was released from jail about 11 o'clock at night. My brother-in-law, Charlie Blair, and my mother-in-law, Mrs. S. J. Case, took me in a taxicab to Pershing, Oklahoma, where we caught a one o'clock M. E. &T. train going to Hominy. After arriving at Hominy, we walked three miles southeast to my home. About two or three days after I got home, about two o'clock in the afternoon, Bill Hale and Ernest Burkhart came to my house. My brother-in-law, Charlie Blair, and my mother-in-law, Mrs. Case, were in the bedroom, and my wife and my sister-in-law, Mrs. Charlie Blair, were in the kitchen. Bill Hale and Ernest Burkhart came into the bedroom.

"Hale appeared to have been drinking a little. After a few remarks, Hale turned to me and said, 'Burt, I got that job done, and a good job of it, and now what I want to ask you to do is not to say anything about what we said to you, for if you did, there would be no way under the sun to keep me from getting hung.'

"Ernest Burkhart spoke up and said, 'Burt ain't going to talk. I knew him when he worked for old man Herrod for six years and knew everything on him and didn't tell nothing on him.' Hale then said, 'Burt, if you ever need a friend or anything just let us know.' Ernest Burkhart then spoke up and said, 'Yes, Burt, if you ever need a friend, money or anything just let us know.'

"Hale then turned to my mother-in-law, Mrs. Case, and said, 'Burt knows enough on me to hang me if he would tell it, but I know that you

folks never meddle with other folks' business, so I can't be worried.'

"My mother-in-law, Mrs. Case, said to Hale, 'It takes all of our time to tend to our own business.'

"In a few minutes Hale and Ernest left my place.

"Some time about the middle of April, 1923, I was in an automobile with Hal Buie, going from Hominy to Ralston by the way of Gray Horse, Oklahoma. Between the Sand Rock schoolhouse and store at Gray Horse, we met Roy Bunch, who was in his car. We stopped and we all got out. Bunch turned to me and said, 'Burt, who is that fellow you have in the car with you?'

"I answered him and said, 'He is just another crook like we are,' referring to Hal Buie.

"Bunch then remarked, 'Burt, you just as well had that thousand dollars as not, you would have got some good out of it on the farm. That damned Kelsie and Bryan will not get any good out of it, they will spend it for women and whiskey. Them crazy sons of bitches, Kelsie and Bryan, said they took the whiskey and strychnine that I gave them to give Henry Roan, and they said they gave it to him and it did not work fast enough so they shot him. I think they drank the whiskey and shot Roan, and I told Kelsie so, and whenever you see him you want to josh him about it.'

"Later on, about a week later, Hal Buie and I were in Fairfax and we met Kelsie Morrison near the corner of the First National Bank. We stopped and got into conversation, and I remarked to Kelsie, 'Roy Bunch is telling a bad tale on you. He said that you took that whiskey with strychnine to give to Henry Roan and drank it, then shot Henry Roan.'

"Kelsie remarked, 'Did that son of a bitch tell you that?'

"I said, 'Yes, that is what he told me.'

"Kelsie said, 'That crazy son of a bitch will tell you anything. I learned one thing in this deal, corn whiskey kills the effect of strychnine.'

"The first part of this year, 1925, I was sent to McAlester State Penitentiary to serve seven years, and then Kelsie Morrison came there as a prisoner with a nine-year sentence. On last Labor Day, while all the prisoners were in the yard, I was walking around with Hal Buie and met Kelsie Morrison near the entrance to the laundry.

"Kelsie remarked, 'I wish I was out of this damned place. I would kill me some more red men if they were not all broke.'

"I said, 'Kelsie, you are going to get yourself in a crack if you don't look out.'

"Kelsie said, 'Oh hell, do it at night like I did the other jobs when nobody can see you.'

"I said, 'I could put my finger on those fellows who did the jobs as soon *as I hear of them being done.'*

"Kelsie said, 'I guess you could after we had talked it over together.'

"I said, 'Yes, and I know who paid you the money and how much they paid you.' Kelsie said, 'Well I don't care for you knowing it for you never did turn anyone in.' I said, 'Well you got good money for the job.'

"Kelsie said, 'Yes, and they're liable to be out a damn sight more before it is over with.'

"Later on I had another conversation in the yard, when there were not many prisoners around and I told Kelsie that he had better be ready to protect himself, that Hale and the Burkharts are liable to frame up on him, and Kelsie said, 'Well I am going to take care of myself.'"

Lawson furnished additional confessions adding more details, implicating himself in the plot and later he confessed that he actually was the person who blew up the Smith residence:

"Some time in September, 1922, I was arrested and put in Pawhuska jail charged with murder, and did not see Bill Hale any more until about three days before Bill Smith's house was blown up, when Hale came to the jail to see me, I was in a cell by myself.

"Bill Hale said to me, 'Burt, you will be needing some attorneys pretty soon and I know you haven't got any money to pay them with, and I want that job pulled. Now I can come and get you out of jail and take you over there and you can do the job, and I can get you back in jail and nobody will ever know the difference.'

"I said, 'All right Bill, I'll pull it.'

"Hale said, 'Well, I'll get everything fixed and be back after you in the next three or four days.'

"Three days after that, about eight o'clock at night, Deputy Sheriff, I think, named Bloyed, or something like that, came to my cell and unlocked it and said, 'Burt, come out here there is a party wants to see you,' and told me to get my coat and hat. He then took me down and out of the north front door and pointed out to a car standing in front of the jail and said, 'The party that wants to see you is in the car.'

"I went out to the car and found Bill Hale in it. He told me to get in, which I did, and he drove off to Fairfax.

"On the road to Fairfax, Hale told me that he had everything fixed and that I could do a good job and nobody will ever know anything about it, and he said, 'As soon as you get through with it, I'll give you $5,000 cash.'

"Hale was driving a big Buick car. We went to Fairfax to Ernest Burkhart's house. When we got there we went in the front room and found Ernest Burkhart there. Burkhart said something about his wife was not at home, and I did not see anyone there but Ernest and Bill Hale. We all sat

down, and Hale told Ernest Burkhart to get us a drink.

"Ernest went out and came back with some whiskey and we all drank. Hale then said that Bill Smith and his family were at a show, and wouldn't be back until late, and told Ernest to go get the box. Ernest went out and was gone a few minutes and came back with a small box about a foot square and sat it down on the floor by us. This box I could see had a jug in it with the neck sticking out through a hole in the top, and had a big roll of white fuse laying on top of the box with one end of the fuse running through a cork in the jug.

"Hale remarked, 'Now everything is fixed fine. This fuse will reach from the cellar in Smith's house, back to the alley.' Hale asked me if I knew anything about Smith's house, I told him yes, that I been by the house many times and knew where the entrance to the cellar was. Hale said, 'Well we will take you in the car and drive you down near the house in the alley and put you out and you then take the box and go to Smith's house before they come home and put the box in the cellar, and then take the fuse and lay it out as far as it will reach, but be sure not to pull it loose from the jug. Then you sit back in the dark and watch and, when Smith comes home and goes to bed, you wait about three quarters of an hour and give him plenty of time to go to sleep, then you touch her off and run like hell and come back here to the house.'

"We then waited quite a while and finally Hale said, 'Well, its time to go.'

"Ernest Burkhart took the box with the fuse and we all went out and got in the car. We drove down to an alley way that leads in behind where Bill Smith lives, and drove down this alleyway a short piece. I got out and took the box and fuse, and Hale and Ernest drove on away. I then went in the back way and into Smith's cellar, and placed the box in the far corner of the cellar, then laid the fuse cut like Hale had told me, and the end of it reached clear out and into the alley behind Smith's house. I then sat down in the dark and waited.

"Finally, Bill Smith, his wife and his hired girl came walking down the sidewalk from the North and went into Smith's house. I saw the lights turned on. I suppose they all undressed and went to bed, for pretty soon the lights went out. I sat there for quite a while. I had no way to tell what time it was, but I would figure it was about three quarters of an hour, and after I thought they were all asleep, I lighted a short piece of fuse that Bill Hale cut off the long piece for me before we left the house and fixed the ends, and touched off the long fuse with it.

"As soon as the long end began to smoke, I beat it as fast as I could for Ernest Burkhart's, going down the alley. When I got to Burkhart's house,

Bill Hale was out on Burkhart's porch waiting for me. I whispered to him and said, 'Well, I touched her off. The fuse was smoking when I left.'

"I went on in the house and Hale remained on the porch. I started to take a drink of whiskey from the bottle setting on the table and about that time I heard the explosion.

"Hale then came into the room and said, 'Well, she went off. Let's all take a drink and I'll rush you back to jail in Pawhuska, and I'm going to take a little trip.'

"Hale and I then went out and got in a Buick car and beat it for Pawhuska to the north entrance of the jail. He blowed his horn, and Deputy Void, or Bloyed, came out of the jail door and Hale told me to go on to him, which I did, and this deputy locked me up again in my cell.

"On the road back to Pawhuska from Fairfax, after the explosion, Hale again mentioned that he was going to take a trip and as soon as he got back, which would be in a few days, that he would pay me for the job.

"Up to this time Hale has never paid me. I have asked him for it several times, and got Hal Buie to write a letter for me to Hale since I have been in the penitentiary, asking him to send me $200 and he wouldn't even answer my letter."

At the time of the Smith murder, Lawson had been confined in jail charged with murdering an old man for his wares, but Lawson's confession to this murder disappeared from the files of the county attorney of Osage County which resulted in his being acquitted. It was assumed that Lawson, described as an unscrupulous criminal, secured high-powered cooperation in defeating his case. The specificity of Lawson's confession was impressive and added to its credibility. An exhaustive investigation was conducted to corroborate or disprove his story.

Agents interviewed the deputy sheriff who, Lawson alleged, released him from prison to blow up the Smith residence. He strenuously denied that he had ever released Lawson from jail. He advanced the argument that Lawson hated him because he had apprehended him and developed the case against him for murdering the old man. He insisted that Lawson's allegations were pure malice, that the story was completely untrue and he was innocent, regardless of what anyone said.

Additional investigation proved Lawson's confession to be a complete fabrication. The Agents developed information that Hale himself had designed the bogus confession believing that, if Lawson were exonerated, he, too, would be cleared since he was out of town when Lawson alleged Hale had gotten him out of jail. He also planned, through Lawson's confession, to place the blame on Roy Bunch for the murder of Henry Roan. Agents located witnesses who stated that Lawson had asked them to swear falsely to verify his untrue confession.

As the schemers had planned, Agents spent days of fruitless work in running out false leads before Lawson's statements were finally disproved.

☞ Chapter 33 ☜

Blackie Thompson Talks

Word was received by the G-men that Blackie Thompson, an inmate of the Oklahoma State Penitentiary, might possibly have information of value concerning the murders. When they talked to Thompson at the prison, he was reluctant to part with the information he possessed, no doubt fearing reprisal from members of the murder ring. However, very slowly and cautiously, bit by bit, he related the following story:

Some time in the summer of 1920 Ernest Burkhart had proposed to him that he go up to Bill Smith's house, stick up Smith and his wife, rob them of their diamonds and kill them. Burkhart told Thompson that he wanted the Smiths killed because he stood to inherit from Mrs. Rita Smith, his wife's sister.

Thompson suggested to the federal Agents that arrangements be made for him to talk to Ernest Burkhart. He said he was sure Ernest would meet him and talk to him whenever he demanded it. He wanted the Agents to plant a recording device in the room where he and Ernest Burkhart would be conversing so they could later give that as the source of their information rather than Thompson in order to protect his identity.

Thompson stated that, if he were brought face-to-face with Ernest Burkhart, he could make him confess. He said he would threaten Burkhart saying, "You have caused others to fall and now you are going to get yours. You tell all about the murders or I'll tell all I know." Thompson told Agents he felt Burkhart would then confess to avoid bringing to light a great number of other crimes in which Burkhart was involved.

Agents, however, preferred to handle Burkhart their own way. They interviewed Ernest Burkhart, confronting him with the meticulous evidence they had gathered. He proved to be the weak link in the Hale organization's chain. He confessed. Burkhart stated to an Agent that, while he realized that his uncle Bill Hale was doing criminal things, he felt that Hale was really a big man and he (Burkahrt) did not know how to refuse to do anything that Hale told him to do.

Burkhart said that Hale had pointed John Ramsey out to him at Henry Grammer's ranch several weeks before Roan's murder and described Ramsey as a man who could be relied on. Hale told Burkhart that Grammer once stole some cattle and got Ramsey to take the blame for it. Ramsey was convicted and served a prison sentence in the Oklahoma State prison for the crime he did not commit

Burkhart continued,

"Some time about one year and a half before Roan's death, Hale took out a policy on Henry Roan's life for $25,000, and told me that the reason he got this policy was on account of the fact that Henry Roan was having family trouble and was drinking very hard and he had made one attempt to commit suicide and he did not figure he would live long.

"After Hale and I left Grammer's ranch, and after he pointed Ramsey out to me, Hale said he would put Ramsey on Henry Roan's trail, that Ramsey would either give him some poison whiskey, or shoot him and lay a gun beside him and everybody would think he committed suicide.

"A few days later Ramsey came down to Fairfax and I was walking down the street and ran into Ramsey and Bill Hale talking something about buying a Ford roadster at Ponca City. Ramsey then left, stating he would go to Ponca by way of Pawnee and Perry over Santa Fe and Frisco.

"After Ramsey left, Hale told me he had given Ramsey the money to buy a Ford roadster as Ramsey had no way to get around to kill Roan and get away, and it would be necessary for Ramsey to steer Roan around and keep up with him and get him to a place where he could bump him.

"In a few days Ramsey returned to Fairfax in a new Ford roadster, which I understand he bought at Ponca City. I saw Ramsey around town in this car for the next few days. About a week before Henry Roan's body was found, Ramsey walked up to me on the street at Fairfax and inquired for Hale. I told him I did not know where he was. Ramsey then told me to tell Hale the job was all right and not to worry, that it happened out in the Sol Smith pasture[34].

"I later saw Hale and told him what Ramsey had said. Ramsey left Fairfax, going to his home at Ripley.

---

[34]Smith 7 Ranch.

"In a few days Ramsey came back to Fairfax, and later went to Grammer's place.

"Shortly thereafter, Henry Roan's body was found dead in his car.

"A few days later Ramsey came back to Fairfax and stayed a short time and went on to Ripley.

"Some time after Roan's body was found, possibly a month later, Bill Hale told me he had paid Ramsey the balance he owed Ramsey for killing Roan, which made the job cost him the Ford car and the balance, being a total of $1,000.

"Some time after Roan was found, I asked Ramsey how it happened. Ramsey said he met Roan on the road running from Fairfax to Burbank and got in Roan's car with Ramsey sitting on the back seat. They drove off and under the hill, with him telling Roan they would take a drink, and when they got to the right place out of sight of the road, he shot Roan. He walked back to the top of the hill where he had met Roan and had left his car, and drove on into Fairfax. He told me he shot Roan with a .45 automatic pistol."

Later the same day Ernest Burkhart discussed the murder of Bill Smith with federal Agents. Burkhart said that, after the difficulties between Smith and Hale over the money Hale allegedly owed Smith, Hale told Ernest Burkhart he believed he would have Smith killed. Burkahrt said:

"Later in conversation, Hale told me that he had either been to see Al Spencer, or thought he would go to see Al Spencer and get him to bump Smith off.

"About this time something happened to Spencer, I don't remember what, and Hale said something to me about not knowing where he was and something about getting Fred Rowe to go with him to see Spencer. Later Hale told me he was going to see Grammer and get him to furnish a man to bump Smith.

"About a week later, Hale told me that Grammer told him that he would have Blackie Thompson do it.

"Some time after that, Hale told me that Blackie could not be found, or was out of the country.

"Just a few days before the blowup happened, Grammer told Hale that Acie — Asa Kirby — would do it. That is what Hale told me. I asked Hale who Acie was, and Hale told me that Acie was one of Grammer's friends.

"I believe the next thing was that Grammer and Hale were going to Fort Worth to the Fat Stock Show, and I understood that Acie lived at Webb City, and John Ramsey lived at Ripley, and John Ramsey knew Acie.

"Just before Hale left, he asked me if I knew Acie, and I told him no. He

said to tell John Ramsey to go to Ripley and get Acie, and, while he, Hale, and Grammer were in Fort Worth, to do the job.

"I got Hale's Buick car and went to Ripley and found John Ramsey. When I found him he was in a blacksmith shop. I talked to him a short while there, and then called him out into the middle of the street and told him that Hale and Grammer were in Fort Worth and that Hale said to have Acie go down and do the job."

"Ramsey said he could not go right then, that he had no chance to get away from his wife, who was sick. Ramsey said that he believed that he would just tell her that he was going up to Grammer's to get a little whiskey. He said he would go then and get Acie.

"I got the car back, figuring it would happen on that day, but it happened on the next night.

"When it happened, I was in bed with my wife.... it shook everything. At first I thought it was thunder, then there were three or four shots fired. I saw a light on the north side. My wife went to the window and looked out and said that Perry King's house was on fire. As soon as she said that I knew what it was.

"My understanding was that Acie was going to shoot Bill Smith, but Acie did not know Smith, and Smith was never out at night and never ran around with a stranger and Acie had no chance. Hale said that Grammer told him that, if he could not get a chance to shoot Smith, that he would have to put 'soup' under the house and blow him up.'

Burkhart added, "Hale showed up in Fairfax about the 12th. Hale asked me about Ramsey, if I knew whether Ramsey was with Acie, or whether Acie did it. I believe he asked me if I had seen Ramsey since the blow up. He, Hale, said to me, 'You don't know whether Ramsey was with him, Acie, or not?' I told him that I had not seen him and did not know whether he was or not. Hale did not tell me that he had registered at the Metropolitan Hotel while he was in Fort Worth, but I would bet you a thousand dollars that he was stopping there, and if you go there, you would find that was where he stayed."

✍ Chapter 34 ☞

The Pieces of the Puzzle Fall into Place

After Ernest Burkhart's confession, the pieces of the nefarious puzzle began to fall into place rapidly. John Ramsey was the next to confess.

"Some time in the early part of 1923," he began, *"the date I don't recall, Bill Hale came to Henry Grammer's ranch where I was working for Grammer selling whiskey. I was in the bunkhouse and Henry Grammer called me. I went out and saw him and Hale standing together. I walked over to them and the three of us walked out several yards to a road and stopped.*

"Henry Grammer turned to me and said that Hale had a little job he wanted done and asked me if I would do it. I said, 'It depends on what the job was.' Grammer said he wanted an Indian bumped off.

"I said, 'That's different.'

Hale, Grammer and I then talked the matter over for a few minutes. I don't recall just what was said, but I remarked that I would look it over and I went back to the bunkhouse.

"In a few days Grammer told me that Hale was getting anxious to have that job done.

"As I remember, the next time I saw Hale was in Fairfax, and we had another talk about the Indian he wanted killed, and I told him I would do the job, but that I did not have any way to get around. Hale said he would see me in a day or two or in a few days.

"I again met Hale at Grammer's ranch and Hale told me he was going to buy me a car, and gave me five hundred dollars. Something was said about where I would buy the car, and I said I would buy it in Ponca City. Something was said about my getting over there, and Hale said he would drive me over to Pawnee, which he did, and I caught the train there and went to Ponca City where I bought a new Ford roadster from the Ford

garage. Before I received the car, I made application and the Ford people secured a license. I drove back to Grammer's ranch.

"At some stage of the game, on the street in Fairfax, Hale pointed out to me the Indian that he wanted killed. I don't remember Hale ever telling me the Indian's name.

"Several days after Hale pointed this Indian out to me, I met this Indian in a restaurant in Fairfax, and he sat down beside me and I smelled whiskey on his breath. We got into conversation about whiskey and I told him I could get him some. He said he wanted some. I told him to meet me out on the road running through Sol Smith's pasture about one o'clock and I would meet him and have the whiskey for him.

"I left him and went to Grammer's and got some whiskey and drove back on the road leading through Sol Smith's pasture and found this Indian sitting in his car waiting at a point near Salt Creek. I drove up and got out of my car and we took several drinks from a bottle I had. I then got in my car and went to Fairfax.

"Several times after that I met this Indian and gave him drinks. This went on for several days, and I was trying to rib up a little more courage.

"Finally, one day, I decided to pull the job, everything being favorable. So, I told this Indian to meet me out on the road running through Smith's pasture, that I would have some whiskey for him. I told him about what point on the road I would meet him. So he went out on one road and I on another.

"We met about the foot of the big hill near Salt Creek. I motioned to him to go up on top of the hill, which he did, and stopped. I drove up and I saw a car coming. I told him to drive off under the hill, which he did. I got out of my car when the car I had seen passed. I then walked down under the hill where I found him waiting for me. He got out of the car and we sat on the running board of his car and drank what whiskey we had. The Indian then got in his car to leave, and I shot him in the back of the head. I suppose I was within a foot or two of him when I shot him. I then went back to my car and drove to Fairfax.

"In a few days I saw Hale and told him enough for him to understand that I had killed the Indian. There was very little said at this time. Some time later I again met Hale and there was something said about paying me the balance of five hundred dollars. Hale said he would pay it a little later as he would have more money then and I told him that was all right, that I didn't need it then. Some time within a month or two Hale paid me the balance due me of five hundred dollars.

"Several days, I don't remember just how long, but something like ten days later, this Indian's body, that I killed, was found. As I remember, that

was the first time I found out that his name was Henry Roan."

The following day Agents questioned John Ramsey again, asking him about the explosion at Bill Smith's house. He said that he wanted to tell all he knew about the killing of Bill Smith and his family.

"As I remember," he began, "before I was hired to kill Henry Roan, through talking with Henry Grammer, where I was then selling whiskey, I knew that Bill Hale wanted Bill Smith murdered and I knew that Henry Grammer was helping Bill Hale to arrange to have him killed. I don't remember right now the different conversations I had with Grammer which convinced me they were going to kill Smith. I can't say for sure whether it was before I killed Henry Roan or after that Grammer told me that he had a man to do the job and told me it was Asa Kirby. In a little while after Grammer told me, Asa Kirby showed up at Grammer's. That was the first time I met him. Grammer was very drunk, and he, in the presence of Asa Kirby, told me Kirby was all right, that he would do that job he wanted done and for me to help Kirby all I could.

"Kirby then talked to me, and asked me what was the job that Grammer wanted done. I told him that he wanted a squaw man killed down near Fairfax by the name of Bill Smith.

"Kirby then said, 'Well, I wasn't figuring on staying here long,' and wanted to know what there was in it for him.

"I told him that I did not know.

"He said, 'Well, I'll see Grammer and talk it over with him.'

"I don't remember now other little details of the conversations, but I do remember that I took Kirby down near Gray Horse where Bill Smith was living on a ranch and pointed out Bill Smith's house to Kirby. The next thing I remember in same way I heard that Bill Smith left the country and had gone to Arkansas. In fact, Ernest Burkhart told me that Smith had gone to Arkansas, but he did not think he would be gone long, and for me to tell Kirby. I told Asa Kirby what Ernest Burkhart had told me. The next thing that followed — and I don't know how long after — Ernest Burkhart came to me and told me that Bill Smith had come back from Arkansas and then took me and showed me a house in Fairfax that Bill Smith was going to move into.

"The next thing that happened Ernest Burkhart came to me at Ripley, where I had my family, and told me that Bill Smith had moved into town, and told me to tell Asa Kirby that everything was ready, or words to that effect, and tell him as quick as I could.

"I told Ernest my wife was sick, and I would go as soon as I could get away. I am not sure whether I went after Kirby that day or the next. I drove

to a little oil town as I remember, either Webb City or Cooper, where Kirby runs a rooming house, and met Kirby and told him everything was ready and I would take him down and show him the house.

"Kirby and I drove to Fairfax and I showed him the house that Ernest said that Bill Smith lived in. Kirby asked me if I knew where there was any 'soup.' He said Henry Grammer had some and he asked me if I knew where it was. I told him I did not. Then there was something said about there being plenty of 'soup' stored in the oil field and there would be no trouble for him to get it if he needed it; that he was not sure whether he would blow up Smith or shoot him.

"As I remember, I went on home, and I suppose Kirby went home. I don't recall exactly when, but soon after that, possibly the next night, Smith's house was blown up.

"At some stage of the game — I don't exactly recall when — before the blowup, I asked Asa Kirby if he needed any help to do the job, and he said, 'No.'

"Some few days later — I don't recall just how long after the Smith blowup — I met Kirby and he told me something about doing a good job. After the blowup I talked with Grammer and he asked me if I had seen the blowup and he said it was a fair or good job.

"In possibly a week after that, I went to Fairfax and saw the blowup. Neither Hale nor Grammer paid me anything for the part I did in this. I was supposed to be just helping out. But at different times since the blowup Hale has given me money and, whenever I needed a little money, I let Hale know and he never failed to favor me.

"Henry Grammer told me that he paid Asa Kirby for the job. I asked Asa if he got a settlement for the job and he said Henry Grammer paid all but a little, that Grammer came up to pay him it all but got drunk and spent a few hundred dollars, but later he paid it all.

"I have made this statement because it is the truth. Before I got mixed up with Henry Grammer I did not think it would be possible to do the things I did do."

⚜ Chapter 35 ⚜

Asa Kirby Meets an Untimely Death

Bill Hale sent for Asa "Ace" Kirby, one of his operatives. Kirby had done many jobs for the "King," in addition to blowing up the home of Bill Smith. Hale explained that he knew of an easy score for Kirby.

Hale unfolded his plan: There was a certain storekeeper who kept a fortune in diamonds and other valuable gems in a chamois bag in his store. Hale had seen them himself. He told Kirby exactly where they were kept and suggested that Kirby break into this store that night. There would be no one there and the job would be a cinch.

Kirby went home and borrowed $80 from the man with whom he was living and then Kirby left the house, saying that some of his friends had a "deal" on and he was going to look it over.

Meanwhile, Hale was doing a favor for someone else. He contacted the owner of the store where the cache of jewels was located and told him that he had reliable information that someone was going to break into his store that night.

At about 2:30 a.m., as Asa Kirby approached the store, the proprietor crouched inside in the darkness with a shotgun ready. As Kirby entered, the store owner blasted him with the shotgun.

Two accomplices helped Asa Kirby home and the man from whom he had borrowed $80 rushed him to a doctor. Kirby was badly shot in the shoulder.

"What happened?" the doctor asked.

Kirby snapped, "That's none of your damned business."

The doctor told Kirby his arm would have to be amputated.

"If you have to do that," Kirby moaned, "just cut my head off."

The doctor treated Kirby and tried to save him, but Asa Kirby died the following day without making a dying statement. There was one fewer witness the King of the Osage Hills had to worry about.

ᔥ Chapter 36 ᔧ

Federal Prosecutors Interview Kelsie Morrison

Special Agents of the FBI felt the time was opportune for inter-viewing Kelsie Morrison and confronting him with the evidence they had gathered regarding his role in the murder scheme. In the face of the evidence the Special Agents had already gathered, Morrison also confessed. Another link in the murder chain was broken.

On the basis of Kelsie Morrison's confession to FBI Agents, one of the federal government's prosecuting attorneys questioned Morrison at Guthrie, Oklahoma.

"Kelsie, you knew Anna Brown during your life?" Kelsie was asked.

"Yes, sir."

"How long did you know her?"

"How long? About six or eight months."

"You also knew W.K. Hale and Bryan Burkhart?"

"Yes, sir."

"How long did you know them?"

"About five years."

"You remember the death of Anna Brown?"

"Yes, sir."

"Were you present when that happened?"

"Yes, sir."

"Who else was present?"

"Bryan Burkhart."

"Did Bryan Burkhart have anything to do with the killing of Anna Brown?"

"Yes, he held her up."

"And you fired the shot, did you?"

"Yes, sir."

"What kind of a place was it where Anna Brown was killed, with reference to a canyon or ravine?"

"It was a ravine, rocky, trees around it and very little water."

"About how far is that from Fairfax?"

"About three miles from Fairfax."

"Is there a spring in this canyon?"

"Yes, sir."

"About how far from the head of the canyon was Anna Brown killed?"

"About 75 yards."

"Do you know how Anna Brown came to be there?"

"Yes. Bryan Burkhart and I took her there."

"Was anyone else with you?"

"Yes, Katherine Morrison."

"She was your wife then."

"Yes, sir."

"Is she known as Katherine Cole?"

"Yes, sir."

"At the time you took Anna Brown down there, what kind of a car were you riding in?"

"A Buick."

"Whose car was it?"

"Ernest Burkhart."

"Who drove the car?"

Bryan Burkhart."

"Were you sitting in the front seat or back seat?"

"The back seat."

"Who was in the back seat with you?"

"Anna Brown."

"When you drove out to this place and stopped the car, how did Anna Brown get out of the car?"

"Bryan helped to take her out."

"What was her condition with reference to being drunk?"

"She was drunk."

"When you took her out of the car, what did you do with her?"

"Took her down in the ravine."

"About how far from the car?"

"About 40 steps."

"After you got there what did you do with her?"

"Gave her a big drink and left her."

"Was she so drunk as to be helpless?"

"Yes, sir."

"What did you do then?"

"Went back and got in the car."

"Where did you go?"

"Rode around two or three hours."

"Did you take Katherine home?"

"Yes, sir."

"And was that when she was killed?"

"Yes, sir."

"At whose instance did you and Bryan Burkhart take Anna Brown out there?"

"Bill Hale."

"Did he request you to kill her?"

"Yes, sir."

"Did he furnish the gun?"

"Yes, sir."

"And did you kill her with Bill Hale's gun?"

"Yes, sir."

"Did he pay you for it?"

"Yes, sir."

"How much?"

"One thousand dollars and what I owed him."

"How much did you owe him?"

"About six hundred dollars."

"After Anna Brown was killed, did you report to Bill Hale?"

"Yes, sir."

"The same night?"

"Yes, sir."

"Where was he then?"

"He was out to the ranch house."

"You mean his ranch house?"

"Yes, sir."

"When did he pay you this one thousand dollars?"

"About thirty days after it happened."

"How did he pay it?"

"He paid it in signing notes at the Osage Bank in Fairfax."

"You mean he signed the notes with you?"

"Yes, sir."

"Did he afterwards pay the notes?"

"Yes, sir."

"Now Kelsie, with reference to the killing of Bill Smith and his family, say whether or not Hale ever talked to you about killing Smith?"

"He did."

"More than once?"

"Yes, sir."

"About how many times?"

"I could not say. Any number of times."

"Did he suggest that he would pay you well for it?"

"Yes, sir."

"Ever give you any figure?"

"No, sir."

"What did you tell him about it?"

"I told him I did not want to do it."

"What way did he suggest that you might kill him?"

"Told me to shoot him."

"Shoot him in the daytime or night?"

"In the night."

"Where?"

"At his home at night."

"Did he ever suggest to you about burning the Smith home?"

Yes, sir."

"What did he want you to burn the house for?"

"He wanted me to set it on fire and when Bill Smith ran out to shoot him."

"Shoot whom?"

"Bill Smith and his wife."

"Did he tell you why he wanted you to kill Bill Smith and wife?"

"No, sir."

"Bill Smith's wife was a sister of Anna Brown?"

"Yes, sir."

"Did you ever hear him suggest that he wanted to get all the estates of those sisters in the hands of Mollie Burkhart?"

"Yes, sir."

"Just how did he express that?"

"Well, he said Mollie would fall heir to the estates, and then Ernest Burkhart would make it right with me."

"Make it right with you for what?"

"For the killing."

"Was that when he suggested to you about killing Rita Smith and Bill Smith?"

"Yes, sir."

"Did you ever discuss the matter with Ernest?"

"No, sir."

"When you refused to do the killing and told Hale you did not want to do the killing, did he say he would get someone else to do it?"

"He said he would get someone else to do it."

﹌ Chapter 37 ﹆

The Net Draws Tight

In 1926, after years of painstaking FBI investigation, the net was drawn tight. Caught in the net were William K. Hale (the King of the Osage Hills), John Ramsey, Kelsie Morrison, Ernest Burkhart, and Bryan Burkhart.

These arrests were made by local authorities since Special Agents of the FBI did not have the power of arrest (or the authority to carry firearms) at that time.

Hale, Ramsey, Ernest Burkhart and Morrison all faced prosecution by state authorities for the Anna Brown murder and the Smith massacre. Hale and Ramsey also faced federal prosecution for the Henry Roan murder.

After it was learned that Bill Hale was the mastermind behind the murders, a lynching party was formed by Osage County citizens who planned to mob the jail and hang him, but cooler heads prevailed and the administration of justice was left to the courts.

With the arrest of these members of the murder ring, Osage County began to regain its self-respect. Witnesses, hitherto non communicative and in fear for their lives, came forth with additional information about the murders and stated that they would be happy to testify against the defendants to rid Osage County of their ilk. The fear was gone. The federal investigators had restored the people's trust in law enforcement. The odds were no longer in favor of the criminal in Osage County. The power of the King of the Osage Hills was broken and the entire populace took a collective sigh of relief.

The defendants made every effort to defeat prosecution. Money was no object. Defense attorneys resorted to every means, legal and illegal, to obtain their clients' freedom. Like adversaries in some great chess game, FBI Agents matched wits with these attorneys. Agents spent long, weary hours of investigation combating the illegal measures to which these unscrupulous attorneys stooped and in trying to keep one step ahead of them.

The investigation conducted by the FBI in connection with the trials of these defendants was as involved and far-reaching as the actual investigation of the murders and was filled with pitfalls, disappointments and danger. During the course of the trials, information was received that a hired gunman was in town who had orders to kill at least one of the Agents. Local officers advised this gunman it would be healthier for him in some other climate.

This investigation to counteract the machinations of the defense attorneys and friends of the Hale faction to manipulate the scales of justice is an interesting story in itself.

While he was in jail, Hale wrote the following poem and signed it, "W.K. Hale":

JUDGE NOT!

Judge Not! the clouds of seeming guilt may dim thy brother's fame;
For fate may throw suspicion's shade upon the brightest name;
Thou canst not tell what hidden chain of circumstances may
Have wrought the sad result that takes an honest name away.
Judge not!

Judge Not! the vilest criminal may rightfully demand
A chance to prove his innocence by jury of his land;
And, surely, one who ne'er was known to break his plighted word,
Should not be hastily condemned to obloquy unheard.
Judge not!

Judge Not! thou canst not tell how soon the look of bitter scorn;
May rest on thee, though pure thy heart as dew-drops in the morn.
Thou dost not know what freak of fate may place upon thy brow
A cloud of shame to kill the joy that rests upon it now.
Judge not!

Judge Not! but rather in thy heart let gentle pity dwell;
Man's judgment errs, but there is One who "doeth all things well."
Ever, throughout the voyage of life, this precept keep in view;
"So unto others as thou wouldst that they should do unto you."
Judge not!

Judge Not! for one unjust reproach an honest heart can feel
As keenly as the deadly stab made by the pointed steel.
The worm will kill the sturdy oak, though slowly it may die.
As surely as the lightning stroke swift rushing from the sky.
Judge not!
— W.K. Hale

THE TRIALS

☞ Chapter 38 ☜

Manipulating the Scales of Justice

The murder trials at Guthrie, Oklahoma City and Pawhuska attracted reporters from virtually all of the Nation's leading newspapers and magazines.

Hale and his attorneys did everything conceivable to thwart the prosecution and prevent the fair and impartial administration of justice. Defense witnesses committed perjury, jurors were bribed, and many of the prosecution's witnesses were intimidated and their lives threatened.

To illustrate the character of some of the witnesses who testified for Hale, shortly after one of these witnesses got down from the stand, an Indian officer arrested him for having stolen from an Indian the very boots which the witness was then wearing.

Agents received a signed statement from one man to the effect that he had been paid $500 by one of the defense attorneys to testify falsely at Hale's trial.

One of Hale's lawyers located two tramps and carefully schooled them in helping to prepare a phony defense for Hale. FBI investigation brought this situation to light as well as the perjured testimony and other illegal manipulations.

In addition to all other obstacles, it was necessary for Agents to guard the prosecution's witnesses to keep them from being harmed by associates of Hale.

On October 6, 1926, a federal grand jury reconvened to hear evidence regarding the impeding of justice and interfering with witnesses. Information developed by Agents showed that Hale's attorneys and some of their detectives had tampered with witnesses. As a result, many individuals subsequently received sentences for perjury, contempt of court and obstruction of justice.

Additional evidence showed that two individuals, one of them a brother of John Ramsey, had perjured themselves at a previous trail in testifying that John Ramsey had been in Ripley, Oklahoma, on January 13, 1923, and the entire preceding week. Agents located witnesses who disproved this testimony.

Bill Hale's half brother was arrested on the morning of January 17, 1929, on a contempt of court charge, for attempting to bribe a prospective juror to whom he had promised enough money to pay off all of his debts and enough to support himself through the remainder of his life.

Matt Williams, a government witness, stated that one of the defense attorneys urged him to sign a false affidavit to the effect that government Agents, while with Williams, had spent as much as $35 per day for whiskey and drank most of it themselves. He was also asked to falsely swear that government Agents associated with lewd and immoral women. Williams said this defense attorney knew all of this to be false.

Agents were advised by another man that defense attorneys furnished money at various times to Dick Gregg, an important government witness, in order to influence Gregg to testify favorably for the defense. Evidence was also developed concerning a conspiracy on the part of the defense, including Bill Hale personally, to kill Dick Gregg and his father, John Gregg. The defense also planned to kill at least one other important government witness.

Another witness advised that he was approached by an attorney and partisan of Hale who told him it would be to the witness' best interests to leave the country and not testify against Hale in his forthcoming trial. This witness told Agents that, in pursuance of this advice, he left Fairfax and went to California. He said he was afraid that, if he testified against Hale, he would be killed.

↝ Chapter 39 ↜

Bryan Burkhart and Kelsie Morrison Arrested

On April 29, 1926, a complaint was filed before the Justice of the Peace at Pawhuska by the county attorney charging Bryan Burkhart and Kelsie Morrison with the murder of Anna Brown. Warrants were issued and Bryan Burkhart was taken into custody and arraigned on April 30, 1926. Morrison was already in custody on another charge.

On May 14, 1926, at a preliminary hearing, Bryan Burkhart was bound over to await trial and was denied bail. Later, however, Burkhart, at a habeas corpus hearing, produced witnesses who swore they were with Katherine Cole, wife of Kelsie Morrison and one of the witnesses against Burkhart, at a tent show in Fairfax on the night Anna Brown was killed. The purpose of this testimony was to show that, if Katherine Cole was at this tent show, it would have been impossible for her to have been with Kelsie Morrison and Burkhart on the night Anna Brown was killed as she had testified.

Investigation by FBI Agents disclosed that not only was there no tent show in Fairfax on the night these witnesses claimed they had attended one with Katherine Cole, but for an entire month prior to the date of Anna Brown's death and one month following it, there had been no tent show in the vicinity.

Kelsie Morrison, brought from the State Penitentiary where he was serving a sentence for a separate crime, admitted at his trial that he had killed Anna Brown. In his testimony he reiterated what he had said at his deposition: that Bill Hale had approached him and tried to get him to kill the Smiths; that he had murdered Anna Brown at the instigation of Bill Hale; and that Bill Hale had promised to give him $1,000, cancel a $600 debt, and buy him an automobile.

Morrison confessed that they got Anna Brown drunk to kill her.

"Bryan Burkhart got the liquor. Bryan had Anna Brown when I got in the car. We had discussed killing her before. Bryan was to arrange things. Anna Brown was pulled up into a sitting position when I killed her. I told Byran how to hold her up then I shot her. She fell over. I did not watch her die, but left immediately."

Morrison testified that he stayed drunk for several days after killing Anna.

Testifying as to what had occurred prior to the murder, Morrison said he told Hale that he was ready to kill Anna Brown. "I told him I did not have a gun," Morrison said, "so he gave me his." After the murder, he and Burkhart then returned to Hale's ranch. "I stayed all night at Hale's home," he said.

"Hale loaned me $600. He said, if I killed Anna Brown, I would not have to pay back the money." Morrison said that Hale had given him $600 two days after the killing. "About three weeks later he gave me a car for the other $400. I later got broke and he signed a note for $1,000 for me. He paid the note. I did not repay him."

Morrison further testified, "Hale said he wanted to get rid of them so Ernest would get the money. He said he wanted to get rid of the whole bunch."

In State court at Bartlesville, Oklahoma, on November 19, 1927, Kelsie Morrison was convicted for the murder of Anna Brown and received a life sentence to the Oklahoma State Penitentiary at McAlester.

❧ Chapter 40 ❧

Hale's Allies "Spin" Ernest Burkhart

In Pawhuska, Oklahoma, at the preliminary hearing of Hale and Ramsey for the Smith murder, Ernest Burkhart remarked to an Agent a few minutes before going on the witness stand that, regardless of anything, he was going to testify to the true facts. When Burkhart took the stand, Hale's attorneys declared before the county judge that they were representing Burkhart and demanded the opportunity of conferring with him. Permission was granted and one of the attorneys and Burkhart retired to the judge's private offices. After a few minutes, one of the other defense attorneys was called into the room. Before this conference was concluded, court adjourned and Ernest Burkhart was taken to the home of W.K. Hale at Fairfax where Hale's friends and members of his family talked to Burkhart for several hours, urging him to do what Hale's lawyers told him to do.

Next morning, Burkhart had another conference in Pawhuska with defense attorneys.

When the preliminary hearing was resumed, Burkhart refused to testify against Hale and Ramsey and was used as a witness for the defense.

The trial of Ernest Burkhart, who was granted a severance from the trial of his co-defendants, commenced on May 24, 1926, at Pawhuska, Oklahoma in the State Court of Osage County. A panel of sixty venire men was drawn, but based on information obtained by Special Agents indicating bribery of members of this panel, the court discharged the panel and ordered a new panel of 100 venire men drawn. A jury was obtained from this second panel for Burkhart's trial.

On June 4, 1926, Blackie Thompson, who was serving a life sentence in the Oklahoma State Penitentiary, took the witness stand to

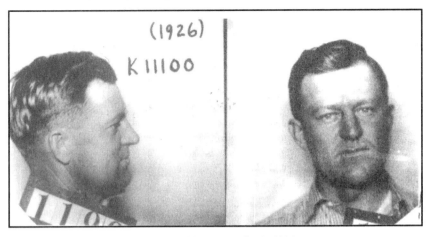

(1926)
K 11100

Ernest Burkhart, March 13, 1926.

testify against Ernest Burkhart. He testified that he and Curley Johnson were propositioned by Burkhart to kill the Smiths. Burkhart said there were diamonds and money in the Smith home and that, in addition to stealing these, Burkhart and Hale would give them a Buick automobile and $1,000. Burkhart reiterated to him several times that he wanted the Smiths killed.

During the entire progress of the trial, Ernest Burkhart seemed to be very restless and nervous. The deputy sheriffs who had charge of him stated that he was unable to sleep.

On June 8, 1926, Burkhart slipped a note out of the jail by a deputy sheriff to one of the prosecuting attorneys, requesting that the prosecuting attorney come to the jail that night because Ernest Burkhart wanted to see him.

When this prosecuting attorney appeared at the jail, Burkhart promptly told him that he was tired and disgusted with trying to go through with the lies which he was swearing to, that he now wanted to tell the truth. He said he wanted to go before the court, plead guilty to the charge, and "take my medicine."

The prosecuting attorney told him he would be unable to advise him in any way, but suggested that Burkhart procure the services of another lawyer and confer with this lawyer before pleading guilty.

When the Special Agent in Charge (SAC) of the Oklahoma City FBI Office appeared in Pawhuska, he was immediately advised that Ernest Burkhart wanted to see him. When the SAC visited him, Burkhart was very much disturbed. With tears in his eyes, he told the SAC that he lied during the trial and that he was now going to tell the truth. He said he considered that telling the truth was always the best course out of anything. He stated that he would not only tell the truth in the Smith case, but he would verify what he had told FBI Agents about the Roan case and would testify in any court in the United States to that effect. Burkhart told the SAC that he had been influenced by Hale's friends and attorneys to deny the truthful statements which he had made previously and swear to lies which would clear Hale.

He said that, when he got on the stand at the Hale-Ramsey preliminary hearing, he fully intended to tell the truth, but when the attorney for the defense made such an objection to his testimony and secured the court's permission to confer with Burkhart, this attorney took him to the judge's chambers and told him, if he testified for the state he would implicate himself. Burkhart said that this attorney did not even ask him what he was going to testify to, but merely stated that, if he testified, he would implicate himself. This lawyer then called in another defense attorney saying, this second lawyer would read the law to him. This second attorney secured a law book and read to Burkhart. They both advised him that he would only get himself into serious difficulty by testifying for the state. After quite an argument, Burkhart promised that he would delay his testimony until the following morning.

They then returned to the courtroom and court was adjourned until the following day. Burkhart said that, even after talking to these attorneys, his intentions were still to testify truthfully, but that one of Hale's close personal friends took Burkhart in an automobile from Pawhuska to Bill Hale's home at Fairfax. That night this man and about twenty of Bill Hale's other friends, including Mrs. Hale and her daughter, Willie, talked to him almost all night, pleading with him not to testify for the prosecution, but listen to the advice of defense attorneys.

The defense attorneys had told Burkhart before he left for Fairfax that they would not accompany him because they thought it best for them not to be seen with him in Fairfax, but that Bill Hale's friends would take care of him. They later told Burkhart what he should say on the stand. Burkhart said, when he got on the stand for the defense, he denied his previous truthful statements and told lies about the alleged abuse he had received from government Agents. He insisted that he received only the kindest treatment from Special Agents. This, as well as the other details concerning his false testimonies, was brought out at the trial.

At 10:00 a.m., June 9, 1926, at the opening of the morning session of court, Ernest Burkhart appeared and stated in open court that he wished to discharge his counsel, and he would henceforth be represented by another attorney, Flint Moss of Tulsa. Burkhart further stated that he wished to withdraw his plea of not guilty and enter a plea of guilty. The court then adjourned until 10:30 a.m. while Moss conferred with the state's attorneys.

When the court reconvened, a plea of guilty was entered for Ernest Burkhart. The jury was then recalled, informed of the guilty plea, and discharged.

On the morning of June 25, 1926, Ernest Burkhart was brought before the judge who, in a few words, sentenced him to the state penitentiary for the remainder of his natural life. As the judge pronounced sentence, Burkhart turned and smiled and there was an expression of relief on his face. He was immediately taken to the State Penitentiary at McAlester.

"As I now look back upon my action," Burkhart told newspapermen, "I feel in my heart that I did it because I was requested to do it by Hale, who is my uncle, and I know that at the time I did it, I did not realize the full consequences of my action.

"I have found in my trial that it is useless to continue against the truth. The truth of what I did, I have told many men and, as I saw it, the honest and honorable thing to do was to stop the trial and acknowledge the truth."

After this turnabout by Ernest Burkhart, many people were alarmed over what might happen to Burkhart. They felt that Hale would have one of his cronies slip Burkhart some poison in his food or kill him some other way to prevent Burkhart from testifying against Hale. Agents had to take precautions to protect Burkhart, one of the government's most important witnesses.

✇ Chapter 41 ✇

Burkhart Worries Defense Attorneys

Ernest Burkhart's repudiation of the lies to which Hale's attorneys had induced him to testify and his indication that he would testify against Hale and Ramsey worried defense counsel. They made every conceivable effort to prevent Burkhart from testifying at a subsequent trial.

Hale conferred with two prisoners at Leavenworth, telling them that he would beat his case by "fixing" Ernest Burkhart through Burkhart's attorney by having Burkhart "forget" some of the things he had testified to at the previous trial.

Burkhart gave Agents a signed statement to the effect that J. I. Howard, an attorney for Hale, sent Duke Burkhart to McAlester, Oklahoma, to visit Ernest in prison in order to persuade him not to testify for the federal government. Ernest Burkhart said, *"On or about October 15th Duke Burkhart, my brother, came to McAlester, Oklahoma, to see me and said that J. I. Howard sent him there to talk to me in regard to what he wanted me to testify to, or to get me not to testify at all. And, if I would agree not to testify, that he would get me out of the pen February or March. And, if he didn't by that time, he would guarantee that he would get me out in less than two years. And he would get any attorney in the state that I wanted and it wouldn't cost me anything and that he, Howard, would come and see me if I would send for him. But he could not come unless I would send for him. He also said, if I would not testify, that he could beat the case and then he would get me out at once.*

"He said that my attorney had not done anything for me and did not aim to do anything, and, besides, he could not do anything; that the governor had told J. I. Howard that he would not do anything for me as long as he was governor."

Howard attempted to get Ernest Burkhart's fellow inmates at

the Oklahoma State Penitentiary to induce him not testify. Howard instructed one of these convicts to tell Ernest Burkhart that, if he did not do as the defense wanted him to do, he would be prosecuted for murder and rape, but if he made certain changes in his testimony which would clear Hale in the Roan case and, if he refused to testify at all in the Smith case, Howard would see to it that the charges of murder and rape were not prosecuted against Ernest, and Howard would get him a pardon.

Frank Pock, an unscrupulous character who had recently tried to hire a man to kill the Chief of Police at Shidler, Oklahoma, and burn his home, was employed by Hale's lawyers. He stated in an affidavit: "Howard brought me three typewritten pages of Burkhart's testimony in the Roan case and had me make pencil notations of the changes Burkhart was to make in case he testified for the prosecution this time against Hale. These changes were calculated to clear Hale, and I was instructed to talk to Burkhart and tell him of the evidence against him in the John Thomas murder and the Mamie Fletcher rape cases, and tell him these cases would be pushed against him if he testified against Hale but not pushed if he did as requested."

Ernest Burkhart turned over to one of the government attorneys this transcript with the proposed changes in his testimony which Pock had furnished to him, adding that Pock had also proposed, on behalf of Howard and Hale, that Ernest escape while out of prison as a government witness and flee to old Mexico. Burkhart was promised that, as soon as the Hale case was over, Howard would procure a pardon for Burkhart and make arrangements so that he could return to this country.

Burkhart told Agents that Kelsie Morrison and Henry Cornett, who were also confined to the Oklahoma State Prison, talked to him every time they met him, prevailing upon him to change his testimony by forgetting some of the things to which he had testified at the previous trial. They told him, if he would change his testimony, Hale's attorney would take a statement from him. Burkhart said he refused to do this and avoided talking to them whenever he could.

A school teacher, a ten-year acquaintance of Hale, visited Hale in June, 1926, at the County Jail during Ernest Burkhart's trial. She said Hale requested her to tell Ernest not to testify against him. Hale said, "If he tells the truth on me, I'm ruined. Whatever you do, you get to Ernest and tell him not to tell the truth because, if he does, I'm ruined."

"W.K. Hale remarked to me," she added, "that, if I would see the boy, Ernest Burkhart, and get Ernest not to appear on the stand against him he, Hale, would get Ernest out of jail." Hale had said to her, "I will guarantee to get him out inside of a year." Hale told her on different occasions that Ernest Burkhart was the only witness he was afraid of. "He appeared worried about Ernest's testimony and wanted me to do anything I could to prevent Ernest from testifying against him." On the day Ernest pleaded guilty, Hale repeated his request, pleading with her, "For God's sake get to that boy and tell him not to open his mouth. If he does and tells the truth, I'm a ruined man."

Dick Gregg, another important Government witness, stated that one of Hale's lawyers had offered Gregg $10,000 if he would take Ernest Burkhart to Mexico so that neither Dick Gregg nor Ernest would be present to testify for the government when Hale's case was brought to trial.

Failing in other efforts, defense attorneys began circulating the rumor that Ernest Burkhart was crazy, that he had been shell-shocked and gassed during World War I and was mentally unbalanced, that he had not even known what he had testified to at the trial. To refute this, Agents produced Burkhart's military record which failed to show that he had been gassed or shell-shocked or that he was mentally unbalanced.

℘ Chapter 42 ℘

Ramsey Changes His Story

Following the confessions made by John Ramsey to G-men, Attorney J. M. Springer requested permission to confer with Ramsey. Ramsey was consulted and he insisted that he had told the government the truth and did not want a lawyer. He refused to see Springer.

Springer then appeared before the judge of the U.S. District Court for the Western District of Oklahoma and claimed that he was John Ramsey's attorney and was being denied the right to confer with his client. The judge promptly permitted him to confer with Ramsey.

Following this conference, Ramsey repudiated his previous confessions and made a new written statement to defense attorneys on November 9, 1926, contradicting the one he had made previously. He provided voluminous detail in an effort to enhance his credibility. The new statement which he made to the defense lawyers exonerating Hale and himself and placing the blame for Henry Roan's murder on Ernest Burkhart, Roy Bunch and Curley Johnson (who was then deceased) follows:

"Some time in the Summer of 1922, the exact date I cannot remember, Curley Johnson, myself and Hank Kidder drove from the town of Ripley to Whizbang in Osage County and went to the hotel of Seth Lewis, where I went to bed soon after reaching there. Curley Johnson did not come to bed until early the next morning. He let Kidder out of the car just before reaching Whizbang. The next morning I got up about 8:00, and went to a cafe for breakfast, and while there, I heard of someone being hijacked the night before, about $30.00 being taken in the holdup.

"I then went back to the room at the Lewis Hotel about 10:00, and found Curley Johnson in bed, but awake, and I picked up the trousers of Johnson, and was fumbling around in the pockets, and I asked Johnson about the hijacking the night before, and told him I thought I ought to have

$15, or half of the $30 that he got in the holdup. Johnson made no reply to this, but in a few minutes he gave me some money, and I went and got a half pint of whiskey and he and I drank this whiskey. Curley Johnson then stated, while still in the bedroom at the Lewis Hotel, that he had a chance to get some long money for knocking off an Indian, but that he had to have some help to get this Indian out of the country; that this Indian lived at Fairfax; and that he (Curley Johnson) was not welcome in Fairfax. Johnson further said that Burkhart and Roy Bunch wanted this Indian (Henry Roan) knocked off, and stated that there was $5,000 in it for whoever would do the job. Johnson wanted to know if I knew Henry Roan, and I said yes, that I had known him a good many years. Johnson then said that I should take him out of town and that he could then knock him off, and we could make this money.

"Johnson went into considerable detail as to why Burkhart and Bunch wanted this Indian killed. I suggested that either Bunch or Burkhart could get him out, and that I was not going to take an Indian or anyone else off to have him killed. Johnson said, no, Roy Bunch was playing Henry Roan's wife, and that he and Roan were on shooting terms, and were not on speaking terms, and that Bunch could not approach him, and that Ernest Burkhart didn't have the nerve to do it.

"I said that I didn't have the nerve to take a man out in the country, thinking he was going to get a drink, and have someone kill him. That substantially ended the talk with him at that time, and I remained there a day or so and either went to Ponca City or to Henry Grammer's.

"Some time later I saw Ernest Burkhart at McInroy's pool hall at Fairfax, saw him either in the pool hall or just in front of it, and Burkhart asked me how I would like to have a little drink. I said, 'Fine, if it's not too little.'

"Burkhart then pointed to his car sitting right in front of the drugstore next to the pool hall, and said for me to get in the car, and I went and took a seat on the front seat of his car. Burkhart went back in the pool hall, and in a few minutes came back out with Roy Bunch getting in the back seat, and the three of us drove out to Bill Trent's hay meadow and went about three quarters of a mile north of the road and into a little swag.

"There was a gallon jug of whiskey hidden in the tall grass, and we all took a drink from this jug, and then Bunch walked away a short distance, and Burkhart asked me if Curley Johnson had mentioned the deal to me, and I said yes he had mentioned something about it.

"Burkhart asked me what I thought about it, and I said I had not thought much about it, that that was not in my line of work. Burkhart said, 'Well it's a cinch. It is just like falling off a log; that that Indian would follow a

John Ramsey, October 20, 1941.

man to hell for a drink of whiskey; and that Curley Johnson was raring to turn the trick if he could get someone that knowed him to get the Indian out of the country. Burkhart said that there would never be a rumble over the killing, that Bill Hale had a life insurance policy on Roan, and that Roy Bunch was in love with Roan's wife, and that one or the other of them would be charged with the killing, but that both could prove an alibi. I told Burkhart I would give the Indian a drink whenever I saw him and he wanted one, but that I would not take him into a death trap. Burkhart said, if I would take him out to where Curley Johnson could kill him, he would pay me $2,000 as soon as it was done.

"Burkhart and me talked 15 or 20 minutes.... Burkhart also told me that Bunch would pay $5,000 to Curley Johnson as soon as he could get it out of the squaw. Bunch came back and joined the two of us, and said that he could pay as soon as he married the squaw and could get his hands on some of her money. This trip was made about good dark or a little after, and it was still warm weather, probably late in the summer of 1922. Bunch, Burkhart and myself then took some more drinks out of the jug, and left the jug at the same place and drove back to Fairfax and got out at the pool hall. I think I saw Curley Johnson again before I saw Burkhart. I again talked the deal over with Burkhart a number of times, in fact almost every time I saw Burkhart the deal was mentioned, and the same was true as to Roy Bunch.

"Some time later Burkhart bought a gallon of whiskey and said he was going to take it and place it where I could have some whiskey to furnish Henry Roan, and also have some to drink myself when I came there. Burkhart took this gallon of whiskey and tied a baling wire to the jug and let it down in an old oil well on a dim road something like a mile southeast from Three-Mile Canyon, east of Fairfax, and told me where it was, and Burkhart and

I went out there and filled a pint bottle and put it under a rock in a dry branch nearby, and shortly after that I took Henry Roan out there and gave him some drinks out of the bottle, and when Roan left going towards Gray Horse, I went back to the oil well and refilled the pint bottle and put it back in the same place.

"After Burkhart and I had gone out in this pasture and had taken some drinks out of this jug, and after I had filled a pint bottle and put it under the rock in the little draw which was dry, I saw Ernest Burkhart at Fairfax and he asked me if I had seen Henry Roan, and I told him no, and he said Henry Roan was raring for a drink, and that he had told Roan I would get him a drink if he could see me, and said Roan was very anxious to see me so he could get a drink, and I did see Roan in Fairfax shortly after that, and took him out there and gave him a drink out of this pint bottle.

"The next time I saw Roan at Fairfax, he again asked me for a drink, and I told him he would have to go to the same place in this pasture, and that he would find this pint bottle in the same place where we had taken a drink a day or two before. The next time I saw Roan he told me he had gone out there and got the pint bottle of whiskey.

"The next time I went with Roan was out in Round Mound pasture south of John Dillinger's, where the whiskey was hid under a flat rock, and I couldn't tell him just where it was. It was my whiskey, but was given to Henry Roan as a part of the deal by which I was to furnish Roan whiskey whenever he wanted it, and following this up, every time I was in Fairfax and would see Burkhart, I would talk with him about killing Roan.

"The third time I furnished Roan whiskey in person was about the same place where he was killed. Curley Johnson had six or seven gallons hidden in this ravine, and had told me about it. Roan and I went out there, and Roan left his car on top of the hill, and we drove down under the hill in the car I was driving, which was a Ford coupe, as it was before I bought my car. This was about two months before the killing of Roan. I let Roan drink whiskey out of a beer bottle filled with whiskey and placed there by Curley Johnson. The whiskey was in a little draw, and when we drank the whiskey, I threw the bottle down in the draw.

"A day or two after the gallon of whiskey was placed in the oil well, Burkhart, Bunch and I went out and pulled up the jug and took several drinks therefrom. I do not recall the exact conversation, but the general run of it was the killing of this Indian. This trip was suggested by Burkhart. An hour or two after supper that evening, he said, 'Let's go out and get a drink,' and the three of us drove out there and he pulled up the jug by the baling wire.

"This trip was before I had given Roan any of the whiskey out of this jug. Bunch said that he wanted this squaw and had made up his mind to have her, and that he and Roan were on killing terms, and that unless Roan was killed, it would mean a divorce between Roan and his wife, and that, if there was a divorce, that Roan would take Mollie Burkhart, as he was in love with her, and Burkhart also stated that, if there was a divorce, Roan would take his wife.

"In the first talk I had with Bunch, I told him that, if he was afraid Roan would kill him, that he could kill Roan much better by doing it some other way, that he could get two or three friends that he knew he could trust, and could meet Roan right in the town of Fairfax at a time when he knew Roan had a gun, and then he could blast him and plead self-defense. I told Bunch to be sure that Roan had a gun before he pulled this kind of a stunt, and that would beat Bunch's way 400 different ways. Bunch said he didn't want to do it that way.

"Burkhart again said that Roan would take Mollie away from him if he ever lost Mary. I again told him I was not favorable to taking this Indian off and making him think he was going to get a drink and then having him killed.

"At the time we were at the oil well taking a drink, Bunch and Burkhart talked about getting me a car if I knew where I could buy a good second-hand car, that it would be lots of help to me in going out and meeting Henry Roan. I told them, if I ever got a car, I was damn sure going to get it myself and not have anybody else mixed up in it.

"The testimony as to how I got the car and how it was paid for, which I testified to in the trial, was absolutely true, and the testimony of Fred Tindell and his wife and Mrs. Hender was true. My testimony about my financial transactions with Bill Hale was absolutely true, and Hale had nothing in the world to do with buying the car, and knew absolutely nothing about the deal or with my giving Roan whiskey.

"I would get whiskey from Burkhart on different occasions to give to Roan, one time a half pint in his barn, another time a pint in Trent's meadow, and another time a pint under a culvert on the Ponca City road west of Fairfax. I took this whiskey on each occasion and gave it to Roan as directed by Burkhart, as a part of the deal that I would place whiskey at certain designated points and tell Roan where it was so he could get it, sometimes in Sol Smith's pasture, sometimes up the railroad track, and other places. I suppose I furnished him whiskey in this way at least twenty times.

"While those negotiations were going on, some time before the death of Roan, I saw Burkhart at McInroy's pool hall in Fairfax, and he asked me if I would give Curley Johnson a gun. I said I would, and Burkhart got a .45 colt automatic and brought it and gave it to me in the telephone booth in *the pool hall. I put the gun in my pocket and started for my car at Spurgeon's Garage, and in the street just south of the First National Bank, I saw Harry Corbett. I think he came from behind and overtook me, and told me that, if that was a bottle causing the bulge in my clothes, I had better get rid of it or it would cause me trouble. I told him it was a gun and that I was going to the garage to put it in my car, and I did put the gun in my car and kept it there until I gave it back to Burkhart the night Roan was killed.*

"After this I went to Ripley and did not see Curley Johnson until Burkhart and Johnson came to Ripley a week or two later. When they came to Ripley they were in a red Buick automobile of Bill Hale's. They came from the south, and Walter Ramsey, Carl Radabaugh and I saw them as they drove up. As they drove in, Burkhart honked his horn and I paid no attention to it. He then drove up by me and asked me if the gun was handy, and I told him not right handy, that it was in the car down at the barn and the barn was locked. Burkhart said all right, he would get it later.

"Burkhart spoke about a farm, and I told him I would be up in a few days and look at it. This talk about the farm was a stall, and was so understood by Burkhart and me.

"The following Sunday I went to Fairfax, taking my wife with me, which was two or three days later, and we stopped at Q. O. Irons'. I did not leave the house during the day, and about supper time, while the folks were at supper, I called Burkhart over the phone and told him I was there and ready to look at that farm. Burkhart said all right, that he could see me the next day.

"The next day Burkhart drove by Irons' house a time or two, and I went out in the yard and talked to him. Burkhart said that the Indian had been missing several days, and that Roy Bunch was then out looking for him. Later on I went to the post office with Evelyn Irons, and Burkhart came out of the post office and came to my car and wanted to know if I would be downtown that night. I told him I would be or else would be at Irons'. Burkhart called Irons' residence after supper, and as I recall, Hazel Irons answered the telephone and called me to the phone. Burkhart asked me if I could come right away, I said yes, and asked him where he was and he said at the pool hall, but for me to meet him in the alley between the Rosa Cafe and the lumber yard.

"I drove down right away, and when I reached the alley, Burkhart stepped out and asked me if I had that gun. I said I did. Burkhart got in the car and told me to drive to Main Street and turn south, which I did, driving to the south end of Main Street where the Teepee filling station is now located, and turned west. Just after turning west, Burkhart said for me to let him drive, that he could drive faster, and he skinned over my lap and

drove.

"*As we were leaving town, Burkhart said that Bunch had just come in from Henry Cornett's and that Curley Johnson had Roan out in Sol Smith's pasture, and wanted Burkhart to get him a gun as soon as possible, as Johnson didn't have a gun with him. Burkhart drove quickly to the top of the big hill in Sol Smith's pasture, and we saw the Ford car of Curley Johnson about 100 yards east. Burkhart stopped the car right in the road opposite the place where Roan was killed, and left the car, taking the gun with him when he got out. We walked to the car of Curley Johnson. When we got to his car, Burkhart whistled, and Johnson whistled from down the hill. Burkhart and I went down the hill, and found Henry Roan and Curley Johnson on the left side of the car. Both had been sitting on the running board, and one or both got up. They had a gallon jug of whiskey there, and when we walked up, one of them said, 'Where are the girls?'*"

"*This was the first I had heard of any girls in connection with the deal, and Burkhart answered and said they were coming out in his car. This was on Monday night, a week and one day before the body of Roan was found. We all then took a drink, and Burkhart said we had better be getting out of there, as the girls would be coming, and Burkhart and I started walking up the hill. As we left the car, Roan was on the left side of the car, and Curley Johnson near him. The jug of whiskey was the same kind of jug which Curley Johnson had hidden there some time prior.*

"*I do not recall the starting of the car, but Burkhart and I were some 15 or 20 steps up the hill when we heard the gun fire, and Burkhart ran rapidly up the hill, and I walked as rapidly as I could to my car, and Burkhart and I got in, and Burkhart started driving north. I asked him where he was going, and he said he was going up there where he wouldn't make any more tracks than possible. He drove 200 or 300 yards up the road, and just as he was turning around, we met Curley Johnson, and Burkhart said for Curley to beat it back to Cornett's and that he and I must be getting away from there as soon as possible, and Burkhart drove back to Fairfax as fast as possible, and got out of the car just a half block from where I had picked him up, and I turned west and drove into the back yard of Quince Irons' place and went on in the house.*

"*There was no discussion between me and Burkhart as to the payment of money, either going out or coming back. Curley Johnson afterwards told me that his gun was either in the house or that he was out of shells that night, was the reason that he had to have another gun to do this killing.*

"*Ernest Burkhart and Curley Johnson both told me afterwards that Curley Johnson refused to let Henry Roan have whiskey at Cornett's that day because he was drinking, and also that while Henry Roan was there, they saw a car down south, which they thought was Roy Bunch, and that Johnson told Roan to go back down in this canyon in Sol Smith's pasture, where he had gotten whiskey from me and Johnson before, and that he would let him have a gallon of whiskey there, and also that they would have some girls out there from Fairfax and get him a gun, that he had an appointment with Henry Roan down in Sol Smith's pasture to give him some whiskey and to meet some girls, and that, if he had the gun, he would kill him.*

"Ernest Burkhart gave me some money, $50 at one time, and at different times small sums. I had a whiskey case at Tulsa in 1924, and had a letter from J. M. Springer, telling me that, if I didn't raise $50, that I would be stuck and my bond forfeited. This was just two days before the case was called, and I went to Fairfax and ran onto Burkhart and told him I had to raise $50. Burkhart put up every excuse in the world and wanted me to wait until the next day. I told him that would be too late, so about eight o'clock he went around and claimed he couldn't find anyone with that much money. I told him I would have to have it, and he went and got it, and said Arch Carroll, who ran the filling station there, had cashed a check for him for that amount.

"In April, 1924, a Fort Worth man shipped in a carload of Jersey cows to Fairfax, and I wanted to buy one. I only had $21 or $22, and Charlie Ashbrook agreed to loan me the balance if I had enough to pay the purchase price of the cow. I bought one cow for $41 or $42. I saw Burkhart there at the auction, and told him what I had done. He said he had some money in his pocket, and, if I could buy another cow that day, he would let me have the money. We went into the barn, and he let me have $35. Either Clark Farmer or a man by the name of Paul was nearby and probably saw the transaction.

"Burkhart would give me money along at different times, in $2, $3, $5 or $10 amounts. When I rented the farm where my family is now living, I was trying to find a team, and I saw Burkhart and told him what I was trying to do, and he told me that the Clay boy at Gray Horse had a damn good team to sell, and that I could probably trade him my Ford car for it.

"I went out that night and looked at the team, and went back the next morning and proposed to trade, and Clay did not much want my car, but tried it out and then offered to trade if I would pay him $75 to boot. I offered him $25 and he refused.

"I came to town and told Ernest Burkhart about the deal, and Burkhart said the shape my car was in I had better trade for this team and harness, that if I kept my car six months it would not be worth as much as the lines on this harness. I asked him to go with me the next morning and look at the team, and as we started to Gray Horse, we met Clay near Salt Creek bridge.

We sparred around awhile and finally agreed to trade if I would pay him $40 to boot. I told him I would give him that if I could get the money. Burkhart said for me to go to the bank and see if I could borrow the money and that he would give me the money to repay it at the bank. He was to wait at Ross' Cafe, and if I borrowed the money, I was to highball him and he would go on, otherwise he would get the money and give it to me.

"I borrowed the money at the bank, and did give Burkhart the highball, and later he gave me the $40 to pay off this note. During the spring and summer of 1924, he gave me $10 a week to make a crop on. He paid me this money for at least three months and possibly longer. I made the notation on a board by the amounts, and kind of feed that I bought, and later on Burkhart gave me a good roping and riding saddle that would cost anywhere from $100 to $125. Burkhart said he was going to help me, that he could give me $200 or $300 at one time, but that it wouldn't look well, and that I was out on a farm and that he would furnish me money from time to time to buy feed, or cows or things of that kind, and would help me get on my feet, and that I would then be in good shape to do for myself. He further stated that he had bought the Brush farm just north and west of Fairfax, and that as soon as Pitts Beatty's lease ran out on this farm that I could move on it and live on it as long as I lived, and it wouldn't cost me a cent except for up-keep.

"We bought a carload of hedge posts, and I was to put them in and build an expensive fence around this farm, and I was to do other work around the farm at a long price which would just about equal the rent.

"Burkhart talked to me repeatedly about the killing of all these Indians who were the heirs of Lizzie Q, so he would have their headrights. He stated time and again that when all of them were killed off but Mollie that she would be the heir, and that he could then kill her. In many of his conversations he would figure about the amount of his income when he was able to draw all the headrights of these Indians.

"On one occasion, a month or two before Henry Roan was killed, Roy Bunch and Amos Tucker drove out to Bill Trent's pasture northeast of Fairfax, together with Bill Revard and myself, to drink some whiskey that Amos Tucker was furnishing or selling. After we got out there Bunch started a conversation which I knew was leading up to the killing of Henry Roan, before Tucker and Revard, I cannot now recall his exact language, but I stepped away as I did not want to hear such talk in the presence of these men.

"On January 4th, the day Ernest Burkhart was arrested, I went to town that morning, and saw Burkhart, I think at McInroy's pool hall, and he said this grand jury was meeting at Guthrie and it looked like it was a *damn cinch they were going to arrest Bill Hale and maybe himself, for this Roan murder. In the conversation Burkhart said it was damn funny that my name had never been mentioned in connection with the killing. I said, 'No, it had not, and it won't be unless you mention it.' Burkhart said he was not going to say anything to implicate me or anyone, that he was going to stand pat, and that, if he didn't tell it, that it wouldn't be told. He said that, if it got to where it looked like he was in a track, that he would damn sure squeeze out of it, and that he and I would then lay all the blame on Bill Hale.*

"Burkhart said he didn't want me to ever mention his name in connection with this killing. We did a part of this talking in Burkhart's car, and then went over to the Buick garage and went back and sat in a storage car and talked the matter over. Burkhart said repeatedly that he wouldn't mention my name in connection with the Roan killing.

"About noon, Bryan Burkhart and I drove out in Bill Trent's pasture and got a drink of whiskey, and late that evening I suggested to Ernest Burkhart that we go out and take another drink. We went out there, and the whiskey was gone, and I asked Bryan about it and he said Tom Boone had gotten it. Burkhart told me at Guthrie after the federal men had talked to him about Grammer, Kirby and Johnson in connection with this killing, that Tom White said to him, 'Ernest, this looks awful funny, the story you are telling. These men that you mention are all dead, and Burkhart said the federal men would agree to help him out if he would give them the names of some live person who could corroborate his statement, and that that was the first time he had mentioned my name in connection with it, as he had made up his mind that the only way out for him and me was for us to put the blame on Bill Hale.

"After the killing of Henry Roan, Roy Bunch talked to me many times and each time said he would fix me up as soon as he could get his hands on something. I told him just to forget it.

"Burkhart and Curley Johnson were both figuring on the killing of Smith. They were figuring with Blackie Thompson on this deal, but when Blackie came back from the penitentiary for stealing Burkhart's car, he went to see Burkhart about getting some expense money, and Burkhart gave him $1.50, saying that he didn't consider that he owed Thompson anything, that they were both taking chances, and that Thompson got stung.

"After Henry Roan was killed, Burkhart talked to me about the death of Anna Brown. Burkhart said he had been having illicit relations with her, and that Anna Brown had been telling Mollie Burkhart (his wife) about his relations with white women, and that this was causing trouble between him and Mollie, and that he had made up his mind that Anna Brown was

*going to separate him and Mollie, and that, if she was killed, that it would
also add to his estate. He said the day that Anna Brown was killed they had
been drinking at his house all day, and that they came into Fairfax late that
evening, drove up in front of Anna Brown's house and honked the horn
and she came out and got in the car and they drove to Three-Mile Canyon
and drove around on the south side of the canyon and stopped the car, and
went down into the canyon to get a drink; that she sat down on a rock and
he gave her a drink and, while she was drinking, he stepped around to the
side and shot her in the top of her head.*

*"Burkhart also talked to me several times about furnishing poison
whiskey to Mollie Burkhart. He wanted me to furnish this whiskey to Mollie.
I told him I wouldn't do that, that I wasn't in that kind of business, and
that he could furnish it as well as anyone else. Burkhart said that he had
started it and that he was going to kill the whole outfit, but was going to
kill Mollie last. He proposed to me to come to his house and ask for him and,
of course, he wouldn't be there, and I could give the whiskey to Mollie with
the poison in it and tell her it was for Ernest, and, if there wasn't more than
a pint, that Mollie would drink it all before he came home. He said she
would be suspicious if he gave her the whiskey, and that he would have to
be away so he could prove his innocence. When I rejected this proposition,
Burkhart then proposed that he could go out on the road either towards
Pawhuska or out in Sol Smith's pasture, and have me and Curley Johnson
hold them up and shoot Mollie, and to be sure she was killed, and also shoot
up the car and shoot him in the leg so it would appear that she was killed in
a hijacking deal. I flatly rejected this proposition, and told Burkhart I would
have nothing to do with it or with killing his wife.*

*"I delivered whiskey to Burkhart at Fairfax many times, by the gallon.
The last time I delivered him whiskey he gave me a check payable to Henry
Grammer for $15, and marked on it for the purchase of a hog. I think this
check shows up in his annual report as guardian.*

*"Burkhart at one time told me that Bill Smith was making so much
talk about the killing of Anna Brown, and was making the statement around
Fairfax that he knew who killed her, that Burkhart figured he would have to
get rid of Smith; that Smith was telling that he had uncovered who killed
Anna Brown, and that was the reason Burkhart had to get him out of the
way."*

As is obvious from this statement, the defense attorneys were
attempting to place the entire guilt on Ernest Burkhart, whose previous confession to FBI Agents had exposed the whole scheme; to
blame Curley Johnson, who was dead; and Roy Bunch, who, from
the very beginning, was being framed for the murder of Henry Roan

because he and Roan were known enemies because of Bunch's affair with Roan's wife.

Ramsey testified that government Agents had forced him to sign a previous confession, but this was later completely disproved.

Ramsey offered as an alibi that he could not have murdered Henry Roan since he was not even in Fairfax at the time. He testified that he was in Ripley, Oklahoma, from January 7 to January 28, 1923. He produced witnesses who perjured themselves in corroborating this phony alibi.

☙ Chapter 43 ❧

Agents Refute Ramsey's Phony Story

Ramsey's new version of his confession required G-men to locate numerous witnesses to disprove it.

John Ramsey's brothers corroborated Ramsey's phony alibi, testifying that John Ramsey had been at Ripley, Oklahoma, continually from January 9 to 10 to January 28, 1923.

An old Indian woman, Fannie Lasley, who had formerly operated a hotel in Fairfax, Oklahoma, recalled renting a room to John Ramsey on January 19 and January 20, 1923. Her testimony was corroborated by the hotel register which bore the signature of John Ramsey under those dates, proving that he could not have been in Ripley as he claimed.

An Osage man advised Agents that the defense attorneys were trying to block Fannie Lasley's damaging testimony. "Some time around 3:00 p.m.," he said, "I was standing just outside of the courtroom in the Federal Building at Guthrie. The court had just taken a recess. A man came out of the courtroom whom I recognized as a lawyer in the Hale and Ramsey case. He introduced himself to me as Attorney Springer and told me he was representing Mr. Ramsey. He took me to one side and asked me if I was a friend of Hale and Ramsey. I told him that I had only spoken to Mr. Ramsey once and that I knew his son, Homer. Mr. Springer told me that a Mr. Murphy had taken Fannie Lasley down to identify John Ramsey and for me to go and tell Fannie Lasley not to identify John Ramsey and say that she did not know him and for her to say that the dates on the hotel register had been changed. I walked away from Mr. Springer and did not tell him whether or not I would do this."

Fannie Lasley was furnished whiskey by one of Hale's lawyers in an attempt to have her change her testimony. This lawyer subsequently received an 18-month sentence in a federal penitentiary for this action.

One witness testified that John Ramsey was working for him in Fairfax doing carpentry work constructing a garage and doing repair work for him late December, 1922, until about January 20, 1923. This man's wife and two other witnesses verified Ramsey's employment in Fairfax during the time he claimed he had been at Ripley.

Two additional witnesses corroborated this testimony and another woman testified that Ramsey was at her home near Fairfax on the evening of January 14, 1923, and on about January 28, 1923, as well as on another occasion between these two dates. Another witness placed Ramsey at Fairfax on January 13, 1923, and at this witness' home west of Fairfax on January 14, 1923. He made the following signed statement to G-men:

"I was called as a witness and went to Guthrie in the Hale-Ramsey case, and after I testified, I was told by Mr. Springer (defense attorney) that I could go home; that they would call me back if needed. I went to Fairfax and the second day later Charlie Hale, Bill Hale's half brother, came and told me they wanted me at Guthrie; that Mr. Springer wanted to see me. We went to Guthrie in Hale's car. At Guthrie I met Mr. Springer after court and in front of the Fed Building and he walked down the street and stopped in a stairway. Mr. Springer then said to me, 'That God damned Bill Taylor came down here and swore that John Ramsey was at your house on January 15 and we can't have it that way. We must change the evidence some way.'

"I said, 'Well, Mr. Springer, that sure was the way it was,' and Springer then repeated, 'We can't have it that way and we got to change it. That is bad evidence.'

"I again told him that was the truth and I would testify to the same thing. Springer got mad and wheeled around and started away. I then asked him if I could go home and he said, 'No!' and left."

Another witness, the Chief of Police at Fairfax, saw Ramsey driving to Fairfax in a new Ford automobile in the early part of January, 1923. Since he suspected that Ramsey was selling whiskey, he and his deputies very closely observed Ramsey's movements. He recalled that Ramsey was frequently seen in Fairfax during the following days of January. He stated that Ramsey definitely was in Fairfax on January 14, 1923. This testimony was corroborated by two other witnesses.

A filling station operator swore that Ramsey drove into his filling station in the early part of January, 1923, and, following this initial purchase of gasoline, visited his place regularly and purchased gasoline as regularly as any other patron residing in Fairfax and vicinity.

Another man testified that he saw Ramsey in a Fairfax cafe, together with Henry Roan, about a week or ten days before Roan was found murdered.

Escape artist Dewey Selph told Agents that, while he was confined at the Guthrie City Jail, in the same cell with John Ramsey, Ramsey told him that he had made a confession to government Agents telling all about the murder of Henry Roan, that Ernest Burkhart had "put it on him" and there was nothing for him to do but tell the truth and tell it all.

Selph, a material government witness, testified at Hale's trial that Hale had hired him to murder Katherine Cole, Kelsie Morrison's wife, a witness in the Anna Brown murder case, but he lost his nerve and did not kill her.

While being held at Guthrie as a material witness, Selph discovered that the bars of his cell had been partially sawed. He broke through these bars and escaped. He was subsequently located by FBI Agents who found him, clad only in his underwear, hiding in a barrel at a pressing shop in Pawhuska, waiting to have his suit pressed. He said he escaped to call on a girl friend, his ex-wife, a full-blooded Osage Indian. Later, Selph made still another escape. He was said to have made the acquaintance of a hotel chambermaid who allegedly helped him escape. He was in the lobby of this hotel with a guard when he requested permission to go to the men's room on the second floor. He was allowed to go, but the guard followed Selph upstairs a few paces behind him, so the guard claimed. When the guard got to the upper landing, Selph had disappeared. A search of the hotel failed to disclose Selph's whereabouts, and an examination of the windows on the second and third floors showed that they were securely locked. Selph's method of escape was never discovered, but he was subsequently recaptured by FBI Agents and returned to testify at Hale's trial. Dewey Selph's next escape attempt, which was made after his return to the Arkansas State Penitentiary to complete a sentence he had been serving there, resulted in his death.

Frank Pock, who had been a hired hand of Hale's attorneys, made the following affidavit:

"*On or about the latter part of November, 1926, J. I. Howard, then of Oklahoma City, came to me at Shidler, Oklahoma, where I was employed* by the Dave Murdock Motor Company, and stated to me that he was in desperate need of some real assistance for getting evidence to corroborate the confession made by John Ramsey.... Howard, at that time attorney for W.K. Hale, gave me a copy of the said confession John Ramsey made, which was the second confession Ramsey had made in this case, Ramsey having made a confession to the Federal authorities previous to said trial, and this second confession being after said trial, and differing materially from the first confession mentioned above.

"To make this clear I will state that John Ramsey made four confessions in this case; the first being to the government before the trial at Oklahoma City, November, 1926; the second being immediately after the said trial which resulted in the conviction of Ramsey and Hale; the third being made at Leavenworth Prison by Ramsey, after he was taken there to serve his sentence; and the fourth being made some time early in 1926, in January, I believe.

"The second confession is the one Howard gave me a copy of in the latter part of November, 1926; this confession stating Curley Johnson was the man who actually murdered Henry Roan.

"Howard informed me he was in desperate need of someone to get affidavits supporting and corroborating this second confession.

"Howard gave me a list of names of persons whom he wanted me to see and secure these affidavits from. At this time I can recall some of the names Howard thus gave me as follows: Ben Hopkins, Bartlesville; Charley Wilson, Seminole; John Million, now at Blackwell; Ray Roy Smith, Burbank, Oklahoma; Carl Rowe and his brother, south of Henry Cornett's place in Osage County, Oklahoma; (First name unknown) Bozarth, Fairfax, Oklahoma; Bill Lucas, Fairfax, Oklahoma; and a number of others whose names I do not at this time recall.

"Howard at that time instructed me that he did not want anything but the truth, but gave me to understand that my business was to get these affidavits to fit said confession, and, if they were not truthful, I was not to apprise him of that fact, and, if the persons' sentiments did not support this confession, I was to not take any affidavit from that person. Some of the persons I interviewed did not make statements fitting the confession, and I took no affidavits from them. Others I had to see several times until they finally made statements that fitted the confession. Then I would make notes, see Howard, who could have the affidavits typewritten and prepared for the person to sign, then I would either send the person in to Howard's office at Pawhuska to sign, or take the affidavit with me and have it signed before a Notary Public and return it to Howard.

"I also questioned other persons, whom Howard had not named, and, *whenever possible, got affidavits from them to fit the confession. In all, I think I got about 25 affidavits in this manner. The plain truth of it is that, while I never asked anyone to state an untruth, I did give them to understand what I wanted them to state, and if they stated it that way, I took an affidavit from them.*

"Howard also took a number of affidavits personally. He got a statement from Dick Gregg a few days before Dick Gregg broke jail at Pawhuska, and also conferred with Dick Gregg several times after Dick Gregg broke jail at Pawhuska, I being present at one conference of this kind between Howard and Dick Gregg at Willison's Ranch, northeast of Pawhuska, where Dick was staying at the time. I did not hear the conversation between Dick Gregg and Howard, but Howard later told me Dick was to stay hid and not appear for the prosecution, and after the trial Howard was to help Dick by preventing him being taken back to Kansas to serve his time in Lansing Prison in Kansas.

"I made a trip and gave Dick Gregg $50 that Howard gave me for that purpose. Carl C. Weaver also told me of him giving Dick Gregg money in this way on two occasions.

"After getting these affidavits, Howard and I conferred and talked the case over a number of times and decided this second confession by Ramsey would not do; would not hold water and that Ramsey should be induced to make a better one.

"Howard said he would see Hale about this as I could not get to Ramsey, myself, and have him do it. Howard and I agreed upon (the) lines (of) the third confession (which was) made by Ramsey while in Leavenworth Prison. This third confession was along the lines Howard and I had agreed upon, and was the most favorable to Hale's interest of any Ramsey had thus far made....

"Of all the affidavits I secured at Howard's direction I am convinced that not one states the truth in the material facts of this case.

"John Ramsey made a fourth confession early this year. Howard gave me a copy of this. I do not know who procured it from Ramsey but surmise it was J. I. Williamson, an attorney at Kansas City employed by Hale, as Carl Weaver told me Williamson had done the fixing to have this case reversed by the U.S. Circuit Court."

❧ Chapter 44 ❧

Defense Lawyers Try to Frame Roy Bunch

Defense counsel were relentless in their efforts to clear Bill Hale of the Henry Roan murder charge by attempting to place the blame on Roy Bunch.

At Hale's trial, defense attorney Howard charged that Roy Bunch "either killed Roan or had him killed." Howard said Bunch began to court Roan's widow three years before the Indian's death. He told the jury that Bunch became intimate with her, and as a result, Bunch and Roan became bitter enemies. "The two engaged in several fights and gun plays," he said. "Bunch made repeated attempts to have Roan killed. When Roan found his home had been broken up, he took to drinking excessively and then attempted suicide twice. A few days after Roan's body was found Bunch married his widow."

Blackie Thompson, an inmate at the Oklahoma State Prison, told Agents that he had several talks with Kelsie Morrison and Henry Cornett, who were both confined in the same prison. They told Thompson that Hale would beat his forthcoming trial because defense counsel had obtained an affidavit showing that the late Curley Johnson had killed Henry Roan at the request and solicitation of Roy Bunch and Ernest Burkhart. They told Thompson that Roy Bunch had been intimate with Roan's wife and that the motive was clear and could be easily proved to clear Hale.

Dewey Selph told Agents that, while he and Hale were both confined at Leavenworth, Hale would give him newspapers to read when articles appeared concerning Hale's trial and Hale talked to him about the trial several times, stating that he had Matt Williams "fixed" and that, if Selph would not testify against him, he had the case beat.

Ernest Burkhart made an affidavit in which he stated in part:

"About two weeks before Hale was arrested in December, 1926, he (Hale) came down to my place and told me that there had been some talk going around that he was going to be arrested, but he thought the blame would be laid on Roy Bunch. He said that he talked to Roy Bunch and told him that he (Bunch) had better leave the country. He said to me, 'You know that Roy Bunch has been going with Henry Roan's wife quite a while,' and I said, 'Yes.' Hale said it would be easy to lay the blame on Roy Bunch because he had been going with Roan's wife.'

J. I. Howard and Bill Hale prepared a statement incriminating Roy Bunch and asked a certain individual to sign this statement and swear that it was true. He informed Hale and Howard that the statement was completely false and he refused to sign it. He gave an affidavit to FBI Agents revealing this information in which he said, 'I never made such a statement or told any such story at any time; none of it nor any part of it is true."

Three witnesses actually did perjure themselves in attempting to vindicate Hale by placing the responsibility for Roan's murder on Curley Johnson and Roy Bunch. This testimony was clearly shown to be false by developments during the trial.

Buster Jarrett, who was serving a sentence for bank robbery in the Oklahoma State Penitentiary at McAlester was subpoenaed by Hale for the trial of the Roan murder case. Jarrett stated that, while he was being held in the Pawhuska Jail as a witness for Hale, Henry Cornett, also a defense witness, was being held there at the same time on a bank robbery charge. Cornett asked Jarrett to testify falsely for Hale to the effect that he was present at Henry Cornett's house in Osage County late in January, 1923, when he saw Henry Roan come there drunk; that he saw the Rowe brothers, Ray Roy Smith, Curley Johnson and Roy Bunch there at the same time. Jarrett was asked to swear that he saw Henry Roan leave Cornett's house by the North road; that he saw Roy Bunch get in front of Roan's car by leaving Cornett's by the south road; and that he saw Curley Johnson following behind Roan's car so that Bunch and Curley Johnson had Roan hemmed in between them.

Buster Jarrett told Cornett that this was not true. Later, Henry Cornett and J. I. Howard came into his cell and stayed for an hour and half or two hours, trying to persuade him to testify to the above facts at Hale's trial. He was asked to testify further that he saw Roy Bunch in Fairfax on that same night paying Curley Johnson some money for killing Henry Roan.

Jarrett finally promised to testify as Cornett and Howard requested, but he told them that his proposed testimony was untrue; that he knew nothing at all about the things to which they wished him to testify. He told them that Cornett would have to testify first in the trial since he was afraid Cornett might not testify to the same facts as Jarrett and Jarrett might thereby get himself in trouble for perjuring himself in federal court. After he returned to prison, J. I. Howard came to see him (while the Hale case was continued) and Howard again asked him to testify falsely. Howard told him that he would "snatch" him out of prison if he testified as they asked him to do.

An Osage County bootlegger and the town drunkard testified for the defense that on the evening of January 27, 1923, at about nine o'clock they drove to Cornett's ranch for whiskey and passed Roy Bunch and Mary Roan on the road.

When Agents interviewed Sol Smith, on whose ranch Roan's body was found, he stated that Springer, one of Hale's lawyers, met him in the lobby of a hotel on July 31, 1926, and asked him if he remembered Curley Johnson and Roy Bunch coming to his ranch house one night in a car with the body of Henry Roan, and didn't he remember showing them where to put the car and body in the canyon. Smith said, "He just asked me if I remembered it and he said, 'You know that car was up there,' and I said, 'I know it was not.' He said, 'You know you saw that car,' and I said, 'I did not see that car.' Well, we had quite a little argument about it."

Smith was asked, "In that conversation, did he tell you that, if you could remember that, there would be $2,500 in it for you?"

"Something to that effect," Smith answered. "I told him there was not enough money in the world to make me remember that, as it was not true and that I did not want him to tell me it was."

Smith pointed out further that it would have been impossible to take a car from his ranch house to the place where Henry Roan's body was found.

Springer had told Smith that two other individuals were going to swear that Johnson and Bunch did come to Sol Smith's ranch house with Roan's body, later taking it to the canyon where it was found. Sol Smith later told an FBI Agent that he was accosted by Springer who placed a pistol against him and told him he would kill him if he mentioned further what Springer had said to him.

One of the individuals who testified falsely that he had seen Roy Bunch, Curley Johnson, and Henry Roan at Cornett's place was questioned by one of the federal government's prosecuting attorneys.

"What time in the day was it that you say you saw Roy Bunch, Mary Roan, and Bill Taylor, riding in a car, go past your house?"

"*It was about five o'clock.*"

"That was in January of 1923?"

"*I could not say what date it was.*"

"Did you know whether it was January or not?"

"*Yes, I think it was.*"

"Do you know whether it was 1923 or not?"

"*Yes, I believe it was in 1923.*"

"Do you know how long it was before you heard of Henry Roan being killed?"

"*No, I do not. About a week though.*"

"Could it have been more than a week?"

"*Yes, it could have.*"

"You say that you had been down to your uncle's, Henry Cornett's, on that day, you and your brother, and helped brand some cattle?"

"*Yes, sir.*"

"And had you got home after branding the cattle before you saw the car pass in which Roy Bunch, Mary Roan, and Bill Taylor were riding?"

"*Yes, sir.*"

"Whose car was the first car you saw pass after you arrived at home?"

"*Roy Bunch.*"

"And who was the next?"

"*Next behind you mean?*"

"Yes."

"*Henry Roan's.*"

"And how far apart were they?"

"*I don't imagine over a half mile.*"

"Were you paying any particular attention as to how far apart they were?"

"*No, sir.*"

"Do you know whether Roy Bunch was out of sight when Henry Roan passed?"

"*Well, I don't think he was.*"

"And what was the next car you saw come along?"

"*Curley Johnson in a Ford.*"

Other individuals were also induced to testify that they saw Mary Roan, Roy Bunch, and Curley Johnson at Cornett's house in January, 1923, while Henry Roan was there. One of these witnesses came to Roy Bunch before the trial and told him that he was going to perjure himself for Hale and would do the same thing for Bunch under similar circumstances. This man testified falsely that he had seen Roy Bunch, Mary Roan, Bill Taylor, and Curley Johnson at Henry Cornett's place buying whiskey some time in January, 1923. Under cross-examination this individual contradicted himself. On redirect examination Hale's lawyer began, "You got yourself a little mixed up on these two dates. I want you to fix one of them. When I asked you a while ago when it was you met this car out there with reference to when Henry Roan's body was found, you said about a week and now you tell Mr. Leahy it was about a week before Christmas, now which one is right? Henry's body was found on the 6th of February?"

"Yes, sir."

"When was it with reference to that? How long was it before you heard of them finding Henry Roan's body?"

"It was about a week."

"That you met this car, is that what you want to say?"

"Yes, sir."

"You told Mr. Leahy you thought it was about a week before Christmas."

At this point the judge interrupted saying, "Tell this jury why, along about the first of February, you were going to lay in a supply of whiskey for Christmas."

"I didn't go out there in February."

Judge: "You say you went out to this place to get your whiskey supply for the holidays?"

"I was selling whiskey all the time."

Judge: "I am asking you if you were getting this for the holidays. Is that true?"

"For a New Year's holiday."

Judge: "Then it was for New Year's?"

"No, sir."

An inmate of the Oklahoma State Penitentiary who was working for Henry Cornett in 1922 told the FBI men that Bill Hale and Henry Cornett asked him to testify that he was at Cornett's house on the day that Henry Roan was murdered and to testify that he saw Roan leave by the north way to the road which led south to Fairfax. He was asked to testify, as the others had been asked, that he saw Roy Bunch and Curley Johnson sandwich Roan between their cars as he left Cornett's. He had advised Hale and Cornett that he had not seen this even though he had been at Cornett's on that day. He refused to testify as they requested. He told Agents that he had seen Roan buy whiskey from Cornett and had also seen Curley Johnson, Mary Roan, Roy Bunch and Bill Taylor, as well as "a lot of other people" buy whiskey from Cornett, but he never at any time saw Roan at Cornett's place at the same time the others were there.

Roy Bunch, in refuting this testimony given by perjured witnesses, denied that he had been to Cornett's place with Mary Roan and Bill Taylor as the witnesses stated. He pointed out that neither he nor Mary Roan even had an automobile at that time. Bunch's testimony was corroborated by both Mary Roan and Bill Taylor.

Taylor said that he had only been to Cornett's place once in his life and that was approximately a year and a half prior to Roan's murder. He commented further that he was not even on speaking terms with Roy Bunch for six months prior to the finding of Roan's body and for a long time thereafter. Taylor's employment record reflected that he was paid for eight hours' work every day from January 1 through March 1. He was not absent from work any time during this period and hence could not have been at Henry Cornett's place with Roy Bunch as the defense witnesses had testified.

Mrs. Myra Johnson, wife of Curley Johnson, told Agents that some time in January, 1926, while she was in Kansas City, she received a telephone call from a friend at Oilton, Oklahoma, advising her that a certain individual wished to see her on some important business, that this individual would send her a train ticket if she would come. Subsequently, he did send her a ticket and she went to Oilton to meet him. He told her someone had told him she had a great deal of information which would help Bill Hale. She answered that she had no such information. He then suggested that she go to Ripley, Oklahoma, to visit her relatives and he would send two men to see her the following Sunday.

In the latter part of July or the first of August, 1926, Mrs. Johnson said, these two men came to see her in Kansas City. They told her that, if she would testify that her husband, Curley Johnson, had killed Henry Roan, she could just name her own price and J. I. Howard, Hale's attorney, would come to see her and she would never have to work again. She told these men that her husband did not kill Henry Roan and she did not know anything about the killing. (Curley Johnson was a small time gambler who had died under suspicious circumstances at Denoya, Oklahoma, on October 17, 1924.)

They told her that she would make a good witness for Bill Hale and since Curley Johnson was dead it could do him no harm and she might just as well make herself seven or eight hundred dollars. She told them she knew nothing about the murder and "they could not pile up enough money" to cause her to take the stand and lie about Curley.

Later, J. I. Howard went to see Mrs. Johnson and repeated what the others had said. Howard attempted to appeal to her better nature, she said, asking her why she ever married a man like Johnson; that she was too good a woman to marry a man of the underworld, et cetera. Mrs. Johnson told Agents that she bawled Howard out "pretty strong" and told him she was tired of them trying to get her to swear to a lie; that the people he was trying to get her to lie for were the individuals responsible for her husband's murder and caused her to lose her job by having her make the trip to Oilton. She told Howard not to bother her any more and ordered him off her property.

Mrs. Johnson told Agents that her husband could not have killed Henry Roan because he was gambling at Whizbang, Oklahoma, at the time of Roan's murder.

A close friend of Curley Johnson verified the fact that Johnson had been gambling at Whizbang when Roan was murdered. This man further remarked that Johnson was a coward who would leave town if he thought there was going to be trouble of any kind and always avoided being involved in any kind of violence.

Agents received a signed statement from a man who resided in Webb City, Oklahoma, as follows:

"On or about May 18, 1928, about 6:00 p.m. at Webb City, Oklahoma, W. W. (Whitey) White told me that he was going to 'promote' some money. I asked him where, and he said he was going to Pawhuska, Oklahoma; that he could get $500 from Bill Hale's attorney for swearing in court that Curley Johnson killed Henry Roan. White said it wouldn't be giving Curley the worst of it — Curley was dead.

"On May 23, 1928, at the O'Hara Rooming House in Webb City, Oklahoma, in the presence of Dora Dock of Ponca City, he made practically the same statement.... He had two new suits of clothes, a used Ford coupe with wire wheels and plenty of money. He said, as he slapped me on the shoulder, 'Well, I didn't do so bad. I am liable to tell those sons of bitches anything for some money.'"

Dora Dock verified hearing Whitey White make this statement.

A man named Ray R. Smith was questioned by one of the prosecuting attorneys after he had stated that he had seen Curley Johnson shoot Henry Roan.

"Where was your business in 1923?" he was asked.

"*I was farming.*"

"Where?"

"*Near Fairfax.*"

"Did you hold a commission as deputy sheriff, or sheriff?"

"*I did, along about that time.*"

"You made some investigation of these Osage murders, did you?"

"*I did.*"

"Who was directing that investigation?"

"*Well, I never could find out, nobody doing anything only Harve Freas; I couldn't tell who was.*"

"Did you report anything to Harve Freas that you found out?"

"*I did.*"

"What did you report to Mr. Freas?"

"*I was standing in front of the Lee-Huckins Hotel. I was talking to Arthur Graves, and Buck Garrett, and my brother-in-law, and Henry Grammer came up and shook hands with me, and about that time Bill Hale came up and he says, 'There is the very man I want to see. Where have you been?'*"

"To whom did he say that?"

"*To Henry Grammer. And he said, 'I want to see you.' They walked from the hotel back this way and I went down through the hall down in the toilet.*"

"Were you in the toilet?"

"*I was in the toilet.*"

"Overheard their conversation?"

"*Yes, sir.*"

"What was it?"

"*Well, it was about this: He says, 'I need a good man.' He says 'I will get you John Ramsey,' something like that.'*"

"Hale said to Grammer, 'I need a good man?'"

"*Yes, sir.*"

"And you reported that conversation to Harve Freas?"

"*Well, I told it kind of that way.*"

"Is that all you ever reported to Mr. Freas?"

"*No, I told him the other day on the street —*'

"Now, you say you know who killed Henry Roan?"

"*No, I don't know who killed him.*"

"What is that?"

"No, I don't know who killed him."

"Didn't you tell me right here that you did know?"

"Yes sir; I was trying to bring this to a close, I was trying to get home."

"You told me you told Howard, the lawyer?"

"I talked with him."

"And you told him that Curley Johnson killed Henry Roan, and you saw Curley Johnson shoot him, and Henry Cornett? Did you tell that to Mr. Howard?"

"Yes, sir. I told him that."

"When did you tell him that?"

"Just a few minutes ago."

"How did you happen to tell him that?"

"Well, there was a man somewhere yesterday between here and Oklahoma City told me; I disremember."

"Told you to say that?"

"Yes, sir."

"Who told you to say that?"

"I don't know, I was drunk. I will tell you what,— they framed up on me."

"There isn't going to be any dispute about what had taken place in this room; everything you are saying is being written down and everything I am saying is being written down. I want to know. You told me not more than 10 minutes ago in the presence of the United States Attorney, Mr. Lewis [sic], in the presence of Tom White, in the presence of Edwin Brown, that you saw Curley Johnson and Cornett kill Henry Roan."

"Well, that is a lie."

"You lied to me?"

"Yes."

"Why did you lie to me?"

"Well, I don't know, but I did."

"Are you a man of good mind?"

"I must not have been at that time."

"I can't understand people lying; if you are of unsound mind I want to know it. Were you drunk?"

"Yes, I was drunk."

"Who was it told you to swear to that story and see Mr. Howard?"

"I don't know."

"You hunted Mr. Howard up to tell him?"

"No, sir. He called me up and said he wanted to see me."

"What did you say to him?"

"He wanted to see me after court."

"And you told me you told him that story?"

"There was a man somewhere between here and Oklahoma City — "

At this point one of the Agents interrupted him and asked, "You know the man?"

"Well, no, I don't know him."

"Did you know this man?"

"I never saw him before in my life. It was somewhere between here and Oklahoma City."

The prosecuting attorney continued, "What was it you told Mr. Howard?"

"Well, I just told him about the same thing I told you."

"I want you to repeat it."

"I told him, 'Let's bring this to a close pretty fast'; I says, 'They have got the wrong man. Curley Johnson killed Henry Roan and Henry Cornett was with him,' and he said, 'Is that so, I want to see you right after court.'"

"Did you tell him that you had seen it?"

"No, I don't believe I told him."

"You told me that you had."

"I don't believe I told him."

"I asked you where you were and you told me you were on the road to Burbank."

"I might have told him that."

"You told me that you saw the whole performance; that Henry Cornett and Curley Johnson did it. Is that so?"

"No, sir."

"How much were you to get?"

"Not a dime."

"How much were you to get?"

"There wasn't no money handed me."

"How much money were you promised to tell that story?"

"There was no money offered me at all."

"You certainly would not want to tell a lie and jeopardize your liberty for nothing?"

"Not a bit, I don't understand why I said it."

"Did you expect to get something in the future?"

"No, I don't want nothing; I want justice."

"Now, let us understand each other. I am asking you a direct question: do you know or have you any information as to the man or men who killed Henry Roan?"

"Well, the best I could believe is it seems to me like that Ramsey must

have done the work."

"Did you see anybody fire the shot that killed Henry Roan?"

"No, sir, I did not."

"Were you in the neighborhood of where Henry Roan was found and hear any shots fired?"

"No, sir, I did not."

"And when you told me, in the presence of these other gentlemen, in response to my question, "Do you know who killed Henry Roan?' and you said, 'Yes', you deliberately lied to me, did you?"

"Yes sir, I did."

"And when I asked you who killed Henry Roan and you said Curley Johnson, that was a deliberate lie?"

"Yes, sir."

"And when I asked you how did you know and you said, 'I saw it done,' that was a lie?"

"Absolutely."

❧ Chapter 45 ❧

Hale Takes the Witness Stand

At his trial Bill Hale took the witness stand and gave a dramatic recital of alleged third-degree methods which he claimed were used by federal officers in an attempt to make him sign a confession. The account rendered by Hale was so dramatic in the extreme to make it fantastic and unbelievable. At times he motioned with his arms and at other times he arose from the witness chair to portray the methods which he claimed were used. He claimed the Agents put him in a chair, put a cap over his head, and then applied charges of electricity to his body, stating that they were going to electrocute him if he did not sign. Hale also stated that guns were pointed at him during the interview to make him confess.

Hale said, "I turned my head while they talked to me and saw a shadow of a gun pointed in my direction through the ground-glass window. About the same time they put a gun on me and told me, if I looked back again, they would beat my brains out. They told me, if I didn't sign, they would give me the hot chair. I wouldn't sign and they put me in the chair. Then they said I would sign or they would electrocute me. I never signed. Then they placed a cap over my head and something like a baseball mask over that. They kept talking about electrocuting me and putting enough juice to me so I could feel it. I refused to sign. Someone then walked out and for an hour or more there was no sound. Then they took the cap off me. One of them said it was about 2:30 am and we should go ahead. I told them to go ahead and do what they pleased. They said they would get me to sign anything they wanted me to. One of them with a gun in his hands told me that, if I went to the stand and testified as to what they had done to me, I would be bumped off within sight of thirty days." Hale repeated this again for emphasis. "At one time during the interval they had me in the chair one of them sniffed the air and asked if I had not smelled burning flesh; that they had electrocuted another fellow and might do the same to me if I did not sign the statement."

The government men were then called to the stand and refuted Hale's testimony. The story of alleged third degree methods was conclusively proved to be a complete fabrication and the judge fully exonerated the federal Agents.

The courtroom was crowded at the afternoon session as court began. An approaching storm, accompanied by occasional thunder, blackened the sky and cast a shadow over the courtroom as Hale explained his business dealings with Henry Roan.

He said, "On small notes I charged him 10 per cent interest and on larger ones 6 per cent interest. We were good friends and he sought me out when in trouble and he needed money."

While on the stand, Hale revealed his disdain for the Osages. He was asked if Henry Roan had been working prior to his death.

Hale asked in return, "Did you ever see an Osage work?"

When asked if Roan spent his money freely, Hale replied, "Don't 99 per cent of them spend their money freely?"

"Were you a deputy sheriff at the time?" Hale was asked.

He answered, "There was only one sheriff that I did not hold a commission under."

Hale had a legal citation to a New Mexico case similar to the Roan case where the federal government was denied jurisdiction on similar grounds. Hale told a man that he felt it would be precedent to show that the federal government did not have jurisdiction in the Roan case.

Hale remarked to him that he was afraid Ramsey "could not stand hitched." This man explained to Agents, "I have never squawked in my life, but Bill Hale is the worst crook and double-crosser I have ever known." He said Hale had rented some grass from him near Lathan in 1925 and brought a lot of stolen cattle along and put them in his pasture. "Some of my neighbors found their stolen cattle in Hale's herd and I returned them to my neighbors." Hale had told him that he had about 185 head of cattle which he had stolen from the Indians and, when he sold them at Kansas City, he had these cattle billed separately from his own under the name of his nephew, Horace Burkhart. Hale propositioned this man that they could steal a lot of cattle and put them in this individual's ranch. He complained that Hale had stolen four steers from him for which he was never paid. This witness was threatened that, if he testified against Hale, he would be killed before he could leave the court-house.

While Hale was confined at Pawhuska in the Osage County Jail, he had a cell with an outside exposure where he could talk to friends. The room in which he stayed, or where he was supposed to have been confined, was left unlocked, and Hale had access to a telephone and other accommodations. He had many visitors while confined at the jail.

While Hale was confined at the Oklahoma City Jail, the jailer found a letter to Hale in his cell from Kelsie Morrison, who, at the time, was jointly charged with Bryan Burkhart for the murder of Anna Brown. This letter was turned over to FBI Agents on October 21, 1926, and was later introduced at Hale's trial:

"Dear Old Friend W.K.,

"You don't know how good I feel because you are going to give that back to me, and old boy, I won't forget you when I am called for witness. I will be there with bells on but please don't think I am taking the advantage of you in asking you for it because I told you I would help you just the same.

"Bill, you know Tillies kidds [sic] are going to have two or three thousand dollars in a few years and I have those kidds [sic] adopted. How can I get possession or control of that money when I get out? You know, I believe I can take those kidds [sic] out of the state and they can't do a damn thing because according to law, they are mine and their names are Morrison, and I was given all rights to them. I am going to talk to Freeing about it. You see, if I take them out of the state, this court in this state would not have jurisdiction, and they could not get me for kidnapping for they are my owns kidds [sic] according to law.

"Mrs. Hale waved at me and said good-by. God I feel sorry for her. Honestly I do, Bill. I'll bet she feels better towards me since I told Judge Cotteral what I did.

"I can't help but feel what I swore at Pawhuska is going to beat them yet. If you win at Oklahoma City, them lies I swore at Pawhuska will win your case over there. I'll burn them down at Pawhuska if I ever get the chance.

"Your true friend, Kelsie"

He added:

"Dear Friend W.K.,

"How are you this morning? I feel some better. Bill, be sure you don't have me subpoenaed as a witness until right on the last. If I had to lay

around in that dirty old jail at Okla City all the time the government is
putting on their evidence. I don't want you to call me until you need me. I
believe you have got them this time. I wish T. J. Leahy would quit just for
the moral effect it would have. John is asleep.

"*Kelsie.*"

(Agents learned of an apparent scheme Morrison was plotting regarding these children. He asked a lawyer if he adopted these boys and they died would he inherit their Osage headrights. The lawyer said this indicated to him that Morrison intended to adopt them and then murder them to inherit their estates.)

At the trial of Hale and Ramsey for the murder of Henry Roan, a motion for a new trial was made by Hale's lawyers based on alleged new evidence set out in affidavits which were attached to the motion.

One affidavit was John Ramsey's (set forth in detail previously) in which he denied that Hale ever had knowledge leading up to the murder of Henry Roan and in which Ramsey alleged there was a conspiracy between Roy Bunch and Ernest Burkhart to have Roan murdered. This affidavit recited the details of the alleged arrangements between Burkhart, Bunch and Curley Johnson to kill Roan. It also gave a pictorial description of the actual murder place supposedly where Curley Johnson shot Roan with a pistol furnished to him by Burkhart in the presence of Burkhart and Ramsey. Ramsey further alleged numerous meetings with Bunch and Burkhart separately and together, and set out details of discussions and numerous money transactions he had with Ernest Burkhart. This affidavit named Bill Revard and Amos Tucker as individuals who were present with Ramsey and Bunch when Bunch discussed murdering Roan. It also named John Morris as the keeper of Burkhart's funds and as being present when Burkhart paid Ramsey a sum of money. It stated that J. O. Evans was with Ernest Burkhart and Ramsey when Burkhart had a .45 automatic pistol. This affidavit contained allegations enumerating numerous details to substantiate Ramsey's association with Burkhart, Bunch and Curley Johnson in the murder of Henry Roan vindicating W.K. Hale.

Other affidavits were from some of Hale's other cohorts, incriminating Burkhart, Johnson and Bunch, and corroborating Ramsey's false affidavit.

Bureau Agents, however, obtained other affidavits which completely refuted these bogus affidavits.

❧ Chapter 46 ❧

Hale's Former Cellmate Talks

Hugh M. Washburn, confined in the Tulsa, Oklahoma, jail on an alleged white slave charge, wrote to the United States Attorney at Oklahoma City, requesting an interview with FBI Agents regarding what Bill Hale had told him while he was confined in the Osage County Jail at Pawhuska. Washburn made an affidavit which read in part as follows:

"Prior to my incarceration in the Osage County Jail, I had never met or known William K. Hale; neither have I ever met nor do I know John Ramsey; neither have I ever met nor know Curley Johnson, and personally, I know nothing of the facts and have never known anything with reference to the facts surrounding the alleged killing of Henry Roan, or the killing of Bill Smith and family or Anna Brown, or any of the other so-called Osage Indian Murders, except what I have heard with reference to the same.

"The first time I saw Bill Hale was when they brought him to the Pawhuska Jail and they placed him in a cell just across from where they had me. I saw a number of people coming in and out and talking to him and once Dick Connor, one of the jailers, was sent downtown by Bill Hale to see a fellow on some business for him. Somebody happened to mention something about it and said that Dick Connor was snitching for Hale, and Demsey, one of the jailers, said he would have to lock Hale up for a few days until it blew over, and they put him in the cell with me, where they had me in solitary confinement.

"Dick Connor, Demsey and old man Hutchinson told him he would have to watch me because I was the worst snitch they had in the jail. Hale told me that they told him that and for him to watch me and not let me know anything, and then I told Hale why they had it in for me — because they found out that I used to be an officer over at Bartlesville.

I told Hale that it was all a mistake and that I was not a snitch, and that, if I had saws in the jail, as they said I had, I would try to break out, and after awhile I seemed to have gained Hale's confidence and he began to talk to me. He asked me once if I could get my former wife up there, whose name is Louisa Washburn, if I would write her to come up right away and she would testify to whatever he wanted her to. I told him I would write for her but I did not write. He told me he would pay me well if I would get up on the stand and swear for him as follows: He wanted me to swear I was living at Shidler, Oklahoma, (where I had never lived in my life) and state as follows:

"'While I were living at Shidler, Oklahoma, I and Curley Johnson were working on my Ford car, and two fellows drove up to where we were at and one of them asked Curley where Ramsey were and, if he had seen him, that he wanted to know if he was going to do that job, and Curley said he didn't know and then Roy Bunch spoke up and said, if he wasn't going to do it, he would get someone that would, and told Curley to come over to Fairfax that next night and I and Curley went to Fairfax and stopped our car in front of the pool hall on the East Side of the street and pretty soon out come Blackie Thompson and ask if we would go and get some whiskey, and we drove East for a ways and then turned south down to a car and there we met two fellows, Ramsey and Roy Bunch, and they were talking of bumping off an Indian and I ask who the Indian was and Curley said it was Henry Roan.'

"Hale wrote the above statement out and gave it to me and I copied it off and then he tore his copy up and destroyed it. I now hand to the United States Attorney a copy of Mr. Hale's statement that I wrote out from his copy before he tore up the same, on which I have placed my initials for identification purposes.

"Mr. Hale told me in the cell one night that he had made a great mistake by getting Ramsey to make way with Henry Roan; that he told Ramsey not to shoot him in the back but to do the job right and shoot him in front, making it appear that Roan had committed suicide.

"While Bill Hale and I were in the cell together, he passed notes to Blackie Thompson, and I, myself, crawled up on the radiator and shoved these notes into a small hole where a radiator pipe went through the ceiling and Blackie Thompson sent a note down to Bill Hale, asking if Hale would help him out, by getting some friend of his to slip him a rod (meaning a six-shooter) and Bill Hale told him he thought he had a friend who would put one in there for him and the next day Blackie Thompson told Bill Hale, if he could get him a rod, he would not testify against him and Bill Hale wrote a note to Thompson and asked him if

he could do a job for him if he would get him a rod. He had reference to a man named Ernest Burkhart, and he told Blackie Thompson in his note that he would not want him killed anywhere around here where they could use his evidence if they found him dead; said he would want him taken across into old Mexico and whatever happened to him over there was immaterial to him, and he told Blackie where he could find this man, said there would probably be a young man with him and to watch his corners as there might be a gun on him, and Blackie told Hale that it would probably take him about three to five days after he hit the ground.

"All the above statements were made by notes passed between Hale and Blackie Thompson through this hole above mentioned. Sometimes Hale would hand me the notes to read, and sometimes I would receive them through the hole and read them, to all of which Hale did not object, after I had gained his confidence.

"Hale asked me if he would get a couple of rods — otherwise six-shooters — if Thompson and I would take the keys and unlock Harry Cornett and Red Ramsey, son of John Ramsey. He wanted us to take all the jailers and himself and lock them up in the basement, and by us taking him and getting hard with him, it would make the thing clear that he had nothing to do with it, and I told him that I would. I told him this to gain his confidence because they had all accused me and told him that I was a snitch and my purpose was not only to gain the confidence of Hale but also the jailers because of the mistreatment they had given me and also for such information as I could get. I had no intention of breaking jail or attempting to, or assisting anyone else in breaking jail.

"I now know Bill Revard and first became acquainted with him in the Osage County Jail at Pawhuska, where he was serving time on a liquor charge. Bill Hale showed me a note he had that was a statement he had procured Bill Revard to make and said he was going to make him an awful good witness; said he had arranged with Bill Revard to testify falsely to the following effect: That Roy Bunch was going out and kill Henry Roan and he said, if Bill Revard would get up and swear that state of facts, that he would make him an awfully good witness. Bill Revard told him in my presence that he would not swear to that at all because he might get himself in a jack-pot, but said he would swear that he heard Roy Bunch ask another fellow to go with him. Bill Hale had in his possession a typewritten statement with reference to what the testimony was that he wanted Bill Revard to swear to, which I got out of Hale's pocket in our cell and copied the same, a copy of which I *now identify by my initials and hand to the United State's Attorney, said statement being as follows, to-wit:*

"'Bill Revard, from my original notes:

"An Indian of Fairfax will testify that he run around with Roy Bunch and Mary Roan for two years before the killing of Henry Roan, that they were on frequent drunken parties together; that he seen Bunch at Henry Roan's house on an average of two or three times a week for a year before the death of Henry Roan; that Roy Bunch would occupy the same room with Mary and that he was very jealous of Mary and was actually in love with her; that one time he and Roy Cook went up to Henry Roan's when Roan was away and Roy Bunch found out about this visit and said you are a God dam fine friend and went so far as to threaten to shoot Revard, and Revard said he thought that he was going to shoot him over the matter, that about a year before Henry Roan was killed, Revard and Roy Bunch were standing in front of Roy Cook's pool hall talking and Henry Roan started to Burbank and Roy Bunch said to Revard that, if he would go with him, that he would go and kill Henry Roan on this trip, and Revard said to Bunch that he would not be a party to a murder. Was out on a drinking party with John Ramsey, Amos Tucker and Roy Bunch; one time a short time before the death of Roan; out on Pawhuska Road, near got to Bill Trent's pasture, Bunch and Ramsey talked of killing Roan.'

"There was also some woman in the Osage County Jail, whose name was Brown, and Hale told me that he had been up to her cell in the jail and stayed up there until about 12 o'clock and said he was going to get her to make him a good witness.

"During the time I was with Hale in the jail, he spent considerable of his time in the women's part of the jail. In fact he had the privilege and liberty of going most anywhere he wanted to most of the time. He had one meal a day in his cell and would leave the cell at 9 o'clock or near that in the (morning) and return at 12 or 1 o'clock that night. The jailers would let people come in at the side door to see him most any time.

"I saw Hale hand money to John Henderson and Dick Connor on different occasions and Hale told me that the information he was getting and the work he was getting done by and from the jailers was costing him plenty, but it was worth the money.

"Every day, Hale was let out of his cell at about 9 o'clock in the morning and was not let back until 12 or 1 o'clock at night, with the exception of sometimes when they would put him in about the noon hour, letting him stay an hour or so and then let him out again, and on

Hale asked Blackie Thompson to kill Ernest Burkhart so he
could not testify against Hale.

other occasions, when they would see someone coming into the jail,
they would put him into his cell until they would leave and then let
him out again. He was always allowed the privileges of the jail when he
wanted them, to go where he pleased and was permitted to use the tele-
phone at his pleasure. On one occasion, I remember, a man came to the
jail that someone said was a federal officer and, when they saw him
coming, they put Hale in the back part of the jail where the jailers sleep
and when this man left they brought him back and put him in the cell."

Blackie Thompson, a government witness, was subpoenaed
by Hale to Tulsa on November 2, 1928, for Hale's hearing on application for bond. Thompson, however, was not put on the stand.
Upon interview afterwards, Thompson stated that when he arrived at Tulsa on November 2, J. I. Howard, Hale's attorney, asked
him if the statement made by Hugh Washburn was true. Thompson said he asked Howard, "Do you want the truth?"

Howard answered, "Yes."

Thompson then told Howard, "What Washburn stated was
true."

Howard then asked Thompson if he would take the stand

and contradict Washburn's testimony. Thompson evaded answering Howard and said that he "would think it over."

Agents discovered that, in addition to the murders already committed, Mollie Burkhart was dying from slow poisoning and was not expected to live very long. Her physician (the same individual who in performing his autopsies of the bodies of Anna Brown and Henry Roan had favored the murderers in every possible way) was allowing her to use narcotics which would probably hasten her death. At this time, her husband, Ernest, who by that time had confessed to his part in the murders and had requested protection from the FBI, was in the care of Special Agents at Hot Springs, New Mexico. Hale's attorneys were making every effort to have Burkhart brought back to Osage County to get him back under his uncle's control, and Mollie's death would have made his return necessary.

Arrangements were made, therefore, with Mollie's consent, to take her and her two small children to join her husband at Hot Springs, New Mexico. When she was removed from the control of Hale's cronies, she immediately regained her health and lived until June 16, 1937.

During the course of the investigation, Federal Agents learned that Mollie Burkhart, who professed the Catholic faith, sent word to a priest that she was afraid of being poisoned at her home. The priest told the Agents that Mrs. Burkhart's husband had kept her from attending church because he feared she might talk to some of the church members.

The Osage wives of Ernest and Bryan Burkhart were in great fear for their lives and contemplated taking their children and fleeing from their husbands. After moving away, they intended to hire a bodyguard to prevent their being killed for their property.

.(Later at the time of the trials, Hale and his conspirators attempted to get Ernest Burkhart under their control again to make him revoke his confession. Ernest himself pleaded with the FBI for protection since he feared that his uncle would have him killed. When Ernest Burkhart took the witness stand at Hale's preliminary hearing, Hale's attorneys claimed that they were representing Burkhart and demanded the privilege of talking to him for a few minutes before he testified. The judge granted this request and, while the lawyers were conferring with Ernest, the court adjourned. He was taken to Fairfax, Oklahoma, where he was pressured by numerous friends and relatives of Hale to comply with the instructions of Hale's attorneys. Later, on advice of Hale's attorneys, Burkhart refused to testify. At a later trial, however, Ernest again testified for the prosecution, explaining that his actions were caused by the influence of Hale's attorneys.)

❧ Chapter 47 ❧

Asa Kirby's Partner Testifies

John Maye, an inmate of the Kansas State Penitentiary and a material government witness, testified, that while he and Asa Kirby were operating a rooming house, Kirby tried to get him to help blow up the Smith home. Maye said he made a trip to the Henry Grammer ranch after the Smith slaying where he saw Grammer give Kirby a roll of bills. When asked why he did not tell about this murder earlier, if he knew about it, Maye said, "I know better. I'd have been murdered, the way the country was then."

The following statement was obtained from Mrs. John Maye, wife of John Maye, indicating that Hale's attorneys were attempting to "fix" Maye's testimony:

"*June 13, 1926. Tulsa.*

"*My name is Mrs. June Maye, the wife of John Maye. I work at the Maye Hotel Coffee Shop as waitress.*

"*About the 28th or 29th of April, 1926, near 8 AM two men came in the Coffee Shop and sit down. The small man with a mustache asked me if I was John Maye's widow. I told him that I was John Maye's wife. He then began asking me when I got off duty and when I was not busy, as he wanted to talk to me. I told him I got off late in the afternoon, but if he came back about ten thirty in the morning, I wouldn't be so busy. I did not at that time know who either of the men were. I asked the small man who they were and he told me they represented Hale and Ramsey, and the tall man with him was Mr. Springer, and his name was Weaver. The tall man, Mr. Springer, said to Weaver not to talk to me there at the Coffee Shop, but make a date with me and talk somewhere else. They both left.*

"*About 10 o'clock that same morning the small man, who said his name was Weaver, came back. He started talking to me, saying he represented Hale and Ramsey and talked as though I knew all about the case, but I told him I knew very little about it and didn't want to know any more about it.*

"He then said 'You know you don't want to see those people go to the penitentiary. You are not that hard-hearted.'

"I told him it was immaterial to me what happened to them; that I was not mixed up in the affair and was not going to get mixed up in it, if I could keep from it.

"He asked me a few other questions, and said that I was their last chance to help save Ramsey and Hale, and he believed I could help. I asked him how he figured I could help them. He said that John Maye made a statement in the preliminary trial about a lot of things, some of which were not true, and we believe you could talk to John and get him to change his testimony. I told him to go talk to John, and he (Weaver) said he couldn't afford to and wouldn't be allowed to. I told him that, if he couldn't go, why didn't he send some of his friends. He said for the simple reason that I would have more bearing on John and John would understand me better than anyone else.

"I commenced to get mad and told him to go on and leave me alone as his conversation did not interest me in the least.

"He then wanted to meet me somewhere or take me out in a car and talk to me, saying he would treat me just like he would his sister or mother. I told him I did not want to talk to him and could do nothing for him, but he said I could after I talked to John and for me to see John. I told him I was going to see John and tell John about him being here talking to me, and Weaver said he wanted me to tell John and that he was to see me and what his business was, and that he, Weaver, would be back Monday to see me. I told him not to come to see me anymore as I did not want to talk to him again. He said I would want to talk to him after I came back from seeing John, as I would understand better, and that he hoped he had not offended me. He then left.

"At the time I told him I did not know anything about the case, and had all I could do trying to work and make a living and pay doctor bills. He (Weaver) said you need not worry about expenses or doctor bills of any kind, for we will fix them up if necessary.

"The following Saturday, May 1, I went to Pawhuska and told John about those two men. I returned to Tulsa Saturday night. John got word to FBI Agents and they came to Tulsa to see me and prepared to catch Mr. Weaver and Mr. Springer if they came back to see me. Mr. Weaver and Mr. Springer never came back to see me."

/s/ "Mrs. John Maye"

Failing to sway Mrs. Maye, the defense attempted other methods. One individual stated to Agents that, while he was employed at the Maye Hotel during the pendency of the prosecution of the murders, a detective from Tulsa came to him and asked him if he would like to make some money. He asked the detective what he had to offer and the man replied, "There is a woman by the name of Mrs. Maye who works in the coffee shop who has some letters or some information and, if you can get it for this man Springer (defense attorney), you can make yourself a piece of change."

A statement was obtained from another man who figured in the manipulations of Hale's counsel:

"On or about May 18, 1926, Bob Ryan told me we could make $150 or $200, but never gave me any details as to how, but told me we would both find out in a day or so.

"On the 20th of May, we met at Ryan's hotel where I met Mr. Elliott, who told us how and what we were to do. Said all we had to do was sign an affidavit that I was at Henry Grammer's ranch house about 16 miles east of Ponca City the last part of Jan. 1923 with some friends of mine, that we drove into the yard and parked. When another car drove up, there was a man and a woman in this car, who was Bill Smith and Laura Tuttle. They were drinking and arguing with one another. The woman said, 'I see you haven't got rid of that squaw of yours yet.' And, 'If you don't give me the money you promised me, I will blow you both to hell.'

"Well, on Friday, May 21, 1926, Elliott called Ryan's hotel. I was there and he told us to meet him in front of the Bliss Building on Third and Main. We met him in front of the Bliss Building and he told us not to tell anyone where we was staying; that he would take care of that, so we went on up to Mr. Springer's office.

"As we went into the office, Elliott said, 'Mr. Springer, these are the boys.' We were told to sit down and Springer asked us what we knew, and I told him the same story as had been told to me by Elliott. Springer said, 'Very good, [except] for a few [other] things they might ask you.'

"So he gave us the descriptions of Bill Smith, Laura Tuttle and Henry Grammer, telling us that Henry Grammer was dead and Laura Tuttle was gone; no one knew where.

"He told us it would be about ten days or two weeks before he could use us, and then asked where we were staying, Mr. Elliott said, 'I know and can find them anytime.' So Springer said he would see us in Pawhuska in a week or so.'"

The other man who had been hired to testify falsely to these same things also furnished a signed statement to Bureau Agents completely corroborating the above story.

❧ Chapter 48 ❧

Hale's Lawyers Try to Convince a Witness to Disappear

Matt Williams, an important government witness, told Agents that he had been approached by a notorious underworld character of Osage County on behalf of the Hale faction. This man, a well-known bootlegger and liquor manufacturer who, at the time, was facing charges by both the Oklahoma State and federal authorities, took Williams to the office of a close personal friend of Bill Hale.

Hale's friend offered to give Williams $2,000 and finance a trip to Mexico if Williams would fail to appear at the trial against Hale. Matt Williams' brother was also approached by this same man, as well as by the County Assessor of Osage County, and requested to use his influence in getting Matt Williams to decline to testify against Hale.

Failing in their efforts to bribe Williams, John Duke, a peg-legged hireling of Hale, threatened to kill Williams. In an affidavit on January 8, 1929, Williams said:

"On yesterday, John Duke stopped my wife, Mrs. Williams, on the streets in Pawhuska and was talking to her relative to her being a witness in the W.K. Hale trial. She left and came across the street, meeting me. Duke hollered over to me, 'Don't you like it? If you don't, come across here.'

"I went across to where he was and Duke then told me about her being a witness in the Hale trial; that he was going to blow her testimony all to hell.

"I said, 'I don't care anything about you being a witness and being subpoenaed in these cases, but I am also witness for the government.'

"Duke said, 'If you take the stand, I'll blow you and your testimony all

to hell.'

"I told him I didn't care to talk with him further in these matters, but I didn't want him to say anything insulting to Mrs. Williams because she was a witness, or to even speak to me again pertaining to this trial.

"This morning he came to the Elks Hotel in Pawhuska. As I started to leave the door of my house, he called my name, putting his hands in his pockets, and stepped back. I engaged in no conversation with him and immediately informed the government Agents and attorney of his mission there. I am satisfied, owing to his mental condition, that he had been ribbed to pick a racket with me in order to kill me. I have known him for a period of about a year and a half. He is a whiskey peddler and for the last six months has served two terms in the county jail here and just recently was liberated."

Mrs. Maude Brown Williams, wife of Matt Williams, was contacted by G-men on January 8, 1929, and she made the following deposition:

"On yesterday, January 7, 1929, my little girl and I was going down West Main Street in Pawhuska, Oklahoma, and just as we started to step off of the sidewalk, there being quite a bit of snow there, my little girl asked me to help her across, saying that she could not step over the wide place in the snow. Just about that time, John Duke came walking up and said, 'I got me a handful of papers this morning.'

"I said, 'I care nothing about your papers.'

"He said, 'Howard sent for me to come up in his office and when I went there he shoved me a handful of papers.'

"I said, 'That is nothing to me' and he said, 'It may mean something to you. My evidence is going to be on you.'

"I said, 'How's that? You know nothing about me.'

"He said, 'I know a plenty of what you have told me.'

"I said, 'Well, I haven't told you nothing.'

"He said, 'You have told me plenty of what Matt Williams has tried to get you to do about the Hale case.'

"I said, 'Matt has not talked to me about it.'

"He said, 'Well, I told Howard this morning just to put me up on the stand and tell me what to say, that I will say anything to keep a man out of jail, but I won't say nothing to put him in.'

"I just turned off and left him there, and then I walked across the street and met Matt on the other corner. That is when he hollered to Matt.

"About one week ago John Duke called me on the phone from some place in Pawhuska and he said, 'Where is that husband of yours?'

"I said, 'I guess he is down in town,' and he said, 'Well, after the 7th, I *am going to have you.'*

"*I said, 'What do you mean?' and he said, 'That husband of yours will be out of the way after the 7th.'*"

This matter was submitted to the United States Attorney at Pawhuska who authorized the filing of a complaint against Duke, charging him with intimidating government witnesses. A complaint was filed before the United States Commissioner[35] on January 8, 1929, at Pawhuska. On the same date Duke was arrested and arraigned and his preliminary hearing was set for January 16, 1929.

Ike B. Ogg of Artesia, New Mexico, was interviewed at Pawhuska where he was appearing as a witness in the Hale case. He said, "*On January 7, 1929, John Duke came to my room number 18, at the Oklahoma Hotel, Pawhuska, Oklahoma, and told Max Billings and myself that Matt Williams, who was a Government witness in the W.K. Hale case, would never live to testify for the government as he, John Duke, was going to kill Williams, the God damned son of a bitch. Charles Davis of Okesa, Oklahoma, and Demsey Smith of Pawhuska was also present and heard John Duke make the above remarks.*"

Duke's preliminary hearing was held before the U.S. Commissioner on January 16, 1929, at Pawhuska and Duke was held for the action of the next grand jury. In default of $2,500 bond, Duke was remanded to the custody of the U.S. Marshal and placed in the Osage County Jail.

On May 7, 1929, Duke entered a plea of guilty before federal court at Pawhuska and was sentenced to serve 30 days in the Osage County Jail on a charge of intimidating a government witness.

---

[35]U.S. Commissioners have since been replaced by U.S. Magistrates.

⚜ Chapter 49 ⚜

State Court Opposes Trying Hale and Ramsey in Federal Court First

Hale and Ramsey were charged by federal authorities with violation of four sections of the Criminal Code. The charge read as follows:

"That in Osage County, Oklahoma, upon a certain restricted allotment of Rose Littlestar, a full-blooded Osage Indian, and within the Indian country on or about February 6, 1923, John Ramsey unlawfully, willfully, feloniously, and with malice aforethought and with premeditation, did kill and murder Henry Roan, a full-blooded Osage Indian, and that William K. Hale then and there did aid, abet, counsel and assist and procure said John Ramsey to kill and murder Henry Roan."

Prior to the presentation of the facts to the federal grand jury at Guthrie, Special Agents made arrangements with state authorities to have Hale and Ernest Burkhart taken into custody by the state on charges connected with the murder of Bill Smith, Rita Smith, and their servant girl, Nettie Brookshire. The reason for this was so the witnesses before the grand jury would be free from intimidation. Hale and Burkhart were arrested in Fairfax and Ramsey at his home in Ripley. Ernest Burkhart and Bill Hale were confined to the Pawhuska Jail on January 6, 1926.

The federal grand jury returned indictments against Hale and Ramsey on February 13, 1926, but the judge pointed out errors in it and quashed it. The grand jury was then recalled and a new indictment was returned on March 1, 1926. Attorneys for the defendants demurred to the indictment on the ground that the allotment of Rose Littlestar was not Indian country and, therefore, the federal government was without jurisdiction. The demurrer was sustained by the

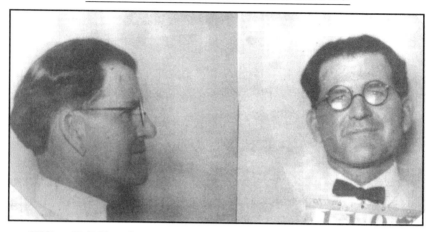

William K. (Bill) Hale, wealthy and influential Osage County rancher and businessperson. (Photo taken March 19, 1926 at Pawhuska, Oklahoma.)

federal judge and Hale and Ramsey were released on $25,000 bond pending appeal by the federal prosecutors.

However, prior to securing their liberty, they were taken into custody on March 5, 1926, by state authorities and returned to Pawhuska to answer the state charge for the murder of Bill Smith, his wife and their servant.

At their arraignment in state court, both defendants seemed to be in the best of spirits and shook hands with several of their friends who were in the courtroom to greet them. The judge read the information charging them with the Smith murders. They then entered pleas of not guilty.

The ruling of the U.S. District Court that the federal government lacked jurisdiction in the Roan case had immediately been appealed to the U.S. Supreme Court by the U.S. government prosecutors. Within the comparatively short period of twenty-five days the U.S. Supreme Court reversed the lower court's ruling on June 1, 1926, holding that the federal government did have jurisdiction over the murder of Henry Roan. When the United States Supreme Court handed down its decision, federal authorities sought custody of Hale and Ramsey from the State of Oklahoma. A fight began over whether the defendants should be tried in State or federal court. U.S. Attorney Roy St. Lewis[36] appeared before Judge Worten and filed an ap-

---

[36]On the strength of his work on the Osage Indian Murder Cases, Roy St. Lewis was named an Assistant Attorney General of the United States. When he left this position he stayed in Washington practicing law. He also became the publisher of Diplomat magazine.

Roy St. Lewis, the federal prosecutor who represented the U.S. Government in the Hale and Ramsey trials.

plication for the delivery of Hale and Ramsey to federal authorities. The letter presented by U.S. Attorney St. Lewis read follows:

"*June 17, 1926*

"Honorable George F. Short
Attorney General of Oklahoma
State Capitol Building
Oklahoma City, Oklahoma

Dear Sir:
"With the supreme significance of its importance, I hope arrangements can be made with you, the County Attorney of Osage County, and the Honorable Jesse J. Worten, District Judge of Osage County, whereby prisoners John Ramsey and William K. Hale be brought to the Western District of Oklahoma in order that they may be tried for the murder of Henry Roan in the United States District Court now in session at Guthrie, Oklahoma.

"Conditions of the docket at this time are such that we are in a position to go to trial as soon as satisfactory arrangements can be made with proper state officials. These arrangements should be made before the Honorable John H. Cotteral is requested to set a date for the (Federal) trial.

"The defendants have been continually in custody either in Guthrie or Pawhuska, Oklahoma, since January 8 of this year, and I feel as if they are entitled to as speedy a trial as possible under the existing circumstances due to the fact that they have been denied bail.

"Federal officials will feel grateful for the valuable service rendered in connection with the investigation of the crimes in the Osage country by members of the Attorney General's Office and other officers and citizens of Osage County, and it is my earnest desire that both Federal and state authorities may continue to work in perfect harmony. The result will be the bringing to justice of the perpetrators of many crimes upon innocent and unsuspecting members of the Osage Tribe of Indians.

"An indictment was returned by a Grand Jury January 9th, 1926, in the District Court of the United States for the Western District of Oklahoma, which indictment charged John Ramsey and William K. Hale with the murder of Henry Roan, a full-blooded Osage Indian.

"On March 1, 1926, a demurrer to the indictment was sustained to the effect that the United States was without jurisdiction, to which ruling exceptions were taken and allowed, and a writ of error was taken to the Supreme Court of the United States. On March 3, 1926, a state charge was filed in Osage County against the two above-named prisoners charging them with the murder of W.E. Smith and on the third day of March, 1926, at 4:00 p.m. the above-mentioned prisoners were taken in charge by the sheriff of Osage County, Oklahoma.

"It so happens that the case pending in the United States Court for this district is the oldest case pending against the above-named men, either in Federal Court or the state court. Consequently, we would like to proceed with the trial of the first case. From the decisions that I have examined I take it that the jurisdiction of the trial court of a cause is not taken away by the allowance of a writ of error, but its power to act in a cause is stayed or suspended during the pendency of the writ of error.

"On June 1, 1926, the Supreme Court of the United States handed down an opinion wherein the ruling of the demurrer above-mentioned was reversed. The mandate of the Supreme Court of the United States has been received and has been spread of record, and this mandate orders the trial court to proceed to trial and this court is now ready.

"The ruling of law seems to be that, where a state court and the court of the United States may each take jurisdiction, one holds it to exclusion of the other, unless its duty is fully performed and the jurisdiction invoked is exhausted, and the ruling applies alike in both civil and criminal procedure. Two or more courts may have concurrent jurisdiction of an offense in which case the one wherein proceedings are first instituted will retain it to the end and the other is not authorized to interfere. The same principal [sic] is declared in many of the state decisions. I realize that the offense charged in the state court is a different offense from the one charged in the United States Court, but the same rule and reason apply which is, that when a *state court and the court of the United States may each take jurisdiction of criminal cases the tribunal where jurisdiction first attached holds it to the exclusion of the other unless its duty is fully performed and the jurisdiction invoked is exhausted and in this connection may I call your attention to the following cases: [Here he cited cases.]*

"*I wish you would please arrange with Honorable Jesse J. Worten, District Judge of Osage County, to release William K. Hale and John Ramsey in order that we may proceed to trial in this district and after the trial on the indictment which is pending in this district which charges the above-mentioned defendants with the murder of Henry Roan, we shall be glad to return the prisoners to the state court where they may be tried for the murder of W.E. Smith. Assuring you again of earnest desire to cooperate with you and the court of Osage County, I remain,*

"*Yours very truly,*
Roy St. Lewis
United States Attorney"

Notwithstanding the U.S. Supreme Court's ruling, the State Court judge for some reason was reluctant to turn Hale and Ramsey over to federal authorities. On June 25, 1926, Judge Worten refused this request. On June 25, 1926, before Judge Worten, arguments were made by Roy St. Lewis for the U.S. government; C. K. Templeton, for the state; and T. J. Leahy, as prosecutor representing the Osage Indians. Their arguments were in favor of the request while those of W. S. Hamilton, James Springer and J. I. Howard, counsel for Hale and Ramsey, and J. Berry King, Assistant State's Attorney, were opposed to the granting of the U.S. government's request.

Judge Worten stated:

"*Gentlemen, I agree with Mr. Leahy's statement and with all of you who have expressed the opinion that this matter is purely a matter of discretion with the court.*

"*The authorities I have read on this subject, which have been few — I have just looked it up briefly — hold that the court which first has prisoners arrested and has jurisdiction over them should keep them until that jurisdiction is exhausted.*

"*It would be the easiest thing in the world for this court, and the thing I would prefer to do, to say to the United States authorities, take these men for it would save this court a great deal of time; and as many of the members of the bar all know, we are pressed for time, our docket is behind; but I will not consider this.*

"*I do not quite agree with some of the counsel; I think the defendants' rights are to be regarded in this case. Of course, from the viewpoint of the state and Government who are standing together, there is no difference in their situation at all. They are together prosecuting these cases, but the State of Oklahoma has completed the arrest of W.K. Hale and John Ramsey on this charge and they have entered their pleas and the issue has been joined. The State of Oklahoma and the defendants have of necessity gone to considerable expense in making preparations in the case of the State of Oklahoma vs. Hale and Ramsey on the Smith charge. They have tried one defendant, with the result that he had pleaded guilty. For the State of Oklahoma at this time to surrender them to the Federal authorities for trial on another charge and then probably come back here again on the Smith case seems to me to be for the state to be doing these men an injustice.*

"I look at this matter from a position standing in the middle of the road looking both ways. I cannot look at it from the one standpoint. If I could look at it from the state's standpoint and regard these men as guilty men and regard it as the court's decision so to do, I would send them down to Guthrie and let them be switched around as they like. But I think the defendants have some rights which are to be considered in these matters. Another thing, it seems to me there is a bare possibility at least of complications arising over this mandate being possibly recalled by the Supreme Court of the United States."

Mr. St. Lewis: "Who would be prejudiced?"

Judge Worten: "They could not try them down there until that was discharged of."

Mr. St. Lewis: "Would not that be to the defendants' benefit?"

Judge Worten: "Probably so, but it means bringing them back here, and probably before we would be ready to try them again you would want them back in federal court again."

Mr. St. Lewis: "They could not kick on that."

Judge Worten: "There is another thing to be considered and that is this: If I understand the procedure, I may be in error about it because I am not very familiar with the Federal procedure, there would be the question of getting these people back to the Western District. I cannot order the sheriff of this county to take them to the Western District of Oklahoma. All I could do would be to release them. Then you would have to get them out of the Northern District of Oklahoma which might entail longer court proceedings."

Mr. St. Lewis: "The government would take care of that, if the court pleases."

Judge Worten: "Yes, I am satisfied you think you could, but it might mean a longer delay. It might not be done before the 20th of September, and thus delay trial in the state court. Take into consideration all of these facts

and the further fact that to release these defendants to the federal authori-
ties, before trial in the state court, might bring on a greater delay in the
trial of the defendants, and in view of the fact that this court has heretofore
ordered the defendants held without bail, I am of the opinion that it would
be an abuse of discretion to grant the request of the United States Attorney;
and the application for the surrender of the defendants to the federal au-
thorities will be denied. I might add, however, that this court invites an
appeal of this matter to the Criminal Court of Appeals for a review of my
jurisdiction, and if the court sees fit to order the delivery of the defendants
to the Federal authorities it will be a great relief to me but, viewing the
situation as I do, I cannot conscientiously make the order which you re-
quested."

A number of delegations of Osage County citizens called on
Judge Worten to plead with him to turn Hale and Ramsey over to
the federal government for trial, pointing out that Hale and Ramsey
could be tried quickly and thoroughly in federal court at Guthrie.
On the other hand, they stated that it would cost the county from
$5,000 to $10,000 to try them and that it would be almost impossible
to get a jury. The case would be dragged through the court for years,
they insisted, and perjured testimony would be submitted to the
state court with the final result that nothing would be gained except
delays, all of which would be beneficial to the defendants.

A writ of *habeas corpus* was then issued by the U.S. District Court,
instructing the sheriff of Osage County to turn these defendants over
to federal authorities and this writ was honored. A U.S. Marshal
and FBI Agents went to the jail to take Hale and Ramsey into federal
custody on July 4, 1926. Hale refused to get dressed and stalled for
time until Special Agents and a U.S. Marshal told him that, if he did
not dress, they would take him in his underwear. Hale insisted, "The
government has no jurisdiction." He demanded to know the amount
of his bond. When he was informed that the charge was not bail-
able, he protested vehemently, saying he could make a million-dol-
lar bond.

Attorneys for the defense continued to wage a legal battle, attempting to have the defendants returned to state court.

As soon as Federal Judge Cotteral decided that the federal authorities had the right to try Hale and Ramsey first, the defense
launched a new attack on the indictment which had been returned
the preceding February by the federal grand jury, alleging that there
were certain irregularities in the grand jury when the indictment
was returned and filing a motion that the indictment be quashed.

On July 10, 1926, after arguments were heard on this motion to quash, it was rejected. The defendants were then arraigned and entered pleas of "not guilty." Trial was set for July 26, 1926.

Application for a severance to try Hale and Ramsey separately was denied by Federal Judge Cotteral when the case opened in federal court at Guthrie.

Ramsey was charged with the actual killing of Henry Roan, while Hale was charged as the instigator and as an accomplice.

Hale and Ramsey appeared in the courtroom early in the morning with their attorneys. Both appeared confident as they listened to questions asked the prospective jurors. Hale chatted occasionally with his attorneys, smiling often. Ramsey appeared to have recently overcome an illness. He said little and silently watched the proceedings. Mrs. Hale sat a short distance behind Hale with their daughter, Willie.

The first sixty jurors drawn from the box were dismissed since FBI investigation revealed that most were the most disreputable kind of characters. An additional sixty men were drawn from the box and they, in turn, were investigated by Agents working day and night. Of this number, approximately three jurors were secured. Next, 100 men were drawn from an open venire and these prospective jurors also were investigated. From this number, a jury was finally selected.

This first trial in federal court at Guthrie, Oklahoma, lasted from July 28 to August 25, 1926, and resulted in a hung jury. This jury was discharged upon failing to reach a verdict after nearly fifty hours of deliberation and sixty-two ballots. Many people speculated that there were friends of Hale on the jury.

At this trial, the foreman of the federal grand jury which had indicted Hale and Ramsey, testified that the statements given by Ernest Burkhart and John Ramsey to Special Agents were not signed when shown to the grand jury. This foreman, a preacher, was later convicted of perjury for this testimony and received an 18-month sentence.

Hale and Ramsey were again tried from October 20 to October 29, 1926, in federal court at Oklahoma City. On page one of its October, 29, issue, the Oklahoma City Times described the courtroom scene the day of the trial:

"W.K. Hale, King of the Osage Hills, and John Ramsey, Fairfax cowboy-farmer, at 3:30 o'clock Friday afternoon were found guilty of murder of Henry Roan, wealthy Osage Indian, in January, 1923. Life sentence was

assessed by the jury in both cases.

"*An immediate appeal will be taken, attorneys for defense announced following the sentencing of the two men by Judge John C. Pollock. A period of eighty days was allowed by the jurist in which an appeal to the circuit court might be prepared.*

"*The verdict came in the fifth ballot taken by the jury following completion of the case at 7:30 o'clock Thursday night when the fate of the two men was placed in the hands of their peers.*

"*Four ballots were taken Thursday night while all of Friday morning was spent in arguing the case. On the fifth ballot a guilty verdict was unanimous, while three hours were spent in determining punishment, only two alternatives being allowed, death or imprisonment for life.*

"*Absolute silence reigned over the crowded courtroom following pronouncement of the sentence, with all eyes turned upon Hale and Ramsey.*

"*Hale remained King of the Osage Hills.*

"*Not for a minute did his characteristic smile of confidence leave his face. Ramsey, silent through the entire trial, became ghastly white, emphasizing the redness of his sleepless eyes.*

"*Ramsey and Hale sat silently as the clerk read, 'We find Mr. Hale guilty of first degree murder without capital punishment. We find Mr. Ramsey guilty of first degree murder without capital punishment.'*

"*Ramsey's mouth twitched as he listened, eyes fixed on Judge John C. Pollock. Hale sat unblinking and apparently unaffected as the verdict was read. Neither were smiling.*

"*Ramsey's son, Homer, who was in the room, shook his head as he heard the verdict. Mrs. Hale and Mrs. Ramsey, who have been beside their husbands throughout the several trials, were not in the courtroom when the jury returned.*

"*Word that the jury was to come in spread rapidly, and the courtroom corridors were crowded to capacity. Hale and Ramsey came in with a jaunty step and seated themselves with their attorneys. As the jury filed in and took their places, no word was said in the crowd, and the tick of the courtroom clock could be heard plainly.*

"*The feeling in the courtroom seemed to grow more tense; Ramsey with a narrow line in his forehead and a strange look in his eyes. Hale, with his chin in a characteristic pose, glanced neither right nor left. No sound, save that of the clock, could be heard as the clerk rose.*

"'*Have you a verdict, gentlemen?' asked Judge Pollock.*

"'*Yes, sir,' the foreman said, handing him the verdict. He glanced at it and handed it to the clerk with instructions to read it.*

"*Standing before the jury, Ramsey, bent and white; Hale, erect and smiling, they listened to Judge Pollock's words. He spoke first to the jury.*

"'Having now discharged your special duty,' he said, 'it now becomes the duty of the court to excuse you. Your duty has been a difficult one, one of the most severe trials in which men can be subjected. This court wants to commend you for the manner in which you have acquitted it. It wants to praise you for your diligent attention both during the hearing and during your deliberations.'

"Hale and Ramsey were then called before the bench and Judge Pollock told them they had been found guilty and that in accordance with the verdict they should be confined in the Federal Prison for life.

"'Have you anything to say?' he asked.

"'Nothing,' said Hale.

"Ramsey did not speak but merely shook his head.

"'You will be turned over to the marshal, commitments will be issued at this time and you will be transferred to the penitentiary.'

"After the verdict finding both men guilty of first degree murder had been read, attorneys at the defense table sat solemn-faced, staring at the court. Hale and Ramsey never moved, but Ramsey's mouth twitched more than when the jury came in.

"'Mr. Hale and Mr. Ramsey,' said Judge Pollock, 'you have been tried before a jury of your peers for a crime of murder of an Osage Indian in such a manner as to make you guilty of murder before the jury. That is their decision. It is the duty of the court to pass sentence. A disagreeable duty has been made easier by a law which gives the jury the power to fix the penalty. They have found you guilty without capital punishment.

"'It is, therefore, the judgment of the court that you be confined in the Federal penitentiary of Leavenworth, Kansas, for the rest of your natural lives.'

"Ramsey said nothing to either the attorneys or friends.

"J. I. Howard, attorney for Hale, asked that his client be allowed to remain in Oklahoma City until November 10, to finish up some business matters which he would have to attend to before he went to the penitentiary. Government attorneys said they had no objection and the court ordered that Hale be kept under guard by the United States Marshal in Oklahoma City until November 10, when he should be taken to the Federal Prison.

"Howard announced that a bill of exceptions were [sic] being prepared that the case would be appealed to the Circuit Court of Appeals in the future....

"Attorneys and friends of the court swarmed around Roy Lewis [sic] to congratulate the United States Attorney who headed prosecution of the murder cases both in the first trial at Guthrie last July when no agreement

Bill Hale, November 17, 1926.

John Ramsey, November 17, 1926 at Leavenworth Federal Penitentiary.

was reached and in the present trial of eight days which brought about conviction of the alleged 'mastermind of the Osage reign of terror' and his cohort.

"Lewis [sic] and his fellow attorneys were jubilant over the verdict.

"'The jury meted out justice. That's all,' said Lewis, [sic] while no words were forthcoming relative to the assessment of life imprisonment rather than death as asked by the Government prosecutors.

"Attorneys for the defense, W. S. Hamilton, J. I. Howard and J.M. Springer (S. P. Freeling being absent) spoke only of the forthcoming appeal.

"'We have not quit. Just put that down,' said Springer. 'We will now devote our entire energy in preparing an appeal to the district court [sic] through which we hope to obtain a new trial and ultimate freedom for our clients.'

Hale's attorneys did immediately appeal this conviction and it was reversed by the U.S. Circuit Court of Appeals for the Eighth

Circuit on the ground that the case had been tried in the wrong district. The federal appellate court ruled that it should have been tried in the district where the murder occurred. The case was remanded for a new trial in the Northern District of Oklahoma. This decision automatically reversed the convictions of Hale and Ramsey.

Hale and Ramsey requested a severance and they were tried separately in the United States District Court sitting at Pawhuska, Oklahoma.

Ramsey was convicted again in the U.S. District Court for the Northern District of Oklahoma sitting at Pawhuska on November 20, 1929. The following day he was sentenced to serve a life sentence in the Federal Penitentiary at Leavenworth, Kansas. Ramsey did not appeal this conviction.

Hale was also retried in the U.S. District Court for the Northern District sitting at Pawhuska. The *Pawhuska Daily Journal*[37] described Hale's appearance in court as follows:

"Hale appeared with his wife and daughter, Willie, as jaunty as ever. Not a gray hair attests to the fact that he has spent a year in a prison shoe factory and there are no lines of worry or grief. With glistening hair, flashing eyes, a dark gray suit and a bright blue necktie, he looked the prosperous rancher he was before trouble befell him about five years ago."

"On January 26, 1929, a guilty verdict was returned and Hale was given a life sentence to be served in the Federal Penitentiary at Leavenworth, Kansas.

"At this point Hale apparently resigned himself to his fate. On May 30, 1929, he sent word from his prison cell at Leavenworth that he wished all appeals on his behalf dropped. His cryptic message read, 'Have decided not to appeal.' This ended what was described as 'the hardest fought legal battle in the State of Oklahoma.'"

With Bill Hale, mastermind of the Osage reign of terror, and his cohorts behind bars, a feeling of relief pervaded Osage County. Citizens walked the streets smiling, confident that it was no longer necessary for them to fear death at the hands of the King of the Osage Hills and his gang of criminals.

The Osage Indians were jubilant over the result of the trials. Principal Chief Fred Lookout, who served the Osage Tribe as Chief for 29 years, called together members of the Tribal Council. He looked from the face of one councilman to the other. The fear was gone, the curse dispelled. Recalling the resolution the Tribal Council had

---

[37]October 1, 1929.

Bill Hale with his daughter, Willie, and his wife at the time of his trials. At the time, 18-year-old Willie was a student at Kidd Key College in Sherman, Texas.

passed in 1923 which brought the federal investigators to Osage Country, it was decided to pass another resolution to perpetuate the gratitude of the Osages to the Special Agents of the FBI and others who were instrumental in sending the murderers to jail. The following resolution was inscribed on the rolls of the tribe:

"RESOLUTION 97

"Being appreciative of the splendid work done in the matter of the investigation of the killing of certain members of the Osage Tribe of Indians, and the trial and conviction of the parties charged with such offenses, the Osage Tribal Council, in session assembled, deems it proper to express the appreciation of the Osage Tribe of Indians, as well as of the Osage Tribal Council, for such services;

"Now, therefore, be it resolved by the Osage Tribal Council, in session assembled, that, speaking for the Osage Tribe of Indians, as well as for the Osage Tribal Council, we express our sincere gratitude for the splendid work done in the matter of the investigating and bringing to justice the

Chief Fred Lookout, who led the Osage Tribe for 29 years.

Chief Fred Lookout and his wife, Julia. He was chief when the murders were
solved and signed a resolution commending the FBI Agents.

parties charged with the murders of…members of the Osage Tribe of Indians…."

As one citizen of Osage County, who was a witness against the
murderers, stated, "I believe the day is past when a man will be shot
down for doing right."

Writer Bill Burkhart, commenting on the victimization of the
Osages by criminals observed:

*"It is a mistake to view these crimes in a different light because the
criminals were white and the victims Indians. This was no race war. Criminals did not prey on the Osages because they were Indians, but because
they had money. Vultures quickly descended on every western boomtown
from California to Kansas, from Montana to Texas. The murderers, card
sharks, dope doctors, thieves, and shyster lawyers in the Osage would have
schemed just as malevolently had their wealthy victims been white, and
they would have succeeded equally as well."*[38]

---

[38]"Osage Oil," Chronicles of Oklahoma, Vol. 41, Fall, 1963.

❧ Epilogue ❧

SUMMARY

The FBI's investigation revealed that Bill Hale, the multimillionaire ranchman and so-called King of the Osage Hills, had orchestrated the murders which were designed to further augment his wealth. The plan was to murder the relatives of Mollie Burkhart so that she would inherit their headrights — entitlements to shares of the tribe's oil wealth — and then eventually murder her so that all her relatives' headrights and the vast oil income they brought with them would be centered in the hands of Mollie's husband, Ernest Burkhart, Hale's nephew puppet. The death of Ernest would place the wealth in Hale's hands.

On the night of her murder, Anna Brown had been plied with liquor by Kelsie Morrison and Bryan Burkhart at the instigation of Hale. While Bryan Burkhart held the drunken Anna, Morrison shot her through the back of the head.

Hale hired John Ramsey, a 50-year-old bootlegger and typical rough-type western criminal, to murder Henry Roan. Hale bought Ramsey a new $500 Ford car prior to the Roan murder as part payment for the deed and paid him $1,000 in cash after the murder had been committed. Ramsey had befriended Roan and gained his confidence by providing him whiskey for several weeks prior to the night he lured him to a remote pasture on the pretext of getting whiskey, He then shot Roan through the back of his head.

Hale hired John Ramsey and Asa "Ace" Kirby to murder William E. Smith and his wife. Acting under instructions from his uncle, Ernest Burkhart pointed out Smith's house to Ramsey and Kirby and told them when the Smiths' house should be blown up. After the Smith massacre, Hale became worried that "Ace" Kirby might disclose Hale's connection with the murders, so he persuaded Kirby to burglarize a store where Hale told him he would find valuable gems. Hale then notified the owner of the store of the planned burglary and, as Kirby entered the store, the owner hit him with shotgun blasts which resulted in his death.

THE TRIALS

The trials of the murders culminated in four life sentences for the killers. William K. Hale and John Ramsey were tried four times for the murder of Henry Roan — twice in the Federal District Court at Guthrie, Oklahoma, once in the Federal District Court at Oklahoma City, Oklahoma, and once in the Federal District Court at Pawhuska.[39] (The United States had jurisdiction only over the place where Henry Roan had been murdered.) They were both convicted and sentenced to life imprisonment in the Federal Penitentiary at Leavenworth, Kansas.

Hale's lawyers employed every device, legal and illegal, to obtain their clients' freedom. Defense witnesses committed perjury and many of the prosecution's witnesses were intimidated and threatened. Many individuals subsequently received sentences for perjury and obstruction of justice as a result of the FBI's investigation.

After all of his appeals, Hale's conviction remained affirmed, and he began serving his life sentence at Leavenworth, Kansas.

Kelsie Morrison was convicted in State Court for the murder of Anna Brown and received a life sentence.

Ernest Burkhart, who was charged jointly with William K. Hale, John Ramsey, Asa Kirby (then deceased), and Henry Grammer (then deceased) with the murder of W.E. Smith, changed his plea from "not guilty" to "guilty" at his trial in the State Court of Osage County and was sentenced to life in prison.

Bryan Burkhart, who turned state's evidence in state court, was never convicted.

TRIBUTES TO FBI AGENTS

The Special Agents who worked on this case made a substantial contribution in shaping the reputation of the FBI because the Osage Indian murder case firmly established the Federal Bureau of Investigation as one of the world's greatest police agencies. Their courage and perseverance in the face of seemingly insurmountable difficulties set the model for future Special Agents.

---

[39]There was no federal courthouse at Pawhuska, but U.S. District Court judges traveled the circuit trying cases at various locations, including Pawhuska.

They drove and hiked thousands of miles through the oil fields day and night in all kinds of weather running out innumerable leads. Their lives were constantly in danger.

Not only did the Osage tribal council pass resolutions expressing appreciation for the service rendered by the FBI in dissolving the vicious murder ring which had preyed on the tribe for many years, but the tribe also adopted the Special Agent who had worked undercover as a medicine man as a blood brother of the tribe. The Yaqui tribe of Mexico also adopted him as a blood brother. The Osage Indians also expressed their appreciation for the work done by one of the other Agents assigned to the case by raising money from their private funds to buy him a new automobile. He graciously refused this very generous gift, explaining that he had done nothing more than his duty.

The Bureau of Indian Affairs of the U.S. Department of the Interior extended splendid cooperation to FBI Agents in connection with the investigation of the murders. From March 24, 1923, when the Commissioner of Indian Affairs first asked for the U.S. Department of Justice's Bureau of Investigation's help in solving the murders until the time the murderers were convicted — a period of approximately six years — thirteen Special Agents were actively assigned to this case at various times. Twenty additional Agents from other offices engaged in a quasi-active investigation of the case since the evidence to convict the guilty parties was gathered from all parts of the country.

A Pawhuska, Oklahoma, attorney employed by the Osage Indians who assisted in the prosecution, wrote a letter to FBI Director J. Edgar Hoover commending the Agents who worked on the case. He said in part:

"It must be highly gratifying to you to know that largely as a result of the efforts of your Agents that one of the greatest criminal prosecutions in the history of the country has been brought to a successful termination. I do not doubt but that more good will result throughout the Southwest over this prosecution than any one of a similar nature that has been had....[Your Agents have] earned the everlasting gratitude of the public."

WILLIAM K. HALE

During the one and one-half years he spent in the Leavenworth Penitentiary while the various trials were pending, Hale had various occupations. For the first two months he worked as a stone cutter. He next developed into a stone planer and then was given the

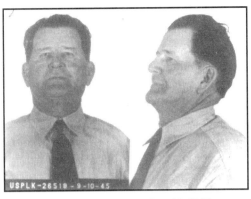

W. K. Hale, September 10, 1945

job of polishing large slabs of Bedford limestone used in the construction of new prison buildings. When the retrial of his case came before the courts, Hale was a shop foreman.

Approximately one year after her father's conviction, Hale's lovely daughter, Willie[40], married an Osage Indian and lived within a few hundred yards of the spot where Anna Brown had been murdered. Willie had two Osage husbands, Willard Oller and Frank Simkins. While Hale was in prison, he befriended an inmate named Sam Cohen. When Cohen was being released, Hale told him to look up his daughter. He did and she became Mrs. Sam Cohen. They lived in Phoenix, Arizona.

On July 31, 1947, at age 72, Hale was paroled from his life sentence at Leavenworth on condition that he take a job in Wichita, Kansas. The Osage Tribal Council called a special meeting to adopt a resolution opposing Hale's parole, but prison officials said that Hale had been a model prisoner and deserved parole.

Hale later moved to Phoenix, Arizona, to be with his daughter, where he lived for 12 years.

On August 15, 1962, Hale, 88 years old, died in a Phoenix nursing home. He was buried in Wichita, Kansas. Surprisingly, a number of citizens from Osage County went to Wichita for his funeral.

JOHN RAMSEY

After his conviction for the murder of Henry Roan, John Ramsey was received at the U.S. Penitentiary at Leavenworth, Kansas, on

---

[40]Her name has been listed in some sources as "Billie."

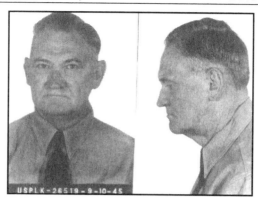

John Ramsey, September 10, 1945.

November 17, 1926, from the Western District of Oklahoma to begin serving his life sentence.

He was paroled on November 10, 1947, and Ramsey took up residence with a son in Idaho.

KELSIE MORRISON

Kelsie Morrison, who at the instigation of Bill Hale was the trigger man in the Anna Brown murder, had received a nine-year sentence on an unrelated charge of "assisting to kill" in 1925. Morrison was brought back to Bartlesville for robbing W. W. "Smoke" Thomason, a federal prohibition officer. In that incident Morrison had taken Thomason's gun away from him and threatened to kill him. At that instant a motorist drove up. As Morrison turned to see who it was, Thomason grabbed his gun back and shot Morrison in the head The wound was apparently superficial because Morrison was confined to the Fairfax jail. However, within a few days, Morrison escaped.

While he was at large he and Blackie Thompson allegedly robbed the First National Bank at Bristow. They were tried for this crime, but were acquitted.

Morrison was then tried for holding up Thomason and he received a seven-year sentence.

While serving this sentence, he was brought back to stand trial for Anna Brown's murder. Following that trial, in 1926, he received a life sentence. To keep him separated from Hale, he was sent to the Federal Penitentiary at Atlanta, Georgia, rather than to Leavenworth. He was paroled from this sentence in 1931.

Subsequently, he was convicted for violation of the National

The jail at Fairfax from which Kelsie Morrison escaped.

Prohibition Act and received a four-year sentence. In 1936 he was again conditionally released from prison and he returned to Fairfax, Oklahoma.

On the evening of May 25, 1937, Morrison was on the streets of Fairfax, drunk and disorderly. A police officer ordered him to go home. He went to his room, but in a short while he returned to the street and confronted the police officer in front of the Hunsaker Funeral Home.

"You're the first man who ever told me to go home," Morrison said, "and I'm not going. What are you going to do about it?"

He then drew a .22 caliber pistol and started firing. More than fifty persons on the street fled for cover. When a second officer, hearing the shots, came to render assistance, Morrison began firing at him. The officer fired two shots, striking Morrison on his left side, an inch apart, piercing his heart. He staggered and fell dead. He was about 40 years old at the time of his death. He is buried in Muskogee, Oklahoma.

ERNEST BURKHART

Prior to his arrest for his part in the murders, Ernest Burkhart had a record of several minor offenses in the Osage County area. He was arrested on March 13, 1926, by state authorities for his part in the Smith massacre. Subsequently, he received a life sentence in state court for this crime and was confined to the Oklahoma State Penitentiary at McAlester, Oklahoma. He began serving this term on October 4, 1926. He was paroled from this sentence in 1937. (His wife, Mollie,[41] who had already divorced him and married a man named Cobb, died that same year.)

His brother, Bryan, had married Lillie Maggie Morrell, a prominent and wealthy full-blooded restricted allottee Osage who was the last surviving member of Chief Pawhuska's White Hair Clan. Lillie had built a new house on an 80-acre tract where she lived with Bryan.

On February 8, 1940, Ernest Burkhart and a woman companion entered the garage of Lillie Maggie Morrell Burkhart and stole two cedar chests containing approximately $7,000 worth of personal property. Since this crime occurred on restricted Osage property under the jurisdiction of the federal government, Ernest was tried in U.S. District Court for the Northern District of Oklahoma. During the trial, both of his brothers, Bryan and Horace, testified against him. On April 24, 1941, Burkhart was sentenced to serve seven years on count two of the indictment and two years on count one, to be served concurrently. Burkhart requested that he not be confined to the Federal Penitentiary at Leavenworth, Kansas, since his uncle, W. K. Hale, who was convicted largely as a result of his damaging testimony, was also confined there. Consequently, Burkhart was sent to the Federal Penitentiary at Atlanta, Georgia.

Ernest was subsequently paroled from this federal sentence, but in 1946 his Oklahoma State parole was revoked and he was confined to the State prison at McAlester.

In 1959 he was paroled again with the stipulation that he never again return to Oklahoma, a pledge he later breached.

Ernest entered prison as a young man of 34 and came out at age 67, a broken down old man in poor health.

Jim Cox, a fellow prisoner, felt sorry for Burkie who seemed to be a misfit in prison. When Cox was released and hired on a ranch near Raton, New Mexico, he talked his boss into hiring Burkhart to herd sheep. Ernest worked at this job for $75 per month plus room and board for six years. Twice a month he would

---

[41]Mollie Burkhart who was born December 1, 1886; died June 16, 1937.

Ernest Burkhart, 50 years after the Osage Murders, in about 1983.

be taken to town for a haircut and to report to his parole officer.

When the book, "FBI Story," by Don Whitehead (which included a chapter on the Osage Indian Murders) was made into a movie, Burkie asked for a ride to town so he could see it. He was not impressed with its accuracy.

In 1965 Burkhart filed a petition for a full pardon. He said he was receiving a pension and had $5,000 in savings. Although it was opposed by the Osage Tribal Council, the Board on a 3-to-2 vote granted Burkhart a pardon.

Toward the end of his life, Ernest Burkhart was interviewed[42] and seemed to be a very bitter man. He claimed that he had been promised immunity if he testified against the others. He commented, "After I explained it and told them..., they said, you won't do a day. We'll turn you right out'."

He complained, *"After it was over, I asked what about it and one of the FBI Agents said he would have to get orders out of Washington before he could do anything. That's the story he told me. They never did tell the truth."*

(Burkhart, of course, was tried and convicted in Oklahoma State Court over which the federal government had no jurisdiction.)

A writer asked, "Well, Mr. Burkhart, you're in your mid 80's.

---

[42]Reported in "Oil in Oklahoma" by Robert Gregory.

Have you any regrets about your life?"

"No. No," he replied. *"I'm making it fine."*

He was asked, "If you had it to do all over again, would you change?"

"I wouldn't talk to the FBI," he said bitterly, *"knowing them like I do. I got no confidence in them at all, none whatsoever."*

"What kind of a man was Bill Hale?"

"Well, I guess you'd say the best you ever saw until after you found him out and knowed him. You could meet him and you'd fall in love with him. Women were the same way. But the longer you stayed around him, he'd get to you. He'd beat you some way. He was smart...had a world of horse sense."

"Before Hale died, he was released from prison before you were. Did you ever see him. Did you ever talk to him?"

"Oh, yeah. He came to McAlester and visited me twice."

"What did he tell you?"

"I don't remember all that was said. He just said that, if I had under- stood what the FBI had planned, I wouldn't have been a witness against him."

"Did he ever tell you what he...?

"He told me, 'I don't blame you at all. I don't hold a thing against you.'"

Ernest Burkhart apparently failed to realize that, as Hale's scheme further evolved after Ernest's wife, Mollie, was eliminated, Ernest would have to be the next one killed for culmination of Hale's plan to acquire all the wealth of Lizzie Q's family.

Ernest returned to Osage County and lived with his brother, Bryan, in Lillie Maggie Morrell Burkhart's home after her death.

Ernest died in Cleveland, Oklahoma.

BRYAN BURKHART

In 1933 Byran Burkhart was arrested in El Paso, Texas, for pos- session of counterfeit ten-dollar Federal Reserve notes and received a two-year sentence from which he was later paroled.

Although Bryan held Anna Brown while Kelsie Morrison shot her, he was never tried for this crime because he turned state's evi- dence.

Bryan had been married previously, but he subsequently mar- ried Lillie Maggie Morrell, a very highly respected and wealthy full- blooded Osage allottee and the last survivor of the White Hair Clan.

When Lillie died she left Bryan a life estate in 160 acres near

Following the death of Lillie Maggie Morrell Burkhart, Ernest and Bryan
Burkhart lived together in this house. Mrs. Burkhart bequeathed it to the
Oklahoma Historical Society for a shrine and research center in honor of her
ancestor, Chief Paw-hui-skah (White Hair). The White Hair Memorial is located
ten miles west of Hominy, Oklahoma, on Highway 20.

Lillie Maggie Morrell Burkhart, last
survivor of the clan of Chief
Pawhuska (White Hair), and wife
of Bryan Burkhart.

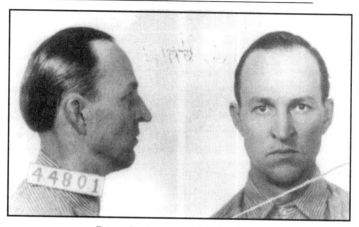

Bryan Burkhart, March 17, 1934.

Gray Horse. (She left her home, where she lived with Bryan, to the Oklahoma Historical Society to be kept as a shrine to her ancestor, Chief White Hair, Pawhuska, together with her headright and the balance of her land for maintenance of the shrine. The White Hair Memorial, an Osage Resource Learning Center, is located 10 miles west of Hominy, Oklahoma off Highway 20.)[43]

Bryan, who had been born in Greenville, Texas, on February 21, 1899, died July 22, 1985.

ROY ST. LEWIS

As a result of the national recognition he gained from his work on the Osage Indian murders, Roy St. Lewis, the United States Attorney who prosecuted Hale and Ramsey, was appointed an Assistant Attorney General of the United States, a position in which he served from 1931 to 1933. After that assignment, he remained in Washington and practiced law. He also later became the publisher of *Diplomat* magazine. A World War I veteran, he served as commander of the National Press Club American Legion Post. From 1930 to 1932 he was vice president of the American Bar Association.

He attended the University of Oklahoma Law School following which he practiced law in Holdenville, Oklahoma. He served as an assistant U.S. Attorney for the Western District of Oklahoma and later became U.S. Attorney. In 1928 he was named a special assistant to the Attorney General of the United States.

---

[43]It is managed by Lillie Maggie Morrell Burkhart's great niece, Billie Ponca.

Bibliography

Books:

Ralph A. Barney, *Osage Indians*. Pawhuska, Oklahoma, The Osage Printery, 1929.
(A short compilation of the many laws enacted by the United States Congress to apportion the land of the Osage Indians. Significant cases tried under these laws are also included.)

Stephen Barrett, *Shinkah, The Osage Indian*. Oklahoma City, Harlow Publishing Co., 1916.
(A story of the home life of an Osage Indian boy, written to give a better understanding of, and to perpetuate the folklore and the sociology of, the Osage Indian.)

Louis Burns, "Reign of Terror," *The Osage*.

William Clark, *Westward With Dragoons*. Fulton, Missouri, Ovid Bell Press, Inc., 1937.
(The journal of William Clark while on expedition to establish Fort Osage; contains a description of the wilderness, and the treaty-making meetings necessary for the construction of Fort Osage.)

Jean Graham, *Tales of Osage River Country*. Clinton, Missouri, Martin Printing Company, 1929.
(A book of folklore of the Osage Indians containing descriptions of the countryside, stories, legends, and yarns.)

Francis LaFlesche, "The Osage Tribe: Rite of the Chiefs; Sayings of the Ancient Men," an article contained in the *Thirty-Sixth Annual Report of the Bureau of American Ethnology*, Washington, U.S. Government Printing Office, 1921, pp. 37-599.
(LaFlesche traces the origin, history, and organization of the Osage Indians, with particular emphasis on tribal rites, together with the sayings, proverbs, and songs of the tribe.)

Francis LaFlesche, "The Osage Tribe: The Rite of Vigil," an article contained in the *Thirty-Ninth Annual Report of the Bureau of American Ethnology*, Washington, U.S. Government Printing Office, 1925, pp. 31-630.
(An explanation of the Rite of Vigil through which the Osage communicated with Wakonda, his God.)

Arthur H. Lamb, *Tragedies of Osage Hills*. Pawhuska, Oklahoma, The Osage Printery, 1935.
(A book revealing the many tragedies which plagued the Osage Indians from the time of their origin. It reveals the deception, thievery, and murder brought about by the finding of oil. It tells also of the work done by the Federal Bureau of Investigation in investigating the murders.)

John Joseph Mathews, *Wah'kon-tah, The Osages and the White Man's Road*. Norman, Oklahoma, University of Oklahoma Press, 1932.
(An autobiographical history of an agent of the Federal Indian Service, Mathews tells of the maltreatment of the Indians as the white man continually moved westward.)

Dennis McAuliffe, Jr. *The Deaths of Sybil Bolton*. Times Books, Random House, 1994.
(A newspaperman investigates his Osage grandmother's death.)

----------, *1872-1972, Osage Indian Tribe Centennial Celebration*. Pawhuska, Oklahoma, Osage Agency Campus, 1972.

Sixty-First Congress of the United States, Second Session, Document 554, *Memorial of Osage Against Enrollment of Tribe*, Washington, May 20, 1910.
(Certain people sought to partake of the Osage wealth through adoption into the tribe. This document was granted to the Osage Indians by Congress to correct such an abuse.)

Victor Tixier, *Tixier Travels on Osage Prairies*, edited by John Francis McDermott, translated from the French by Albert J. Salvan. Norman Oklahoma, University of Oklahoma Press, 1940.
(The travels of a Frenchman through the vast expanse of Osage territory; depicts the life, habits, customs, and traditions of the Osage Indians.)

William E. Unrau, *The Kansa Indians*. University of Oklahoma Press, Norman and London, 1971.
   (This study of the Kansa Indians also chronicles their dealings and battles with the Osages.)

Don Whitehead, *The FBI Story*. Random House, 1956, Chapter 9.
   (A survey of famous FBI cases.)

Terry Wilson, *"The Osage, The Richest People in the World."* (date unknown.)

Periodicals:

Estelle A. Brown, "Our Plutocratic Osage Indians," *Travel*, Vol. 39, p. 19, 1922.
   (A picture of the Osages before and after the discovery of oil. Relates how the Osages spent their money and what they bought with it. It tells also of the benefits of money, and its miseries.)

Nolen Bulloch, "Indian Murders Recall Terror of '20s," *Tulsa Tribune*, August 20, 1953.

----------, "Osage Hills 'King' Dead," *Tulsa World*, August 20, 1962.

----------, "FBI Agent in Dillinger, Osage Murder Case Dies," Associated Press, *Tulsa World*, December 26, 1961.

Bill Burchardt, "Osage Oil," *The Chronicles of Oklahoma*, Vol. 41, Fall, 1963.

Rev. J. Owen Dorsey, "Osage Indians, An Account of War Customs," *American Naturalist*, Vol. XVIII, No. 2, February 1884, pp. 8-133.
   (A discussion of the war customs of the Osage Indians, including dances, costumes, and formation before 1890.)

William R. Draper, "Depression in Osage," *Outlook*, Vol. 160, January 27, 1932, p. 113.
   (Shows how, with the aid of some white men, the Indians spent their money freely and foolishly.)

Robert Gregory, "Richest Indians in the World," Oil in Oklahoma.

Fred Grove, "Oil and the Osage Murders," *Twin Tercloves* Times, date unknown.

William Irwin, "Richest People on Earth," *Colliers*, Vol. 76, August 22, 1925, p. 5.
(A history of how the Osage Indians acquired oil lands in Oklahoma, and the marriage laws which prevented undue inheritance of oil holdings by the white man or nonmembers of the tribe.)

Kenneth Jacob Jump, "The Legend of John Stink," Pawhuska, Oklahoma, 1977.

Nicole Marshall, "Dark Post Illuminated," *Tulsa World*, September 18, 1994.

Elmer T. Peterson, "Miracle of Oil," *Independent*, Vol. 112, April 26, 1924, p. 229.
(The discovery of oil and its subsequent effects on the Osage Nation.)

Billie I. Ponca, "Osages, Oil and Murder," *White Hair Memorial*, Ralston, Oklahoma (unpublished).

----------, Folder, *The White Hair Memorial*, P.O. Box 185, Ralston, Oklahoma 74650, 918-538-2417.

----------, "The Once and Future Kingdom," *Oklahoma Monthly*, April, 1978.

Sherman Rodgers, "Red Men in Gas Buggies," *Outlook*, Vol. 134, April 28, 1923, pp. 629-632.
(Another story of how the Osage spends his money.)

Bill Sansing, "Oil Rich Osages Figured in Oklahoma's Most Heinous Crimes in Early Statehood," Associated Press, published in *Tulsa World*, April 24, 1957.

THE OSAGE INDIAN MURDERS   281

----------, "Famed Osage Death Trial Attorney Now Publisher," *Tulsa World*, April 14, 1960.

----------, "Osage Death Ring Figure Seeks Mercy," *Tulsa World*, August 24, 1959.

----------, "Osage Bombing Figure Paroled," *Daily Oklahoman*, October 27, 1959.

----------, "Death of W.K. Hale Recalls Osage Slayings," Associated Press, August 20, 1962.

William G. Shepard, "Lo! The Rich Indian," *Harpers*, Vol. 141, June 1920, p. 723.
(A descriptive story of the Indian and his wealth; how he got it and what he did with it.)

----------, "Richest People Per Capita on Earth," *Current Opinion*, Vol. 74, June 1923, p. 740.
(A statistical survey of the wealth of the Osage Indians after the discovery of oil.)

----------, "The Black Curse of the Osages," *Literary Digest*, Vol. 89, No. 1, April 3, 1926.
(The tragedies of the Osage Indians, the direct result of the discovery of oil and new-found wealth.

----------, "Osage Oil Wealth Fading," *Literary Digest*, Vol. 113, May 14, 1932, p. 43.
(Statistical article pointing out the decline of wealth in the Osage Indian Nation.)

----------, "The Osage Murders," *Literary Digest*, Vol. 88, January 23, 1926, p. 11.
(Quotes newspaper accounts of the Osage Indian murders.)

----------, "Phillip Nolan of the Osages," *National Republic*, Vol. 22, December 1934.
(The pathetic story of John Stink, an outcast Osage.)

Pearl Wittkopp, "Osage Will Figure May Have Feared for Her Life," *Tulsa Tribune*, August. 24, 1973.

ABOUT THE AUTHOR

LAWRENCE J. HOGAN, an attorney, teacher and businessperson, served with the Federal Bureau of Investigation for ten years. He is a former member of the Maryland Commission on Law Enforcement and the Administration of Justice. For six years he served as a member of the U.S. Congress during which he was the leading architect of the District of Columbia Court Reorganization and Criminal Procedures Act (D.C. Crime Bill) and served on the Subcommittee which revised the Federal Rules of Evidence. For four years he was the elected County Executive of Prince Georges County, Maryland.

For many years he has taught law courses at various educational institutions and since 1982 he has been developing and delivering training programs for the Federal Emergency Management Agency's National Emergency Training Center.

Mr. Hogan received Bachelor of Arts (dual majors in history and philosophy) and Juris Doctorate degrees from Georgetown University and a Master of Arts degree in communications from the American University.

He is married and the father of six children. He resides in Frederick, Maryland.

What the Media is Saying About Lawrence J. Hogan's
"THE OSAGE INDIAN MURDERS"

"...The Osage saga is gripping. It's about the FBI's first major homicide probe in the 1920's after the discovery of oil on the reservation in Oklahoma made the tribe very, very rich. The white man cheated them every way they could with swindles and false claims and then came up with the scheme of marrying into the tribe, killing all the relatives, then killing their wives so they could inherit..."

The Washington Post

"Many, many Osage Indians died in the 1920's from explosions, gun shots and even poisoning with the killers walking away freely. The Osage Tribe pleaded with the federal government to intercede, and when they did, federal agents were dispatched to Osage County, Oklahoma. FBI Agents, some of whom worked undercover as a medicine man, cowboy, an oil prospector and insurance salesmen, conducted a dangerous, painstaking investigation for several years which finally resulted in the conviction of the murder ring's leaders. A new book by former FBI Agent and former U.S. Congressman Lawrence J. Hogan chronicles the investigation and the four trials which eventually resulted in life sentences for the perpetrators in spite of the fact that some witnesses were killed, others disappeared and still others were bribed to perjure themselves."

The Pawhuska, OK *Journal Capital*

"I half expected ghosts to step out of The Osage Indian Murders...[F]rom the author's chapter-and-verse narrative and bare bones prose comes a haunting look back at a lawless time and place...
"Apart from business owners who upped their prices when an Osage was buying, white thieves routinely got their hands on Osage money...A man could have an Osage declared incompetent, have himself made legal guardian then help himself. Or a man could marry an Osage woman, have her killed and inherit her headright...
"Author Lawrence J. Hogan—a former FBI Agent and former U.S. Congressman—did voluminous research for this book. He quotes from original documents, interviews and confessions and organized an interesting bibliography.
"The photographs in the book are astonishing. Old black and white photos of Indians and outlaws, murder scenes and city streets evoke the time and place in ways that words never can. The people in the photos bring the story to life. They look straight out of the page and their eyes speak volumes. After a while it sinks in: they were real people and they really did those things!"

The Hanford, CA *Sentinel*

"...The Osage Indian Murders is the true story of a multiple murder plot to acquire the estates of wealthy Osage Tribe members. One of the darkest episodes of Osage history, the conspiracy to exploit through murder at least 17 members of the Osage Tribe...is a chilling true-life crime story that is more dramatic than anything to come out of Hollywood movies. The Osage Indian Murders is a recommended addition to Native American supplemental reading lists, and will thoroughly engage the interest of anyone with an interest in true-life crime stories. Highly recommended."

The Midwest Book Review

"The book takes us through the history and culture of the Osage Indians, their customs, rituals, their distinctions from other tribes, their buffalo hunting and the impact horses had on the tribe. Hogan tells the chilling and uncomfortable tale of these murders in a forthright and matter-of-fact way. He intersperses the factual telling with informative footnotes, testimonies, photographs and records...
"Countless ways were devised to cheat the Indians out of their money...One of the ways was ruthless murder...The story is a fascinating and horrifying tale of marriage for inheritance, of barbarous murder and of extraordinary cover-up."

Ponca City, OK *News*

"Here's another fascinating book about native Americans. It's a true story written by a Frederick, Maryland lawyer, Lawrence J. Hogan who served 10 years with the FBI and served in Congress...
"When oil was discovered in Oklahoma, Osage Indians became wealthy. Outlaws and con men invaded their reservation to swindle them as best they could, while known criminals were marrying Osage women so they could kill off Indian relatives and acquire their shares of the wealth. It's a fascinating story..."

Naples, FL *Daily News*

"Greed, murder and history all combine to make a grisly tale of man's inhumanity to man...Marriage plots became a way for many unscrupulous white men, and a few white women, to obtain some of the vast Osage wealth. It was when the marriages began to end in murder that suspicions were aroused."

Frederick, MD *News* **and** *Post*

WHAT THE MEDIA HAS SAID ABOUT
THE OSAGE INDIAN MURDERS

"Nothing so far-reaching in murders has ever before been known in the United States," one of the Federal prosecutors stated, *"A condition has been revealed that will astound the nation when the details are known." Seventeen of that little tribe of Indians have bitten the dust ... when the white man wants what he wants. They have been shot in lonely pastures, bored by steel as they sat in their automobiles, poisoned to die slowly, and dynamited as they slept in their homes. All because of the curse that has fastened itself upon the tribe."* ... *[S]eventeen of the innocent Indians have gone to their happy hunting grounds by methods that would have made Sitting Bull seem like an angel administering mercy.*

Literary Digest

The murder of two or three heirs to bring a fortune or a title into the hands of a scoundrel is a familiar theme with fiction writers. But even lurid fiction pales beside the story of these Osage murders.

New York World

The [Osage] Indian is the plaything of clever lawyers, the fair game of anybody who can beat him out of his possessions.

Grand Rapids Press

The Osage Indian murders ... one of the blackest chapters in the history of the white man's dealings with the American Indian.

...[A]sk an Indian ... to tell you why the Osages were murdered and who murdered them and he will cringe in terrified silence. Take him to the middle of a field with no cover for eavesdropping; make oath to him that his name or his news will never be disclosed; and still he will say nothing. "No, no," he mumbles, "if do, me be next." ... Finding themselves in this situation, the Osages, still child-like and usually uneducated, have recourse to their superstitions. They believe their white enemies to be vested with hypnotic powers. They are confident that white men invoke the Evil Spirit and are, therefore, immune from punishment....

Those Government detectives who have come to the Osage wilds to track down the facts in a score of mysterious killings are up against more than tangled clues. They must pry from frightened Indians evidence against the Evil Spirit. What will it turn out to be this Evil Spirit? A group of white traders banded in a murder compact? A band of greedy Osages who have slain their relatives for the headrights which they desire to inherit? Or will it be the black taciturnity of the Osage scene itself which in the end will defeat all attempts to solve the enigma?

St. Louis Post-Dispatch